Career Track English

STUDENT BOOK

Ⅰ. Liberal Arts & Humanities

Ⅱ. Social Science & Business

Ⅲ. IT, Engineering & Natural Science

저자: 정성희, 송은혜, 복은임

감수: 베어드교양대학 글로벌 소통과 언어 원어민교원

YoungMin Publishing Company

Preface

본 교재는 인문, 교양, 사회, 비즈니스, IT, 공학 등을 전공한 학도들이 출중한 영어능력을 가지고도 자신의 전공을 추후 직업이나 비즈니스 업무에 활용하지 못하는 어려움을 극복하도록 도움을 주기 위한 Career 활용 전문 교재입니다. Career Track English (CTE) 교재는 학습자들이 직업 업무에 투입되었을 경우 사용 가능한 **영어의 기본 논리 구조와 틀을 잡아 전공 콘텐츠를 활용하여 산업계 전반에 걸친 다양한 비즈니스 영역에서 실제 업무 영어로 활용 하는 영어능력을 배양할 수 있도록** 고안되었습니다. 총 열 개의 Unit으로 구성된 본 교재를 통해 콘텐츠 **융합 지식활용 능력, 문제해결 능력, 통합적 사고력을** 향상시킬 수 있습니다.

이 책의 활용

Ⅲ 대학교 전공 콘텐츠와 연계한 전문 영어, 프레젠테이션 교육을 위한 전문 ESP 과목 교재로의 활용

본 교재의 **활용 방법**은 아래와 같습니다. 첫째, 본 교재를 대학 ESP 교양필수 혹은 선택 교양영어 과정으로 활용할 수 있습니다. 이를 통해 **실제적인 전공 관련 최근의 이슈와 트렌드를 익혀 추후 업무에 활용할 수 있는 전공 내용 프로젝트 발표 능력 배양 뿐만 아니라 아래와 같이 교수자와 학생 간의 상호작용을 극대화하는 과정**을 통해 학생들의 영어능력이 최적화되는 효과를 얻을 수 있습니다.

각 장마다 주어진 영어논리 구조 완성하기, 전문 지식 영역 읽기 실습 후 전공 관련 지식 함양, 콘텐츠 중심 영어표현, paraphrase, 주제 문장 및 뒷받침 문장쓰기, 표절 없는 제대로 된 인용하기, 데이터 및 샘플 분석과 읽기 실습 이후 주어지는 글쓰기 실습 페이지를 활용하여 학습자들은 초고를 만듭니다. 그 후 교수자와 동료의 일차 피드

백을 받아 다시 수정하는 과정을 거쳐 영어로 작성한 이메일 및 과제 활동의 부족한 점을 보완하게 됩니다.

교수자의 이차 점검 및 최종 점검, 피드백 제공 과정에서 학생들의 초고는 수정되어 실제 업무에 사용되어도 손색이 없을 정도의 수준에 이르게 됩니다. 이때 교수자는 Final Engaged Learning Writing Submission 페이지에 학생들이 최종본을 작성하게 하여 최종 정리 과정을 거치거나 혹은 제출하게 하여, 평가 과제로도 사용할 수 있습니다.

III 다양한 전문 비즈니스 상황을 영어로 문제해결, 실제 상황을 준비하고자 하는 대학생, 취업준비생, 직장인들의 핸드북, 참고 서적으로의 활용

둘째, 본 교재를 스스로 학습하고자 하는 대학생 및 취업준비생 혹은 영어로 전공관련 프로젝트를 해 보고 싶은 대학원생 및 직장인이라면 각 장에서 주어진 **현대 산업 사회에 핫한 이슈를 활용한 전문 비즈니스 발표 상황에 필요한 영어 프로젝트 작성하기 실습 적용과 학습**을 활용할 수 있습니다. 특히 전문 콘텐츠 영어 사용 능력 및 상황대처 능력을 아래와 같이 향상 시킬 수 있습니다.

우선 Unit 1 부터 Unit 5 까지 영어 표현과 논리를 익혀 흥미있는 콘텐츠 주제와 프로젝트 모델을 탐구하고 흥미영역을 설정합니다. 그 후 실제 자신이 그 업무에 종사하여 전문 프레젠테이션을 한다는 가정하에 Unit 6에서 보여주는 영어표현, 좋은 이메일 샘플을 참조하여 유사하게 써보며 프로젝트로 완성합니다. Unit 7 에서는 Liberal Arts & Humanities 영역, Unit 8 에서는 Social Science & Business 영역, Unit 9 에서는 IT, Engineering & Natural Science 영역에서 자신의 최종 탐구 주제를 설정합니다. 이를 통해 Unit 10 에서 전문 프레젠테이션 연습, 실전을 위한 준비 및 발표와 영상 촬영과 피드백을 통해 자신의 부족한 점을 발견하고, 향상, 보완하여 최종적인 Problem-Solution & Achievement 단계를 성취하여 현업에 투입되어도 손색없을 수준을 갖추게 됩니다.

맺음말

국제화, 세계화 이슈를 능가하는 인공지능의 출현이란 이슈로 인해 인간이 영어로 된 정보를 비판적으로 취사 선택, 독해하는 능력이 더 중요해졌음은 두말할 나위 없습니다. 이러한 시대에 발 맞추어 이제는 영어라는 매체를 통해 전공 영역을 영어로 프로젝트화 하는 능력, 프레젠테이션하는 능력, 비판적 사고능력을 활용한 콘텐츠 취사 선택과 문제해결 능력을 어떻게 종합적으로 발휘할 것인가가 시대적 요구사항입니다. 현 상황의 흐름에 발 맞추어 AI와 경쟁하는 시대가 요구하는, 산업사회의 인재상에 한 걸음 다가설 수 있도록 본 교재가 밑거름이 되기를 소망합니다.

끝으로 CTE 교재를 활용한 비전을 제시하고 선제적인 융합영어 교양교육의 틀을 만들어주신 숭실대학교 장범식 총장님, 숭실대학교 영어교육에 관심과 애정을 주시며 늘 격려를 아끼지 않으시고 응원해 주시는 숭실대학교 법인 박영립 이사님, 이덕실 이사님, 김재철 이사님과 문태현 동문회장님 이하 동문회와 두나회 회원님, 실제 필요한 콘텐츠와 내용 선정에 전문성 향상으로 도움을 주신 서울대학교 기계항공공학부 여재익 교수님, 전기전자공학부 문태섭 교수님과 사랑하는 FIP교우 여러분들, 또한 좋은 교재를 만들기 위해 불철주야 밤낮으로 같이 일해 준 CTE 개발팀에 감사드리며 이 책에 대한 소개를 마칩니다.

숭실대학교 베어드교양대학 글로벌소통과 언어 CTE 개발팀 드림

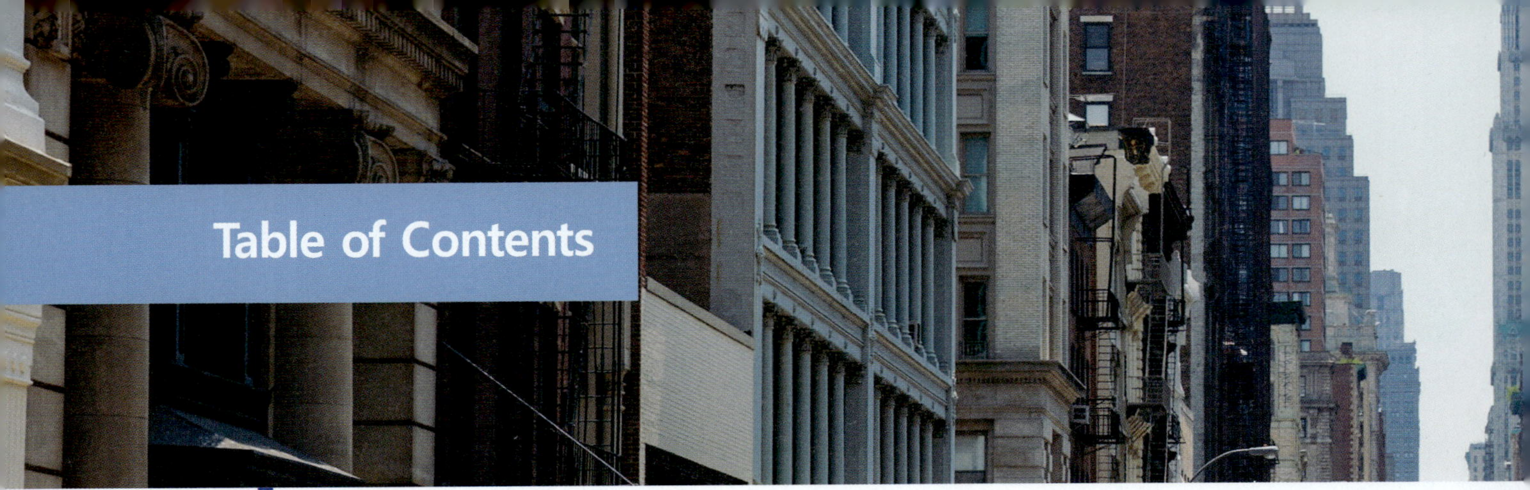

Table of Contents

LEARNING OBJECTIVES	IN THIS UNIT STUDENTS WILL ...
PERFORMANCE & TASK	create their own professional introduction narratives.
CRITICAL THINKING SKILLS 1	examine the nuances of effective verbal and non-verbal gestures.
CRITICAL THINKING SKILLS 2	identify their self-introductions' strengths and needs for improvement.
COMMUNICATION SKILLS	communicate effectively about themselves.
PRESENTAION SKILLS	record and critically asses their work in order to improve presentation skills.

UNIT 01

Self-Introduction for Academic & Professional Purposes

[Chapter 1]
Self-introductions in Business Settings

BRAINSTORMING

This unit deals with making an effective self-introduction. **Non-verbal factors** mean **physical gestures** that make a good impression during a self-introduction. As a group, select three non-verbal factors and explain why they are important for giving positive impressions to the audience. Refer to the following examples using the sample sentence format.

Language Focus

Example Format & Requirements

Use because, as, since + S + V. as the sample sentence shows.

1) **Smiling face** of the speaker is important **because it shows** the positive attitude of the speaker to the audience.

   → S + V because S + V.

2) **Because smiling face shows** the positive attitude of the speaker to the audience, it is an important factor in the presentation.

   → Because S + V, S + V.

1) Three important non-verbal factors (Use the sample sentence format)

(1) ______________________________

____

(2) ______________________________

____

(3) ______________________________

____

Video & Note-taking Activity

Watch a video about **self-introduction**. While watching the video, take notes and answer the following questions.

1) Is it a good or **bad self-introduction**? Why do you think so?

2) What are the factors of a **bad self-introduction**?

Watch another video about **self-introduction**. While watching the video, take notes and answer the following questions.

1) Is it a good or **bad self-introduction**? Why do you think so?

3) What are the factors of a **good self-introduction**??

Nonverbal Factors

Non-verbal factors in a self-introduction mean the use of physical manners that include Factors 1, 2, 3, and 4. Refer to the following factors required for an effective self-introduction in academic as well as business settings.

1) Non-verbal Factor 1: Smiling Face

(1) Be natural.

(2) Practice makes perfect.

2) Non-verbal Factor 2: Eye Contact

(1) Do not stare at your listeners too intensely.

(2) Do not blink too much.

(3) Look at the central points between peoples' eyebrows.
→ MiGan Contact = 미간 = 眉 間 in Korean

(4) Focus back onto people only after looking around for a few seconds.

(5) Maintain eye contact but be sure not to stare at one person for a long time.

(6) Have a conversation with yourself in front of a mirror.

3) Non-verbal Factor 3: Natural Hand Gestures

(1) Don't point directly with your finger.

(2) Gesture with an open palm facing upwards.

(3) Do not point at somebody's face.

(4) Do not point with your feet.

4) Non-verbal Factor 4: Posture

(1) Do not sway.

(2) Do not slouch.

(3) Do not lean on the podium.

Writing Activity

Answer the following questions to check your understanding of non-verbal factors from 1 to 4.

1) What are the most useful non-verbal factors that you would like to remember for your own self-introduction? Write two or three factors that make your self- introduction better.

(Use the sentence format of S+V because S+V. or Because S+V, S+V.)

VERBAL FACTORS

Verbal factors in a self-introduction mean the use of good verbal manners including Factors 1, 2, 3, 4, and 5. Refer to the following factors to make an effective self-introduction in academic as well as business settings.

1) Verbal Factor 1: Volume

(1) Speak at an appropriate volume (not too loud or quiet) for your audience.

(2) Use a microphone if your voice is not loud enough.

2) Verbal Factor 2: Tone of Voice

(1) Use a consistent and comfortable tone.

(2) A gentle and soft tone is better than a high-pitched tone.

3) Verbal Factor 3: Speed & Use of Pauses

(1) Speak at an appropriate speed (not too fast or slow) during your presentation.

(2) Speaking slowly with good pauses is better than speaking fast.

4) Verbal Factor 4: Intonation

(1) Use appropriate and clear intonation (up & down) during your presentation.

5) Verbal Factor 5: Pronunciation

(1) Speak with correct and clear pronunciation.

(2) Be careful of pronouncing words starting with **p-f, b-v, r-l**.

Writing Activity

Answer the following questions to check your understanding of verbal factors from 1 to 5.

1) What are the most useful verbal factors that you would like to remember for your own self-introduction? Write **two or three factors** to improve your self- introduction. (Use a complete sentence format)

(1) ______________________________

____

____

____

(2) ______________________________

____

____

____

(3) ______________________________

____

____

____

PROFESSIONAL SPEAKING SKILLS

For your self-introduction, think about your unique characteristics. Please include any information that would **make yourself unique or different from others** using the self-introduction categories in the box.

Self-introduction Categories

Seven Categories

(1) Name and age

(2) Major

(3) Why you selected this major

(4) Where you are from and where you live

(5) Favorite ways to spend your free time
(e.g., Provide details about activities, foods, pets, songs, movie genres, game titles, etc.)

(6) Unique things about you (e.g., past experience of success or failure, travel, achievements, talents, etc.)

(7) Your goal (e.g., What you want to learn from this class)

Check-up Questions

Fill in the blanks with the **correct category numbers**. Then write one specific **self- introduction** paragraph (**seven to ten sentences)** to explain your unique characteristics using the seven categories.

Example Writing with Self-Introduction Categories

Hello, nice to meet you.

(***1—Name and Age***) *I am YunJu Jeon and I am 21 years old.*

( ) *I am from Gwangju, Jeolla Province in Korea, which takes almost four hours by bus.*

( ) *My major is Computer Science because*

( ) *I am good at coding and interested in developing my own games.*

( ) *I go to Department of Convergence IT Technology, in Department of IT, at Soongsil University in Korea.*

( ) *I like playing role play games online while I have free time.*

( ) *My favorite thing is watching pet-tube in online because I am a animal lover.*

( ) *Even though my hometown is Kwangju, I live in University Dormitory now and I am very lonely.*

( ) *Therefore, I want to make good friends in this class and improve my speaking ability in English.*

Speaking Activity

Using the following seven categories, please do a pair-work activity with your partner. Let your partner ask the questions in the box and you are supposed to answer and fill in the blanks.

Number	Categories	Your partner's question	Your answer (In complete sentence)
1	Name and age	What's your name?	e.g., My name is Jimin and I am 22 years old. You can call me ______ **Your answer** ______________________________
2	Major	What's your major? What are you studying?	**Your answer** I am majoring in ______________ at Soongsil University. My major is ______________. I am studying ______________.

3	Why you selected this major	Why are you studying that major? (e.g., Korean literature, Computer science, politics)	e.g., I am studying computer science because I am good at coding and programming. **Your answer** I am studying Korean literature (e.g., English, Bio Engineering, etc.) because ______________________.
4	Where you live	Where do you live? How long does it take from your house to university?	e.g., I live in Incheon and it takes one and a half hours from my house to Soongsil University. **Your answer** I live in ______________ and it takes ______________.
5	Favorite ways to spend your free time	What are your hobbies? What are your favorite activities when you have free time?	e.g., My hobbies include playing soccer and watching online videos. **Your answer** My favorite activities are ________. because ______________. I like cooking during my free time because ______________. My favorite movie is Parasite because ______________________.
6	Unique things	What are you good at? What is a memorable experience from your past?	e.g,) I am good at singing and dancing because ______________. **Your answer** I am good at ______________ because ______________. I had a good experience ________ because ______________.
7	Your goal in this class	What do you want from this class? What is your goal in this class?	e.g., I want to make a lot of new friends in this class because ________. **Your answer** My goal in this class is ________ because ______________.

ACADEMIC WRITING SKILLS *(**Double space if necessary.)*

Writing Activity: Self-introduction First Draft

Feedback Activity

Using the seven categories, receive <u>two pieces of feedback</u> from your group members. Use a complete sentence format (S+V because S+V. or Because S+V, S+V.).

Peer Feedback 1 (Three things done well and two things to improve)

Peer's Name:

Peer Feedback 2 (Three things done well and two things to improve)

Peer's Name:

Writing Activity: Self-introduction Second Draft

Using the two pieces of feedback from your group members, rewrite the first draft of your self-introduction. Your second draft should now be ready for your professor's feedback.

Professor Feedback

Video & Presentation Activity

For your self-introduction, please record a practice video. Follow the tips and strategies provided in the box below. Watch the video-clips of your group members and write feedback about each clip during the next activity. After that, **select the best clip** from your group members' work. Write the **reasons and details** to support your decision in complete sentences.

Video Guidelines

(1) Using the second draft, read it aloud more than five times to prepare for your effective self-introduction in front of the audience.

(2) Using a smart-phone, have your self-introduction recorded in order to check your eye-contact, smile, and other positive non-verbal factors.

(3) After recording, watch these videos together. Then give feedback to each other in the blanks below.

Feedback from your members

(1) ______________________________

____

____

____

____

(2) ______________________________

____

____

____

____

(3) ______________________________

____

____

____

____

Group Discussion & Video Analysis

From these self introductions with your group members, please **select the best one** with your group and write your reasons below. The reasons should include **this unit's language focus and should be written in complete sentences.** (Use because, as, or since)

Use this page to rewrite your final draft if necessary.

ENGAGED LEARNING PROJECT 1

FINAL SUBMISSION

Title of This Project: ________________

Class Day, Time: ________________

Student ID: ________________

Name: ________________

LEARNING OBJECTIVES	IN THIS UNIT STUDENTS WILL ...
PERFORMANCE & TASK 1	observe the rules of punctuation in formal writing and practicing the guidelines in academic contexts.
PERFORMANCE & TASK 2	follow academic formatting guidelines and apply indentations/block style paragraphs in their essays.
CRITICAL THINKING SKILLS 1	express ideas more clearly in academic writing.
CRITICAL THINKING SKILLS 2	maintain clarity and academic standards in essay writing.
WRITING SKILLS 1	use clauses and conjunctions effectively and write a variety of complete sentences.
WRITING SKILLS 2	produce standardized and professionally presented information.

UNIT 02

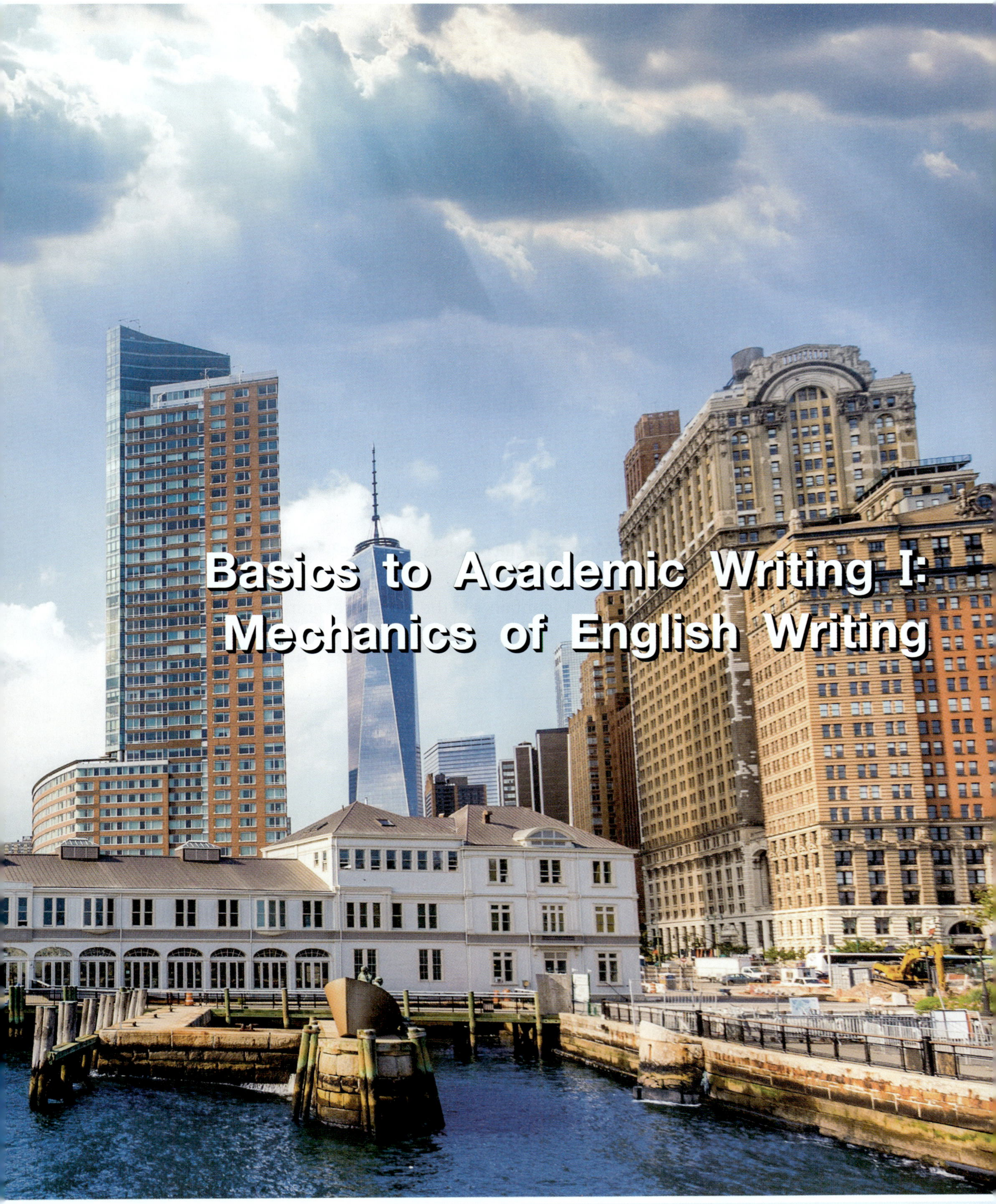

Basics to Academic Writing I: Mechanics of English Writing

[Chapter 1]
Formal English Writing Rules

ACADEMIC WRITING SKILLS

Complete & Incomplete Sentences

What is a Complete Sentence?

A complete sentence includes a subject and a verb. Additionally, it may have a complement or object depending on the verb in the sentence. A simple sentence is a sentence with one independent clause (subject, verb, complement(s), or object(s)) that expresses a complete idea.

What is an Incomplete Sentence?

When a sentence does not contain all the sentence components such as subject, verb, complement(s), or object(s), it is **an incomplete sentence**, which is called a sentence **fragment**.

Check-up Questions

Decide whether each of the following is a fragment (F) or a complete sentence (CS). Write your answer in the space provided and then compare with your partner.

______ 1. By using an autonomous car, people their life more convenient.

______ 2. Excessive use of disposable products can lead to environmental pollution, global warming, and depletion of resources.

______ 3. Augmented reality (A.R.) the digital graphics that convey real-time information to live footage technology and is activated by an open-source video tracking software.

Incomplete Sentence: Misuse of 'Because'

Because + S + V. (X)

A dependent clause, especially with 'Because', cannot be written without an independent clause. This is a common mistake.

– Vehicles are now entering into the era of 'big data'. **Because the on-board computers in cars are creating large amounts of data. (X)**

How to Correct: Because + S + V. (X)

A dependent clause alone cannot be a sentence. In order to make a sentence, there needs to be an independent clause. There are two ways to write a sentence using 'because'.

Correction 1: S + V ~ [no comma] **because + S + V.**
[Independent clause] + [dependent clause]

– Vehicles are now entering into the era of 'big data' **because the on-board computers in cars are creating large amounts of data. (O)**

Correction 2: Because + S + V **[comma],** S + V ~.
[Dependent clause] (Comma)(Space) + [independent clause]

– **Because on-board computers in cars are creating large amounts of data,** vehicles are now entering into the era of 'big data'. **(O)**

TIPS

* There are other dependent clauses, which begin with a subordinating conjunction, such as **when, since, as, although, even though, if, unless, after, before,** etc. These subordinating conjunctions also follow the same rules as above.

* See the **references 1 & 2** for more explanation about 'because of', 'in spite of' and 'despite of'.

Check-up Questions

Decide whether each of the following is a fragment (F) or a complete sentence (CS). Write your answer in the space provided and then compare with your partner.

_____ 1. Datasets continue to grow exponentially. Because they include big data in areas such as complexity and volume.

_____ 2. Because they can gather all the necessary information for an operation inside their field of vision without turning their heads.

_____ 3. Their domain of use in language differs even though both are computer programs that imitate hardware because a hypervisor is not the same as an emulator.

Step-up Optional Activity

Rewrite the following fragments to make them complete sentences.

The Veblen effect refers to a type of product that is in demand simply because of its price This generally creates products that are liked by people Because the product is very expensive For example many people luxury cars Because they are so expensive to buy

Formal Language Style: Contractions & Acronyms

What are 'Contractions'?

A **contraction** is a reduced form of a word, syllable, or word group generated by omitting internal letters and sounds from the spoken and written forms. In formal writing, do not use contractions. Instead, use complete forms as shown below:

- can't → cannot
- don't → do not
- wasn't → was not
- shouldn't → should not
- It's → It is

(Its = A possessive pronoun meaning 'belonging to')

What are 'Acronyms'?

An **acronym** is a word formed from the first letters of a longer name or phrase, commonly using individual first letters, such as EU (European Union). When writing for the first time, do not use acronyms alone **(e.g., EU (X))** but write them with the full words or phrase with the acronym in brackets immediately afterwards. From then on, only the acronym is required. Check the following examples.

- The **European Union (EU)** is a political and economic union consisting of 27 countries mostly in Europe. The United Kingdom left the **EU** on January 31, 2020.
- Limiting global warming to 1.5 degrees Celsius is the safety threshold that has been set by the **Intergovernmental Panel for Climate Change (IPCC)**.

Check-up Questions

Read the following passages. Find the contraction or acronym mistakes and correct them. Compare answers with your partner.

1. Blockchain technology and the IoT have gained immense hype but have also shown that real-world implementation and adoption of these new technologies have been slower than anticipated.

2. Removing carbon dioxide from the atmosphere and achieving net zero emissions may result in all worldwide GHG emissions being counterbalanced.

3. Gatekeeping refers to a type of filtering system used when communicating information to others. Generally, gatekeeping is the act of regulating what can and can't be said or used by someone in a publication, broadcast, the Internet, or any other type of media.

4. In the 1990s, VR technology seemed to transport users into immersive virtual worlds. Unfortunately, limitations of early VR associated with resolution, graphics, and user experience led to disillusionment and a failure to achieve widespread adoption.

Formal Sentence Style

FANBOYS + S + V (X)

'FANBOYS' represents '**For**', '**And**', '**Nor**', '**But**', '**Or**', '**Yet**', '**So**', which are coordinating conjunctions. Coordinating conjunctions should be used in the middle of a sentence to connect two independent clauses.

In academic and business writing, a sentence should not **start with any usage of 'FANBOYS'**.

– The price of the Big Mac is standardized worldwide. **So the cost of the Big Mac is almost the same everywhere. (X)**

How to Correct: FANBOYS + S + V

1) The incorrect sentence above can be written *correctly* as shown below:

– The price of the Big Mac is standardized worldwide, so **the cost of the Big Mac is almost the same everywhere.** (O)

2) At the beginning of the sentence, instead of 'FANBOYS', use other formal connectors as shown below:

(1) And (X) → **In addition,** ~ / **Moreover,** / **Furthermore,** / **Additionally,**

(2) But (X) → **However,** ~ / **Nevertheless,**

(3) So (X) → **Therefore,** ~ / **As a result,**

– The price of the Big Mac is standardized worldwide. Therefore, the cost of the Big Mac is almost constant anywhere. (O)

Check-up Questions

Decide whether each of the following is formal (F) or informal (IF). Write your answer in the space provided and then compare with your partner.

_____ 1. Ever-present mobile computing can be used as a purchasing system on buses and trains. And it can also be used to get food from mobile vendors.

_____ 2. Scientific computing provides an incoming of new knowledge. And this has come about through numerous concepts such as high-performance computing (HPC).

_____ 3. Over ten years ago, many scientific breakthroughs would not have happened. But now things are changing because of scientific computing that is making these breakthroughs possible.

Step-up Optional Activity

Rewrite one of the informal sentences above to make it formal.

____

____

____

____

____

____

____

____

____

Capitalization Rules

Cases Where Capitalization Should be Used

1) **The first word of a sentence**

– gatekeeping refers to a type of filtering system used when communicating information to others. (X)

→ Gatekeeping refers to a type of filtering system used when communicating information to others. (O)

2) **Proper nouns: Specific names of people and places** (e.g. English, the North Pole, First Street)

– In the 1980s, all korean films were filtered through the korean government before being shown in the movie theaters. (X)

→ In the 1980s, all Korean films were filtered through the Korean government before being shown in the movie theaters. (O)

3) **Acronyms**

– Combine information technology (it) infrastructure so that it is in a more integrated and manageable ecosystem. (X)

→ Combine Information Technology (IT) infrastructure so that it is in a more integrated and manageable ecosystem. (O)

TIPS

* Do not capitalize after using formal connectors (In addition, Therefore, etc.)

– Therefore, ~~D~~evelopment in technology affects human society. (X)

→ Therefore, development in technology affects human society. (O)

* Except for proper nouns or acronyms

– Therefore, Korean technology development affects human society. (O)

* **See the reference 3 for more explanation about capitalization rules.**

Check-up Questions

Read the following sentences. Find the capitalization mistakes and correct them. Compare answers with your partner.

1. a business might decide to handle an erp system from its private cloud.

2. bring down expenses when it comes to IT energy/power consumption.

3. additionally, It allows services to be accessed at any place and at any moment, and the infrastructure can be built up in a fast and simple way as any business's requirements change.

4. cameo refers to a brief appearance in a film by someone with celebrity status. for example, song, kang-ho making a small appearance in a marvel movie would be considered a cameo to a south korean movie watcher.

Punctuation Rules 1: Run-on Sentences

Definition of 'Punctuation'

At the end of each sentence, there should be end punctuation. For example, a period (.), question mark (?), or exclamation point (!).

Definition of 'Run-on Sentences' (No correct punctuation)

A run-on sentence is not grammatically correct as there is no proper punctuation (no comma, period, etc.). It confuses the reader because important punctuation is missing between phrases in a run-on sentence.

– The price of the Big Mac is standardized worldwide so the cost of the Big Mac is almost the same everywhere **(X)** (No comma and period)

How to Correct Run-on Sentences

Run-on sentences can be corrected with the use of a comma, period, and/or semicolon, etc.

1) Use of Comma, Period, Semicolon

– The price of the Big Mac is standardized worldwide, **so** the cost of the Big Mac is almost the same everywhere. **(O)**

– The price of the Big Mac is standardized worldwide; the cost of the Big Mac is almost the same everywhere. **(O)**

Check-up Questions

Decide whether each of the following is a run-on sentence (RS) or a complete sentence (CS). Write your answer in the space provided and then compare with your partner.

_____ 1. The price of the Big Mac is standardized worldwide Therefore the cost of the Big Mac is almost the same everywhere

_____ 2. A swing voter refers to a person who is not on any particular side of any bill or candidate that is being voted on but whose decision will be a deciding factor on which side wins or which bills are passed

Step-up Optional Activity

Rewrite one of the run-on sentences above to make it complete sentences.

1. The price of the Big Mac is standardized worldwide Therefore the cost of the Big Mac is almost the same everywhere

____

____

____

____

2. A swing voter refers to a person who is not on any particular side of any bill or candidate that is being voted on but whose decision will be a deciding factor on which side wins or which bills are passed

____

____

____

____

Punctuation Rules 2: Use of Periods (.) & Commas (,)

How to Use Periods (.)

1) At the end of each sentence, a period should always be used.

– As cars become more and more technologically savvy, they will be able to share that data with other cars through cloud computing (X)

→ As cars become more and more technologically savvy, they will be able to share that data with other cars through cloud computing. (O)

2) If a sentence is not a statement, a question mark (?) or an exclamation point (!) should be used at the end.

– Will this lead to safer conditions on the road It's probably too early to know for sure. (X)

→ Will this lead to safer conditions on the road? It's probably too early to know for sure. (O)

How to Use Commas (,)

1) Do not use a comma between an independent clause and a dependent clause.

– Mike needs to be on campus all day because he has many classes on Monday.

[Independent clause] + [dependent clause: because]

2) However, use a comma between a dependent clause and an independent clause.

– Because Mike has many classes on Monday, he needs to be on campus all day.

[Dependent clause: Because ~] + [comma] + [independent clause]

3) Use a comma after conjunctive adverbs (e.g. finally, therefore, however, nevertheless, consequently). However, do not use a comma after 'Then'.

– Finally, Mike finished his last class on Monday.

4) Use a comma in front of coordinating conjunctions (FANBOYS) to separate two independent clauses.

– Mike has many classes on Monday, **but** Stacey does not have a class on Monday.

5) Use a comma to separate items in a series. Put 'and' before the last item in the list.

– Mike has many classes on Monday. For example, APE1, Computer Science 101, Math 101, and History 101.

Check-up Questions

Put the correct punctuation (comma) in the following sentences. Compare answers with your partner.

1. These high-tech hanging gardens show us ways we can save space water and the climate on such an overpopulated planet.

2. However fashion is an important part of a person's life because it is a way to bring out individual personalities it boosts people's self-esteem and it makes people happy by buying clothes or something they like.

3. A flash mob refers to a group of people who suddenly start doing some sort of performance in a public area without prior notice. Flash mobs are planned out via telecommunications social media or viral emails and rehearsed ahead of time in private so as to surprise people when it does happen.

Check-up Questions

Put the correct punctuations (commas and periods) in the following sentences. Also, correct the capitalization. Compare your answer with your partner.

1. Datasets continue to grow exponentially because of big data in areas such as complexity and volume making their analysis archival and sharing one of the diverse challenges of the 21st century Therefore it should not be a surprise that large scale systems, which can help find answers to these grand challenges, have become harder and harder to design and manage

2. The placebo effect refers to the positive or negative effects that people may experience after getting 'fake' medical treatment that they believe to be genuine people may begin to actually feel better if they are told that the shot they received will help them recover from a cold

3. On-board computers are now making many parts of your car automated from the stereo and navigation to the brakes and accelerator vehicles are now entering into the era of "big data" Because just like the desktop computer, the on-board computers in a car create a large portion of data most of this data collection is about things like how people operate their vehicle And it can be used to find trends and correct problems that might be present.

Formatting 1: Indentation & Block Style

Indentation

Indent the first sentence of a paragraph by pressing the **'space bar' five times** or **'Tab' once**.

However, fashion is an important part of a person's life because it is a way to bring out individual personalities, it boosts people's self-esteem, and it makes people happy by buying clothes or something they like. (X)

↓

    However, fashion is an important part of a person's life because it is a way to bring out individual personalities, it boosts people's self-esteem, and it makes people happy by buying clothes or something they like. (O)

Block Style

Do not start each new sentence on a new line (in order to make it **block style**). After 'period', do not use the **'Enter'** to change to a new line.

However, fashion is an important part of a person's life.
This is because it is a way to bring out individual personalities.
It boosts people's self-esteem.
It makes people happy by buying clothes or something they like. (X)

↓

However, fashion is an important part of a person's life. **This** is because it is a way to bring out individual personalities. **It** boosts people's self-esteem. **It** makes people happy by buying clothes or something they like. **(O)**

Formatting 2: No Extra Line Spacing Between Paragraphs

Example of Incorrect Line Spacing

For instance, smartphone applications such as Gokemon For and Znatchap filters are two of the most popular examples of contemporary AR applications. Moreover, this technology has been developed by the most powerful computing hardware as well as the software system known as ComTool that can be used as one of the most adaptive tools in health care, education, fashion, business and manufacturing.

(X)

In addition, AR technologies can be applied in the health care sector. Surgeons can use digital images and other necessary information in 3D which AR produces while performing a procedure (...)

Example of Correct Line Spacing

For instance, smartphone applications such as Gokemon For and Znatchap filters are two of the most popular examples of contemporary AR applications. Moreover, this technology has been developed by the most powerful computing hardware as well as the software system known as ComTool that can be used as one of the most adaptive tools in health care, education, fashion, business and manufacturing.
In addition, AR technologies can be applied in the health care sector. Surgeons can use digital images and other necessary information in 3D which AR produces while performing a procedure (...)

Check-up Question

Choose the correct answer to identify the formatting mistake(s) in the following passage. Compare your answer with a partner.

1.

> Socialtainer is a term that is a combination of the words social and
> entertainer
> and refers to celebrities who speak out
> in support of numerous social issues.
> This is very familiar in Western cultures,
> but a relatively new thing
> in many Eastern cultures,
> such as Korea.

① Indentation mistake

② Block style mistake

③ Line spacing mistake

④ Indentation and block style mistake

Sum-up: Key Points & Rules about Formal English Writing

There are different rules between formal and informal writing, as shown below.

1. Sentence vs. Fragment

1) Write a sentence that includes a subject and a verb. It may have a complement or object.

2) Do not write a fragment.

e.g., [Because + S + V + period] (X)
→ S + V ~ [no comma] **because + S + V.**
→ Because + S + V **[comma],** S + V ~.

2. Formal Language Style

1) Do not use contractions.

e.g., don't → do not
wasn't → was not

2) Write the acronyms with the original name or phrase first **(e.g., European Union (EU)**. From the second reference onwards, write the first letters only **(e.g., EU)**.

3) Do not start a sentence with FANBOYS, which are not formal.

e.g., And → In addition, ~
But → However, ~
So → Therefore, ~

3. Capitalization

1) Capitalize the first letter of a sentence.

2) Capitalize the first letter of proper nouns (specific names and places).

e.g., english → English

3) Capitalize all the letters of acronyms.

e.g., eu → EU
unesco → UNESCO

4. Punctuation

1) Put the correct punctuation at the end of a sentence (e.g., Period (.)).

2) Use a comma to separate two independent clauses, items in a series, and after a conjunctive adverb (e.g. Therefore, ~).

5. Formatting and Indentation

1) Indent the first sentence of each new paragraph by pressing the 'space bar' five times or 'Tab' once.

2) Do not start each new sentence on a new line (in order to make it block style).

3) There should be no extra line spacing between paragraphs.

Review Check-up Questions (Chapter 1~ Chapter 3)

The following passages contents many mistakes in terms of formal writing. Find all of the mistakes and correct them. Write your answer in the space provided and then compare with your partner.

1. according to the cisco visual networking index mobile data use will rise by 18 percent between 2011 and 2016 this is due to the fact that numerous systems in urban realms use a large networking infrastructure gigabit-bandwidth backbones high-speed relays and unlimited power and recharging capabilities

2. an experimental farm located in el paso, texas is pictured above it is helping to bring about a reduction in water and fertilizer waste Because crops are growing

3. the master of vertical farming techniques dickson despommier came to have such a title because his students were upset at columbia university in new york city dickinson despommier lectures on parasitism and environmental disruption

4. glen kertz, ceo of valcent, (a tech company found in el paso, texas that is attempting to incorporate vertical farming as part of its business ventures) says, "Vertical farming could allow food to be grown locally and sustainably."

5. gatekeeping refers to a type of filtering system used when communicating information to others generally gatekeeping is the act of regulating what can and cannot be said or used by someone in a publication broadcast the Internet or any other type of media

6. galápagos syndrome refers to how some products evolve differently when considering where the product was developed for example, japaense 3g mobile phones became very popular in japan because of specialized features that Japanese people liked But the product was not successful in other countries Because the features were only appealing to the Japanese

Reference 1: Incomplete Sentence: Misuse of 'Because of'

Because of + S + V. (X)

As 'of' is a preposition, after 'because of', it is impossible to write a subject and a verb. This is a common mistake.

- Because of intelligent mobile systems have been created. (X)
- Because of AI functions have been more advanced. (X)

How to Correct: Because of + S + V. (X)

As 'of' is a preposition, after 'because of', write a noun (or a gerund (~ing)).

Correction: **Because of + noun (O)**

- Because of their heavy social media use, depression and other mental disorders often occur in teens. **(O)**
- Depression and other mental disorders often occur in teens because of their heavy social media use. **(O)**

Check-up Questions

Decide whether each of the following is a fragment (F) or a complete sentence (CS). Write your answer in the space provided and then compare with your partner.

_____ 1. Because of big data in areas such as complexity and volume continue to grow exponentially.

_____ 2. Climate change could cause disease problems because of climate change induces the migration of animals to their habitats.

_____ 3. The more frequently they use smartphones for solving something, the harder it will be to think creatively because of they may just search for other's idea on the Internet.

Step-up Optional Activity

Rewrite one of the fragments above to make it a complete sentence.

Reference 2: Incomplete Sentence: Misuse of 'In spite of' & 'Despite'

In spite of + Subject + Verb (X)

It is wrong to write a subject and a verb after 'in spite of'.

– In spite of there were many external databases. **(X)**

How to Correct

After 'in spite of', write a noun or a gerund (~ing).

Correction: In spite of having many external databases, **(O)**

Despite of (X)

It is incorrect to write 'of' after 'despite'. It is also incorrect to write a subject and a verb after 'despite'.

1) **Despite ~~of~~ (X)**
   – Despite of artificial intelligence, solving problems was not simple. (X)

2) **Despite + Subject + Verb (X)**
   – Despite artificial intelligence is the ability. (X)

How to Correct

After 'despite', do not write 'of' and write a noun or a gerund (~ing).

Correction: **Despite + noun** (or **~ing** (gerund) (O)

– Despite artificial intelligence, solving problems were not simple. (O)

TIPS

In spite of + noun (or ~ing)

Despite + noun (or ~ ing)
Although + subject + verb, subject + verb
Even though + subject + verb, subject + verb

Check-up Questions

Decide whether each of the following is a fragment (F) or a complete sentence (CS). Write your answer in the space provided and then compare with your partner.

_____ 1. In spite of 3D printing has made significant advancements in health care, the limitations in speed caused the initial expensive advertisement.

_____ 2. Despite of 3D printing's significant advancements in health care, the limitations in cost lead the initial expensive advertisement.

_____ 3. Even though automated cars could dramatically help make the driver safer, it still faces some obstacles that will need to be figured out.

_____ 4. Although 3D printing's significant advancements in health care, the limitations in cost lead the initial expensive advertisement.

Reference 3: More Capitalization Rules

Capitalization of the Titles of Paragraphs, Essays, Books, and Films

1) Always capitalize the first letter of a title

– new AI Coding Assistant

→ New AI Coding Assistant

2) Capitalize the important words of a title (e.g. noun, adjective, adverb, etc.)

– the Elements of Statistical Learning

→ The Elements of Statistical Learning

3) Do not capitalize articles (a, an, the), prepositions (to, in), and conjunctions (and, but) in the middle of the title. However, capitalize if they are the first letter of the title.

– artificial intelligence: foundations of computational agents **(X)**

→ Artificial Intelligence: Foundations of Computational Agents **(O)**

Capitalization of Organizations

1) The name of specific schools, companies (e.g. Google), and organizations (e.g. the United Nations) must always be capitalized.

– Go to the home page of the university of london for the online application. (X)

→ Go to the home page of the University of London for the online application. (O)

– boston university is in Boston, Massachusetts. **(X)**

→ Boston University is in Boston, Massachusetts. **(O)**

Capitalization of the Days

1) The name of days of the week, months, and holidays, must always be capitalized. However, do not capitalize the name of seasons (e.g. spring, summer, fall, winter).

– The **f**ourth of **j**uly is **i**ndependence **d**ay, which is a federal holiday in the United States. (X)

→ The **F**ourth of **J**uly is **I**ndependence **D**ay, which is a federal holiday in the United States. (O)

Check-up Question

Read the following sentences. Find all capitalization mistakes and correct them. Compare your answer with your partner.

The book, chatgpt code interpreter: do data science In minutes, was published in march of 2023 by standford university.

LEARNING OBJECTIVES	IN THIS UNIT STUDENTS WILL ...
PERFORMANCE & TASK	paraphrase content supporting sentences and produce academically sound written work.
CRITICAL THINKING SKILLS 1	distinguish between proper and improper paraphrasing and examine various writing.
CRITICAL THINKING SKILLS 2	prevent academic misconduct and demonstrate citations or reported speech correctly.
COMMUNICATION SKILLS	evaluate and improve the quality of paraphrased sentences by comparing original texts with paraphrased versions.
WRITING SKILLS	replace words with appropriate synonyms and/or altering words or phrases and recreate ideas and evidence from other text.

UNIT 03

Basics to Academic Writing II: Academic Integrity

[Chapter 1]
Academic Integrity & Misconduct

BRAINSTORMING

Discussion

This unit deals with academic integrity in writing. The word 'integrity' means being honest and fair. As a group, discuss three examples of what violates the rules of 'academic integrity' (e.g., copying someone else's ideas).

Video & Note-taking Activity

Watch a video about 'academic integrity.' While watching the video, take notes and answer the following questions.

1. What is 'academic integrity'?

2. What are some examples of 'academic integrity'?

3. What are some examples of 'academic misconduct'?

____

____

____

____

ACADEMIC WRITING SKILLS

Type of Academic Misconduct 1: Using Generative Artificial Intelligence (AI) or Electronic Translation Tools

The use of generative artificial intelligence (AI) tools (such as ChatGPT and bard) or electronic translation tools (such as Papago and Google Translate) IS NOT permitted for any assignment in this course for the following reasons:

1) It is NOT students' own work.
2) It is considered to be cheating.
3) It can lead to a loss of meaning because AI or translation tools cannot comprehend the context.

Type of Academic Misconduct 2: Plagiarism

What is plagiarism?

In an academic setting, using another author's ideas or expressions without proper acknowledgment is called **plagiarism**, which is academic theft. Possible consequences of plagiarism include a failing grade on the assignment, expulsion from the class, and/or dismissal from the institute.

What are common forms of plagiarism?

1) Submitting someone else's work as your own
2) Copying and pasting five or more consecutive words
3) Rewriting someone's ideas without a proper citation
4) Providing a proper citation, but failing to rewrite the ideas

How to avoid plagiarism?

1) Paraphrasing: Rewriting someone else's ideas using different words to what the author originally wrote them AND
2) Citing: Giving the author(s) credit when paraphrasing

Check-up Questions

Answer the following questions to check your understanding of plagiarism.

1. Using someone else's idea as your own is best defined as:
   ① citation ② paraphrasing
   ③ academic misconduct ④ plagiarism
   ⑤ cheating

2. Which of the following must be cited? Select all that apply.
   ① charts/ tables/ pictures ② paraphrased ideas
   ③ your original ideas ④ summarized ideas

3. All of the following are forms of plagiarism EXCEPT:
   ① submitting someone else's work as your own
   ② providing citations without paraphrasing
   ③ copying and pasting more than five consecutive words
   ④ paraphrasing someone else's ideas with proper citations

[Chapter 2]

A Guide to Academic Integrity

ACADEMIC WRITING SKILLS

Avoiding Plagiarism 1: Paraphrasing

How to Paraphrase a Text

1) Rearrange the sentence by changing the order of the words and phrases instead of copying the structure of the original.

[Original sentence] Though social networks allow huge opportunities, an increase of these brings new risks.

[Changing the order of the words] An increase of social networks brings new risks though they allow huge opportunities.

2) Then try to substitute the original words with their synonyms.

[Using synonyms] A growing use of social networks may lead to unexpected problems in spite of their positive aspects.

TIPS

* Remember both 1) and 2) to avoid the risk of being accused of plagiarism.
* Retain key terms (e.g., social networks) since changing them may not convey the same meaning.

Check-up Questions

For the given original sentence below, match the paraphrase with the correct strategy.

> Intellectual property grants exclusive rights to the creators, ensuring they can control and benefit from their creations.

1.
Intellectual property gives sole privileges upon the inventors, guaranteeing their ability to manage and profit from their innovations.

2.
Sole privileges are bestowed to the inventors, guaranteeing their ability to manage and profit from their innovations.

3.
Exclusive rights are granted to the creators through intellectual property, ensuring they can control and benefit from their creations.

- changing the order of the words
- using synonyms
- changing the order of the words + using synonyms

Avoiding Plagiarism 2: Inserting an In-text Citation

How to Insert an In-text Citation

1) In-text citations are citations within the main body of the text.
2) In-text citations must be included when paraphrasing ideas taken from another piece of work.
3) In-text citations include the **last name(s)** of the author(s) and date of publication only. Examples are as follows:
   (1) One author:
   - According to Watson (2023), ...
   - Watson (2023) states ...
   - ... (Watson, 2023).

(2) Two authors:
- According to Watson and Miller (2023), ...
- Watson and Miller (2023) state ...
- ... (Watson & Miller, 2023).

(3) Three or more authors:
- According to Watson, Miller, and Boyd (2023), ...
- Watson, Miller, and Boyd (2023) state ...
- ... (Watson, Miller, & Boyd, 2023).

TIPS

* When there are three or more authors, all names should be listed for the first citation as above, but for further ones:
  - According to Watson, et al. (2023), ...
  - Watson, et al. (2023) state ...
  - ... (Watson, et al., 2023).

Check-up Questions

Read the following sentences. Please cross out any errors with the in-text citations and provide the correct version in the blank space. There might be more than one error in one sentence.

1. Recent advancements in artificial intelligence have revolutionized the way companies analyze data, enabling them to make more informed decisions and gain a competitive edge in the market (David Schultz, 2023).

____

2. In her recent article, Fisher (April, 2017) stated that companies have implemented a comprehensive digital marketing strategy, leveraging social media platforms and influencer collaborations in response to changing consumer preferences.

____

3. Mendes & Chen (2020) argued that the recent cybersecurity breach at a multinational corporation highlights the pressing need for organizations to fortify their network defenses and regularly update their software to safeguard sensitive customer data.

---

4. Secondary batteries, such as lithium-ion cells, have become increasingly popular due to their ability to store and release energy multiple times, making them essential for portable electronic devices like smartphones and laptops (Rhymes, B. and Emerson, D. 2018).

Reporting Verbs

Reporting Verbs

Whenever a citation is used, it should be introduced using a reporting verb.

1) Reporting something the author(s)/research <u>did</u>:
   analyze, assess, conclude, demonstrate, examine, find, identify, investigate, prove, report, show

2) Reporting something the author(s)/research <u>stated</u>:
   comment, describe, discuss, point out, note, remark, write

3) Reporting the author(s)'s <u>opinion</u>:
   advocate, argue, assert, believe, claim, contend, deny, maintain, propose, recommend, reject, suggest, view

TIPS

* These verbs are not always interchangeable, so make sure to read the resource carefully and understand the author's claims before choosing an appropriate verb.

Check-up Questions

Read the following research abstract and fill in the blanks with one of the reporting verbs.

This research paper ____________ the impact of Social Networking Sites (SNS) on individuals' engagement in political activities. Through a comprehensive analysis of user behavior and attitudes, this study describes how SNS platforms influence political participation, encompassing activities such as sharing political content, discussing social issues, and interacting with political candidates. By employing both quantitative surveys and qualitative interviews, the research shows that SNS serve as vehicles for political mobilization, information dissemination, and fostering civic engagement. Based on the findings, researchers ____________ that understanding how SNS affect political engagement is important for improving democratic participation in the digital era.

ACADEMIC READING

Pre-reading Activity

Read the definitions of the key vocabulary found in the example paragraph. Fill in the blanks with the correct form of the words in bold.

transmit (v) to send or pass something from one person, place or thing to another
contribute to (phr. v) to help to make something happen
emission (n) the act of sending out light, heat, gas or other substances
substantial (adj) significant in size, amount, or importance
release (v) to set free, let go, or allow something to be liberated from confinement or control
generate (v) to produce, create, or bring into existence
staggering (adj) extremely surprising
worrisome (adj) causing worry
awareness (n) consciousness, knowledge, or understanding of something
imperative (adj) crucial, essential, or mandatory to be done or followed

1. The company's profits showed a ____________ increase of 300% in just one year, leaving both investors and analysts in awe.

2. Public service announcements play a vital role in raising ____________ about the importance of regular exercise and healthy lifestyle choices.

3. The software developer decided to ____________ the updated version of the app, addressing several user concerns and improving its overall performance.

4. Volunteering at the local food bank can ____________ alleviating hunger and supporting vulnerable members of the community.

5. Using renewable energy sources is crucial to ____________ sustainable electricity and reduce our carbon footprint.

6. The sharp increase in pollution levels is ____________, as it poses a serious threat to the environment and public health.

7. The research findings provided ____________ evidence to support the effectiveness of the new treatment in managing the disease.

8. The satellite is responsible for ____________ data and images from outer space back to the Earth's research centers.

9. Investing wisely and diversifying your portfolio is ____________ to minimize risk and maximize potential returns in the unpredictable world of finance.

10. The new regulations aim to reduce harmful ____________ from vehicles, thereby improving air quality and public health in urban areas.

Reading Activity

Read the following example paragraph first. Then carefully examine five ideas found in the paragraph and their paraphrases. Identify whether each idea is well-paraphrased or not. Write "WP" for a well-paraphrased idea. If an idea is not well-paraphrased, write the reason(s) for that.

Transmitting data through the internet can be harmful to the environment. In fact, it **contributes to** 4% of greenhouse gas **emissions**. This happens because its process requires millions of physical servers in data centers all over the world, and it takes a **substantial** amount of energy to run them. Much of this energy comes from sources that **release** carbon dioxide into the air. To put it another way, browsing the internet or using social media leads to carbon emissions. Some people may say that one individual's use **generates** only a small amount of carbon. However, the total carbon footprint of global digital usage is **staggering** and **worrisome**. Unfortunately, there seems to be a lack of **awareness** of the problem. Suppose that 150,000,000 emails are sent in one minute. This releases approximately 600,000 kg of carbon dioxide, which is equal to burning 232,258 kg of coal every minute. While technology is and will be an essential part of people's daily lives, it is **imperative** that individuals become more environmentally conscious and try to find ways to minimize their contribution to the world's digital carbon footprint.

Retrieved and modified from: https://www.viessmann.co.uk/en/company/blog/the-worlds-digital-carbon-footprint.html

a. Transmitting data through the internet can be harmful to the environment.
→ Transmitting data through the internet can be bad to the environment.

---

b. Its process requires millions of physical servers in data centers all over the world.
→ Its procedures takes a lot of physical helpers in data places all over the world.

---

c. Browsing the internet or using social media leads to carbon emissions.
→ Carbon is being emitted whenever an individual uses the internet or social media.

---

d. Some people may say that one individual's use generates only a small amount of carbon. However, the total carbon footprint of global digital usage is staggering and worrisome.

→ Some might say that one person's use makes only a little amount of carbon dioxide. On the contrary, the total amount of carbon footstep in the world is a lot and worrying.

---

e. It is imperative that individuals become more environmentally conscious and try to find ways to minimize their contribution to the world's digital carbon footprint.

→ It is essential for individuals to raise their environmental awareness and to take actions to lessen their influence on the global digital carbon emissions.

ACADEMIC WRITING

Writing Activity

Write the letter of the idea which was not well paraphrased (plagiarized) from the previous Reading Activity. Then paraphrase it with a proper in-text citation using the information below.

> 1) Authors: Joseph Maxwell & Sandra McKay
> 2) Year of publication: 2022
> 3) Use one of the reporting verbs as needed

1. Paraphrase for <u>a</u>

Maxwell and McKay (2022) remarked that the environment can be adversely affected by sending data via the internet. OR The environment can be adversely affected by sending data via the internet (Maxwell & McKay, 2022).

2. Paraphrase for ___

3. Paraphrase for ___

Feedback Activity

For each of your paraphrases and in-text citations, receive feedback from your group members and the professor.

1. Paraphrase for ___

Peer Feedback

Done by: ___________________

Professor Feedback

2. Paraphrase for ___

Peer Feedback

____

____

____

____

Done by: ______________

Professor Feedback

____

____

____

____

Rewriting Activity

Based on the feedback, complete your paraphrased sentences with a proper in-text citation in the following page for submission.

ENGAGED LEARNING PROJECT 2

FINAL SUBMISSION

Class Day, Time: ________________

Student ID: ________________

Name: ________________

LEARNING OBJECTIVES	IN THIS UNIT STUDENTS WILL ...
PERFORMANCE & TASK	develop the ability to revise topic sentences.
CRITICAL THINKING SKILLS 1	understand the organization of well-constructed paragraphs and improve clarity and coherence in their writing.
CRITICAL THINKING SKILLS 2	recognize the significance of a topic sentence, draft a topic sentence with a controlling idea, and prioritize its role in expressing the main idea of a paragraph.
COMMUNICATION SKILLS	share peer reviews, getting feedback, and adjust topic sentences.
WRITING SKILLS	identify the structure of model paragraphs and examine its three parts in reading passages.

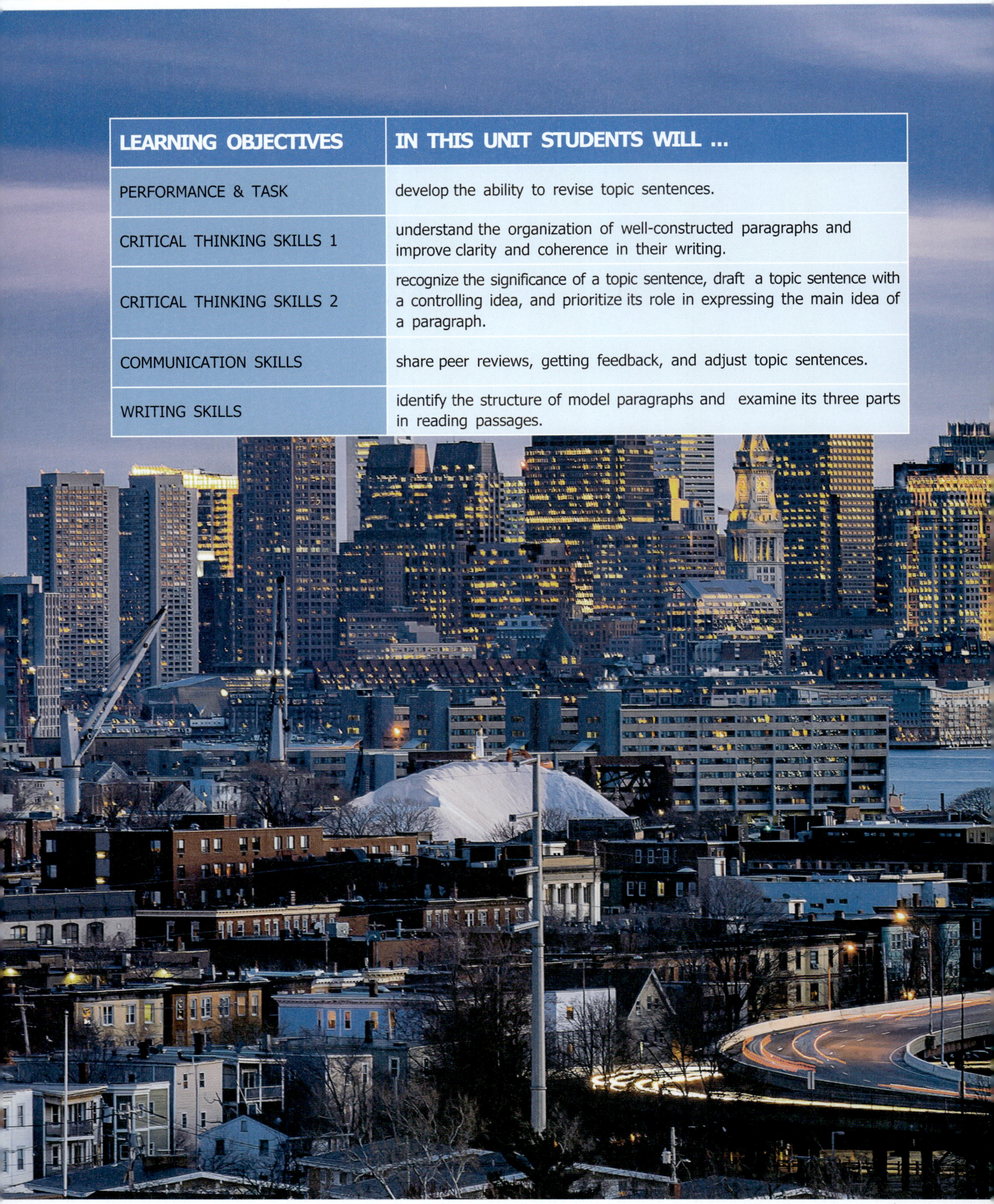

UNIT 04

Writing a Paragraph I: Paragraph Structure & Topic Sentence

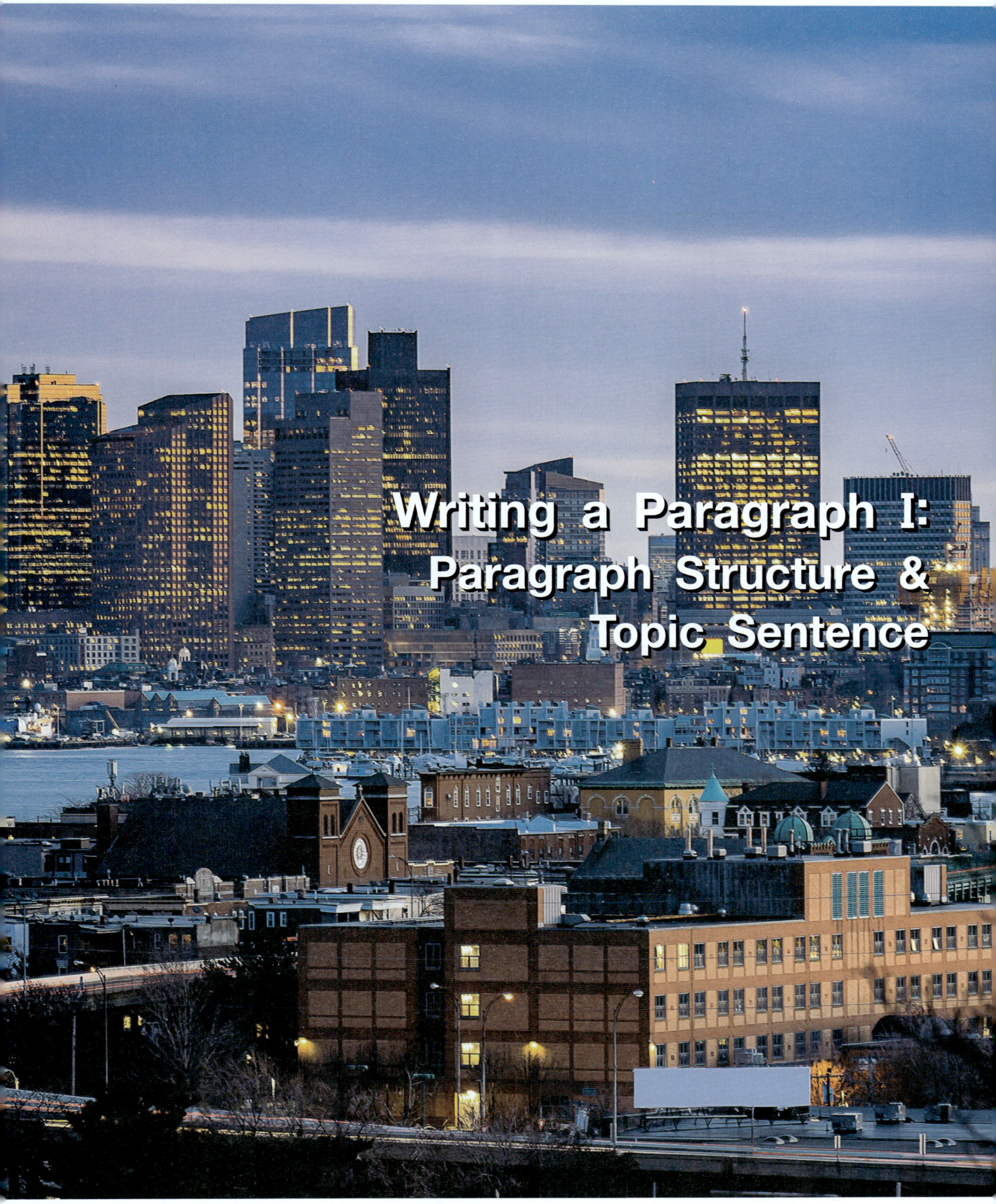

[Chapter 1]
Presenting Ideas in a Logical Manner 1
How to Write a Topic Sentence

ACADEMIC WRITING SKILLS (Part 1)

Presenting an Idea in a Logical Manner: A paragraph

Read the following resource: **Organizing a Paragraph**.

Take brief notes about how to present ideas in English in a logical manner. Please (1) pay close attention to the basics of delivering one main idea (or main point), (2) see how the first sentence may work as an appropriate topic sentence that suggests the main idea, and then, (3) practice writing the topic sentence following the basic components.

Organizing a Paragraph

The Paragraph Structure

When presenting ideas, speakers or writers should organize the main idea or main points in a logical manner. A **paragraph** refers to the **basic unit of organizing one main point**.

A paragraph normally includes several sentences (7-13 sentences) consisting of three parts as follows:

1) **Topic Sentence** (**T.S.**): Usually, the first sentence
2) **Supporting Sentences** (**S.S.**): The chunks of sentences between the T.S. and C.S.
3) **Concluding Sentence** (**C.S.**): The last sentence that summarizes the T.S.

Look at **the paragraph structure** as follows:

(1) Topic Sentence (**T.S.**)	**Topic + Controlling Idea (C. I.)**
(2) Supporting Sentences 1 (**S.S.**) (2) Supporting Sentences 2 (**S.S.**)	Facts, Examples, Reasons
(3) Concluding Sentence (**C.S.**)	Summarizing & Reminding

The Topic Sentence (T.S.)

1) Is the most important sentence in a paragraph.
2) Is usually, the first sentence in a paragraph.
3) Is used when **presenting the main idea for the first time**.
4) Consists of two parts:
   (1) **Topic (=subject=theme=what)** of the sentence
   (2) **Controlling idea (C. I.: how / why / what about / reasons)** of the sentence
5) Needs **one topic** in **one paragraph**.
6) Introduces **one controlling idea** to **limit, guide, and control** what you are discussing.

Some examples of topic sentences are:

Fields	Topic: What, Theme	Controlling Idea (C. I.): How, Why, What about & Reasons
Bio & Health Science	Gene-editing technology has led in a new era in biotechnology	because it has initiated detailed changes to a live organism's DNA and has the potential to decrease disease by altering genes.
IT & Engineering	Battery module packs consisting of high-density lithium ion cells have attracted huge attention in the IT industry.	since they are used in various fields such as grid-scale energy storage devices and commercial applications.

Writing Activity

Please review **Organizing a Paragraph** (p. 72) and summarize in your own words. How is a paragraph normally composed of?

In your opinion, what are the **two most important technologies** that have changed human history or influenced our lives? Why? Referring to the T.S. examples (p. 73), please **select two different fields** and write **a topic and a specific controlling idea**.

Fields	Topic: What, Theme	Controlling Idea (C. I.): How, Why, What about & Reasons

How to Organize a Good Topic Sentence

1) Don't forget to **write a clear controlling idea** (C.I.).
→ Include "how" and "why".

Gene-editing technology is very helpful for humans.
→ Is it a **good T. S**? Why or why not?
Your answer is:

____

2) Should not be **too general or vague**.

Gene-editing technology has developed human history.
→ Is it a **good T. S**? Why or why not?
Your answer is:

____

3) Should not be **too specific** while stating **particular examples and details**.

The gene-editing technology research has been continuing since 1980.
→ Is it a **good T. S**? Why or why not?
Your answer is:

____

4) Should include **one appropriately specific controlling idea** that helps the audience to **limit, guide, and control on their own** as you introduce your main point.

Gene-editing technology has led to a new era in biotechnology since it caused **changes in life expectancy by altering genes**.
→ Is it a **good T. S**? Why or why not?
Your answer is:

____

Check-up Questions

Please write whether you think the following example sentences are **excellent, good, bad, or terrible** and give your reasons (S+V because S+V. or Because S+V, S+V.).

1) Augmented reality (A.R.) **means digital graphics**.

→ Is it a **good T. S.**? Why or why not?

Your answer is:

____

2) Augmented reality (A.R.) **conveys real-time information to live footage technology**.

→ Is it a **good T. S.**? Why or why not?

Your answer is:

____

3) Augmented reality (A.R.) **is activated by open-source video tracking software**.

→ Is it a **good T. S.**? Why or why not?

Your answer is:

____

4) Augmented reality (A.R.) refers to **digital graphics** which convey **real-time information to live footage technology and is activated by open-source video tracking software**.

→ Is it a **good T. S.**? Why or why not?

Your answer is:

____

5) In the highly-connected global world of YouTube and SNS, the K-pop explosion **has broken down cultural barriers** as well as **played a remarkable role in the country's growing economy**.

→ Is it a **good T. S.**? Why or why not?

Your answer is:

____

6) Gene-editing researchers at Soongsil University independently **discovered a bacterial immune system known as CELLISPR in 2013**.

→ Is it a **good T. S.**? Why or why not?

Your answer is:

---

7) Gene-editing technology **has raised ethical questions**.

→ Is it a **good T. S.**? Why or why not?

Your answer is:

---

8) Gene-editing technology **has raised ethical questions** ever since research in this field started in 1980.

→ Is it a **good T. S.**? Why or why not?

Your answer is:

---

9) Human gene-editing technology has raised **ethical questions in regard to using it for reproductive purposes**.

→ Is it a **good T. S.**? Why or why not?

Your answer is:

---

10) Gene-editing technology has led to a new era in biotechnology since **it has changed life expectancy by altering human genes**.

→ Is it a **good T. S.**? Why or why not?

Your answer is:

[Chapter 2]
Academic Reading in Content Area
PROFESSIONAL READING SKILLS (Part 1): IT & Engineering

Pre-Reading Activity

Read the definitions of the key vocabulary found in the example paragraph.

convey (v) to transmit or communicate
footage (n) film/video sequences
contemporary (adj) present-time; modern
application (n) a formal request or a software program
adaptive (adj) able to adjust to situations
manufacturing (n) large-scale goods production
surgeon (n) a medical specialist in surgery
precision (n) accuracy and exactness
consumer device (n) electronics for personal use

Fill in the blanks with the correct form of the words in bold.

1. The _______ algorithms used in the new software make it superior to older versions.
2. The software team reviewed the video _______ of their product demo to confirm all features were presented correctly.
3. In networking, protocols are used to _______ data between devices efficiently.
4. The _______ for the graphic design tool has become more popular among designers and artists.
5. A medical _______ often uses robotic tools which demand programming and precise control.
6. In engineering, _______ in measurements is vital; even a slight variation can lead to a product malfunction.
7. The _______ nature of modern AI algorithms allows them to improve their performance based on real-time feedback.
8. The _______ of computer chips requires a clean environment to ensure no defects.
9. Smartphones, the most commonly used _______, are constantly updated to include the latest technological advancements.

Reading & Analyzing Activity: Augmented Reality-AR

For a topic sentence analysis, read the paragraph below. Then carefully examine, underline the topic and controlling idea, and think about **any important information that makes the sentence a T.S.** in this paragraph.

Augmented Reality & Application in the Real World

[T.S.] Augmented reality (A.R.) means the digital graphics [Topic], which **conveys** real-time information to live **footage** technology [Controlling Idea]. and is activated by open-source video tracking software. This technology helps people superimpose digital content, using images, texts, audial & visual images over a real world environment.

[S.S] For instance [Transition], smartphone apps such as Gokemon For and Znatchap filters are two of the most popular examples of **contemporary** A.R **applications**. Moreover, this technology has been developed by the most powerful computing hardware as well as the software system known as ComTool that is one of the most **adaptive** tools in gaming, education, business, design, construction industry, **manufacturing,** marketing, branding, advertisement, travel, sports, fashion, beauty, and makeups.

In addition, AR technologies can be applied in the health care sector. **Surgeons** can use digital images and other necessary information in 3D which AR produces while performing a procedure. This can enhance **precision** and convenience for surgeons since they have access to all critical information needed for an operation within their field of view without having to look away.

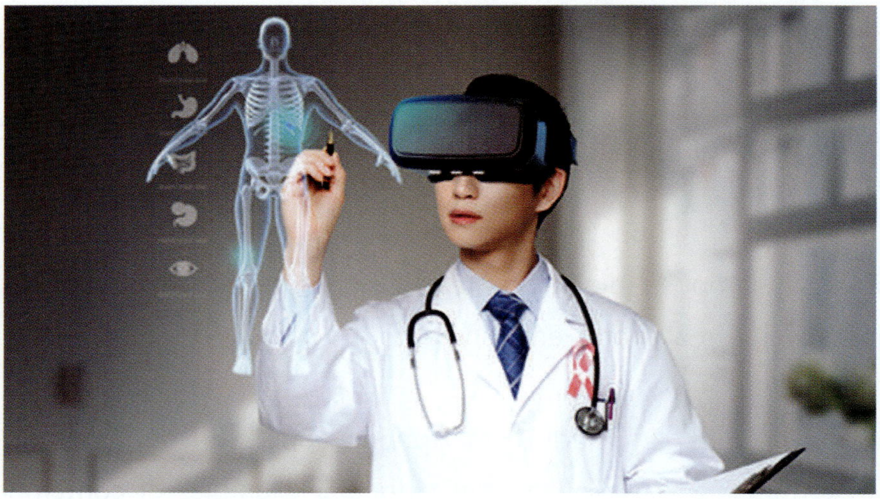

To conclude[C.S-Transition], A.R has exerted a great deal of impact on our lives and can be found in everyday **consumer devices** such as smartphones, T.Vs and game machines.

Retrieved and modified from: https://www.softwaretestinghelp.com/augmented-reality-examples/

Topic Sentence Analysis Activity

Please refer to the resources about Topic Sentences and analyze the following Topic Sentence in the box according to the directions for each question.

An Example of a T. S.

Augmented reality (A.R.) means digital graphics, which convey real-time information to live footage technology and is activated by open-source video tracking software.

1. Is the T.S. in the box a good topic sentence? Why or why not? Please explain your reasons and details referring to the resources about T.S.

Step 1)

My Reasons (Write the reasons in a complete sentence.)

2. If the T.S. in the box is a good topic sentence, please rephrase the T.S. in your own words using linking verbs that imply the same meaning.

Step 2)

My Topic Sentence First Draft (Paraphrase the example in the box.)

3. Please analyze the **first draft** of your topic sentence focusing on two parts: **topic** and **controlling idea**. If your T.S. does not include a clear topic and C.I., it is recommended that you should rewrite your T.S..

Step 3)

Analyze the **Topic** and **Controlling Idea** in My Topic Sentence

PROFESSIONAL READING SKILLS (Part 2) : IT & Engineering Pre-Reading Activity

Vocabulary Check-up Questions : Battery Technology

Match the original (A-F) with its paraphrased sentence (1-6) by focusing on the similar word or phrase in bold.

Original Sentences:

A. The new software **boasts** advanced encryption techniques.

B. Regular **maintenance** of the server ensures smooth operations.

C. The results of the experiment were **consistent** with the engineer's initial predictions.

D. After the introduction of 5G, the demand for high-speed internet **skyrocketed**.

E. The project's cost was **estimated** to be around 1 million dollars.

F. With the growing concern about the environment, many tech companies are focusing on the **eco-friendliness** of their products.

Paraphrased Sentences:

1. ______ The project's cost was predicted to be approximately 1 million dollars.

2. ______ The new software is proud of its modern encryption features.

3. ______ Ensuring the server gets regular checks helps it run without having minor problems.

4. ______ The demand for faster internet rose quickly with the arrival of 5G.

5. ______ The outcome of the test reliably matched what the engineer had originally thought.

6. ______ Consideration for the environment is now a priority for numerous technology firms.

Vocabulary Check-up Questions : Battery Technology

Before reading, circle the correct definitions for the words in bold.

1. The new software **boasts** advanced encryption techniques to keep user data secure.
   a) complains about
   b) features or possesses
   c) ignores

2. Regular **maintenance** of the server ensures smooth operations and reduces unexpected downtimes.
   a) celebration
   b) dismantling
   c) upkeep or routine care

3. The results of the experiment were **consistent** with the engineer's initial predictions.
   a) variable
   b) in contrast with
   c) in agreement with

4. After the introduction of 5G, the demand for high-speed internet has **skyrocketed**.
   a) declined slowly
   b) remained stable
   c) increased dramatically

5. The project's cost was **estimated** to be around 1 million dollars, but final expenditures may vary.
   a) guessed roughly
   b) fixed exactly
   c) ignored

6. With the growing concern about the environment, many tech companies are focusing on the **eco-friendliness** of their products.
   a) cost-effectiveness
   b) electronic compatibility
   c) environmentally friendly nature

Reading Activity

For a topic sentence analysis, please read the paragraph below. Please underline the topic and controlling idea and think about **any important information that makes the sentence a T.S.** for the paragraph.

Car Business Battery Package Change

[T.S.] Battery technology [Topic] plays an important role in the energy transition between electronic devices and a critical backstop for intermittent power generation. However, in the 21st century, even though Lithium-ion, or Li-ion, **[Controlling Idea]is the most prolific battery** in the world while facilitating decarbonization, this technology may not end up carrying a good relationship among the market sharing competitors.

[S.S.] Actually, the Lithium-ion battery **boasts** high energy density relative to older nickel-cadmium batteries. High energy efficiency and zero **maintenance** have made Lithium-ion batteries a valuable proposition up to now. By contrast, the absence of a memory effect on this technology may cause the battery packs to lose storage capacity with continued usage. Also, major consumers of batteries such as the U.S.A. and E.U. mostly rely on Chinese and Korean imports to produce various electronic devices.

[S.S] For example, **consistent** demand of Li-ion batteries are the reasons for the increasing usage of AI devices, smartphones, smart watches, laptops, electronic-vehicles, and energy grids. The incessant need for this technology has **skyrocketed** both in terms of applications and face-value. To be specific, a recent ***Frost and Sullivan report*** **estimated** that in the next ten years, the global lithium industry will cross USD 100 billion. The table below shows the voltages, typical applications, and other characteristics of the six lithium batteries.

Chemical Name	Abbreviation	Voltages	Application
Lithium cobalt oxide	LCO	3.60V nominal; typical operating range 3.0- 4.2V/cell	Cell Phones, Cameras & Laptops
Lithium iron phosphate	LFP	3.20, 3.30V nominal; typical operating range 2.5-3.65V/cell	Power tools, Medical, Electric Vehicles
Lithium-Ion Manganese Oxide	LMO	3.70V (3.80V) nominal; typical operating range 3.0-4.2V/cell	Power tools, Medical, Electric Vehicles
Lithium Nickel Cobalt Aluminium Oxide	NCA	3.60V nominal; typical operating range 3.0- 4.2V/cell	Grid Storage and Electric Vehicles
Lithium Nickel Manganese Cobalt Oxide	NMC	3.60V, 3.70V operating range 3.0-4.2V/cell, or higher	Power tools, Medical, Electric Vehicles
Lithium titanate	LTO	2.40V nominal; typical operating range 1.8- 2.85V/cell	Grid Storage and Electric Vehicles

[C.S.] To conclude [C.S-Transition], the most popular battery technologies, Lithium-ion and Li-ion batteries, have contributed to the convenience and **eco-friendliness** of our lives.

Retrieved and modified from: https://www.batterypowertips.com/difference-between-lithium-ion-lithium-polymer-batteries-faq/

Topic Sentence Analysis Activity

Please refer to the resources about Topic Sentences and analyze the following Topic Sentence in the box according to the directions for each question.

An Example of a T. S.

Battery technology plays an important role in the energy transition between electronic devices and a critical backstop for intermittent power generation. However, in the 21st century, even though Lithium-ion, or Li-ion, is the most widely used prolific battery in the world while facilitating the decarbonization, this technology may not end up carrying a good relationship among the market sharing competitors.

1. Is the T.S. in the box a good topic sentence? Why or why not? Please explain your reasons and give details referring to the resources about T.S..

Step 1)

My Reasons (Write the reasons in complete sentences.)

____

____

____

____

____

2. If the T.S. in the box is a good topic sentence, please rephrase the T.S. in your own words using linking verbs that imply the same meaning.

Step 2)

My Topic Sentence First Draft (Paraphrase the example in the box.)

____

____

____

____

____

3. Please analyze the **first draft** of your topic sentence focuing on two parts: **topic** and **controlling idea**. If your T.S. does not include a clear topic and C.I., it is recommended that you rewrite your T.S..

Step3)

Analyze the **Topic** and **Controlling Idea** in My Topic Sentence

____

____

____

____

____

PROFESSIONAL READING SKILLS (Part 3): Humanities & Social Science Pre-Reading Activity

Vocabulary Check-up Questions : K-Pop & World Influence

Before reading, circle the correct definitions for the words in bold.

1. The population **explosion** in urban areas led to significant challenges in city planning.
   a. a rapid and sudden increase
   b. a method of measuring density

2. Socio-economic **barriers** often limit access to quality education for many communities.
   a. structures built for community gatherings
   b. obstacles or hindrances

3. Different **genres** of literature offer insights into various cultural and historical contexts.
   a. ancient writing tools
   b. categories or kinds

4. The dancers moved **synchronized** to the rhythm, reflecting the community's deep-rooted traditions.
   a. in coordinated or matched timing
   b. in random or chaotic patterns

5. The **choreography** of traditional dances often tells stories of a community's past.
   a. the sequence and design of movements in dance
   b. the materials used to design costumes

6. The campaign used a **catchy** slogan to raise awareness about social issues.
   a. complex and hard to understand
   b. easily remembered or appealing

7. The politician spoke **sophisticatedly** about the nuances of international relations.
   a. with frequent pauses and hesitations
   b. in a complex or refined manner

8. Nelson Mandela remains an **inspiration** for many who advocate for civil rights and freedom.
   a. a source of motivation or admiration
   b. an ancient method of communication

9. With the **burgeoning** interest in social sciences, universities are expanding their courses.
   a. rapidly growing or developing
   b. slowing down or diminishing

10. The 1960s saw a **fad** of peace and love movements across Western countries.
   a. a historical event of great significance
   b. a trend popular for a short period

11. The speech had a deep **resonance** among the audience, touching on shared experiences and emotions.
   a. a strong emotional or meaningful connection.
   b. a repetitive pattern of sounds.

12. The **aesthetics** of ancient civilizations can be studied through their art and architecture.
   a. the science of building structures.
   b. principles and appreciation of beauty and taste.

Reading Activity

For a topic sentence analysis, please read the paragraph below. Please underline the topic and controlling idea and think about **any important information that makes the sentence a T.S.** for the paragraph.

K-Pop and Its Influence on the World: Culture & Business Report Change

[T.S.] In the global world of being connected through YouTube and SNS, the K-pop (Korean pop music) **explosion** [Topic] breaks cultural **barriers**. [Controlling Idea-C.I.]

[S.S.]
More than anything else, various **genres** challenged by K-pop artists include a wide range of musical performances, colorful costumes and perfectly **synchronized choreography**. Besides hip hop, pop, rock, electro-pop and R&B, the musical effects also include **catchy** tunes, music videos with eye-catching visual effects and **sophisticatedly** elaborate storylines. The K-pop industry has made every effort to export their music by getting some attention and **inspiration** from the Western world while demonstrating English cover-songs in order to keep up with contemporary trends that help western people break their cultural bias and barriers. Many K-pop fans have become interested in learning the Korean language, which was once regarded as a barrier to entering Korean culture.

[S.S.] When digging into historical trends for some of these top cities, we see that while all cities trended negatively on YouTube, most cities climbed across Instagram and Spotify. More than anywhere else, Mexico performed the strongest, showing large growth in both Instagram (817 percent) and Spotify (68 percent) metrics since March. This is unsurprising given its large multi-cultural population. Conversely, as a smaller city, Lima performed the weakest, declining on Instagram (-75 percent) and Spotify (-22 percent) over this 5-month period. Los Angeles, São Paulo, and Santiago saw mild growth over this period, likely due to K-Pop's saturation in these markets.

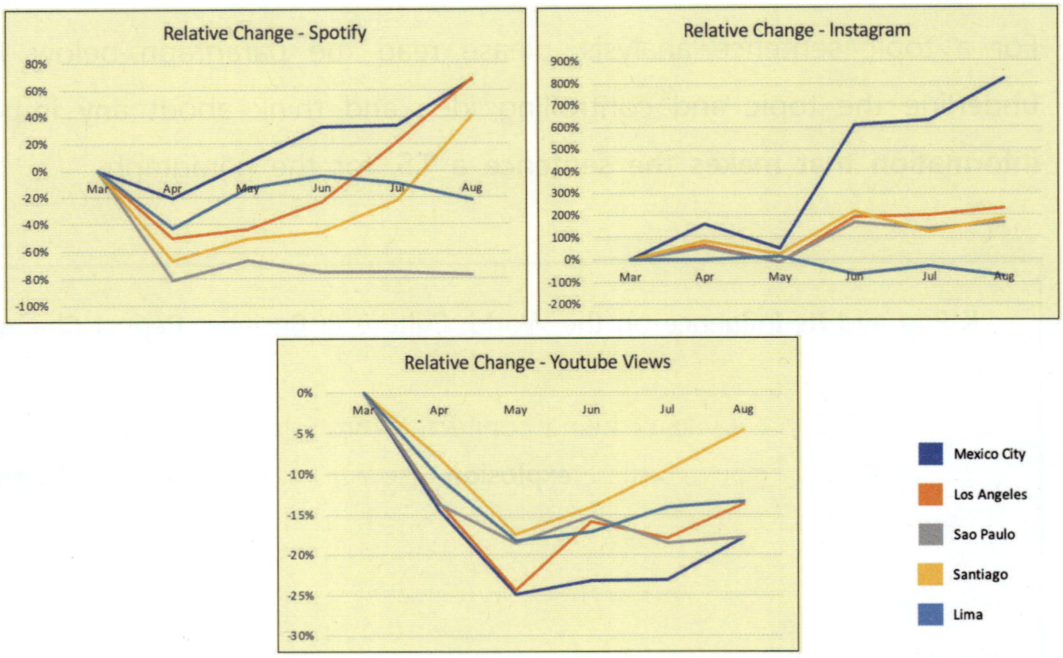

[C.S.]

Even though the **burgeoning** genre's popularity may seem like a **fad**, the rise of K-pop has had greater cultural **resonance** through its reach, records, and **aesthetics** in Western society.

Retrieved and modified from: https://blog.chartmetric.com/why-is-k-pop-popular/

Topic Sentence Analysis Activity

Please refer to the resources about Topic Sentences and analyze the following Topic Sentence in the box according to the directions for each question.

An Example of T. S.

In the global world of being connected through YouTube and SNS, the K-pop (Korean pop music) explosion breaks cultural barriers.

1. Is the T.S. in the box a good topic sentence? Why or why not? Please explain your reasons and give details referring to the resources about T.S..

Step 1)

My Reasons (Write the reasons in complete sentences.)

2. If the T.S. in the box is a good topic sentence, please rephrase the T.S. in your own words using linking verbs that imply the same meaning.

Step 2)

My Topic Sentence First Draft (Paraphrase the example in the box.)

3. Please analyze the **first draft** of your topic sentence with focusing on two parts: **topic** and **controlling idea**. If your T.S. does not include a clear topic and C.I., it is recommended that you rewrite your T.S..

Step 3)

Analyze the **Topic** and **Controlling Idea** in My Topic Sentence

PROFESSIONAL READING SKILLS (Part 4) : Bio & Health-Care Pre-Reading Activity

Vocabulary Check-up Questions : Bio & Health-Care Science

Read the key vocabulary found in the example sentence. Fill in the blanks with the correct form of the words in bold.

1. The **integration** of software and hardware is essential for a smooth-running system.
2. The transition from wired to wireless communication is an example of a **paradigm shift** in technology.
3. As smartphones became prevalent, many older cell phone models became **obsolete**.
4. Artificial intelligence is having a **transformative** impact on the way we process data.
5. The software update will **accompany** a detailed user guide.
6. The programmer had a **slew** of bugs to fix before the product launch.
7. Some people have a **predisposition** to understanding complex algorithms quickly.
8. The error message was **fleeting**, disappearing before the user could read it fully.
9. The benefits of upgrading the server were immediately **tangible** in terms of speed and efficiency.
10. The **makeup** of the committee responsible for cybersecurity should be a team of skilled professionals.

a. __________ (n) a fundamental change in approach or underlying assumptions.

b. __________ (adj) able to be clearly seen, touched, or felt; real.

c. __________ (adj) outdated or no longer in use.

d. __________ (n) bringing separate elements into a unified whole.

e. ________ (adj) creating a marked change.

f. ________ (n) a large number of something.

g. ________ (n) the physical constitution of an individual.

h. ________ (adj) lasting for a very short time.

i. ________ (v) to be with or occur at the same time as something.

j. ________ (n) of being put together or composition.

Reading Activity

For a topic sentence analysis, please read the paragraph below. Please underline the topic and controlling idea and think about **any important information that makes the sentence a T.S.** for the paragraph.

Bio & Health Care Science

[T.S.] The **integration** of biological science and healthcare, often referred to as [Topic] bio-healthcare, is revolutionizing the medical field by offering treatments that are more personalized and effective. [Controlling Idea-C.I.] This **paradigm shift** ensures that medical care is personalized to an individual's specific genetic makeup, greatly improving the potential for successful outcomes.

[S.S.] Bio-healthcare offers new treatments like gene therapy, which may leave traditional methods **obsolete**. Dr. Rebecca Hanlon, in her work The Dawn of Bio-healthcare, explains the **transformative** potential of this approach. One of the most groundbreaking advancements is in gene therapy, where scientists can replace or modify a patient's genes to combat or even cure genetic disorders. Traditional treatments, often **accompanied** by a **slew** of side effects, might become **obsolete** as these therapies promise precision and minimal adverse reactions.

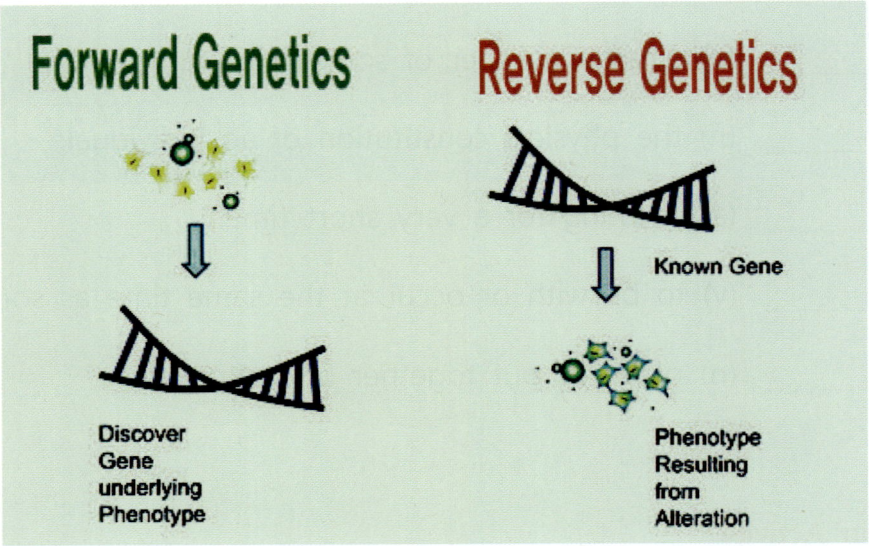

Bio-healthcare also examines personalized nutrition. By understanding an individual's genetic **predisposition**, nutritionists can construct diets that not only enhance well-being but also prevent potential diseases. As Hanlon notes, "Understanding one's genetics can be the difference between prevention and treatment."

[C.S.] Consequently [Transition], bio-healthcare is not just a **fleeting** trend but a significant step forward in medical care. As research increases and more breakthroughs emerge, patients worldwide will experience the **tangible** benefits of treatments specifically designed for their own unique biological **makeup**.

Retrieved and modified from: https://www.vigyanstudy.com/2020/05/what-is-genetics-.html

Topic Sentence Analysis Activity

Please refer to the resources about Topic Sentences and analyze the following Topic Sentence in the box according to the directions for each question.

An Example of T. S.

The **integration** of biological science and healthcare, often referred to as [Topic] bio-healthcare, is revolutionizing the medical field by offering treatments that are more personalized and effective. [Controlling Idea-C.I.]

1. Is the T.S. in the box a good topic sentence? Why or why not? Please explain your reasons and give details referring to the resources about T.S.

Step 1)

My Reasons (Write the reasons in complete sentences.)

2. If the T.S. in the box is a good topic sentence, please rephrase the T.S. in your own words using linking verbs that imply the same meaning.

Step 2)

My Topic Sentence First Draft (Paraphrase the example in the box.)

3. Please analyze the **first draft** of your topic sentence focusing on two parts: the **topic** and **controlling idea**. If your T.S. does not include a clear topic and C.I., it is recommended that you rewrite your T.S..

Step 3)

Analyze the **Topic** and **Controlling Idea** in My Topic Sentence

Vocabulary Check-up Questions : ESG

Read the definitions of the key vocabulary found in the example paragraph. Fill in the blanks with the correct form of the words in bold.

a) criteria (n) – standards for making judgments.

b) sustainability (n) – the ability to last without harm.

c) ecological footprint (n) – a measure of environmental impact.

d) carbon emissions (n) – release of carbon into the air.

e) pivotal (adj) – crucially important.

f) stakeholders (n) – interested parties in a company.

g) reputation (n) – general opinion about something.

h) commitments (n) – promises or obligations.

i) resilient (adj) – quick to recover from difficulties.

k) adaptable (adj) – able to adjust to changes.

1. To be chosen as our main supplier, companies must meet certain ________ that we've set based on quality and reliability.

2. In today's business landscape, ________ is often seen as a key factor in long-term success.

3. Many organizations are working to reduce their ________ by implementing more environmentally-friendly practices.

4. Due to growing environmental concerns, our company has set a goal to reduce ________ by 25% over the next decade.

5. The introduction of digital marketing was a ________ moment in the advertising industry.

6. It's crucial for a company to engage with its ________ regularly to understand their needs and concerns.

7. Maintaining a positive ________ online is essential for businesses in today's digital age.

8. It's crucial for companies to honor their ________ to customers to build trust and loyalty.

9. Despite facing numerous challenges last year, our team proved to be ________ and managed to exceed sales targets.

10. As market trends continuously change, the most successful companies are those that are ________ to shifts in consumer behavior.

Reading Activity

For your topic sentence analysis, please read the paragraph below. Please underline the topic and controlling idea and think about **any important information that makes the sentence a T.S.** for the paragraph.

Business & Marketing: Environmental, Social, and Governance

In recent years, businesses worldwide have recognized the significance of environmental, social, and governance (ESG) **criteria** in their operations. These criteria not only promote **sustainability**, but also shape a company's impact on society and its governance structures. [T.S.] For businesses, [Topic] prioritizing ESG is not only ethically significant but also crucial for a company's long-term prosperity. [Controlling Idea-C.I.]

[S.S.] Firstly, the environmental component encourages corporations to assess and reduce their **ecological footprint**. This means companies are taking actions to decrease **carbon emissions**, manage waste efficiently, and ensure sustainable resource use. According to The Global ESG Benchmark Report by Thompson & Clark (2020), firms that actively incorporate environmental measures witness a 15% increase in their market value within five years. Such data underscores the financial benefits tied to eco-friendly practices.

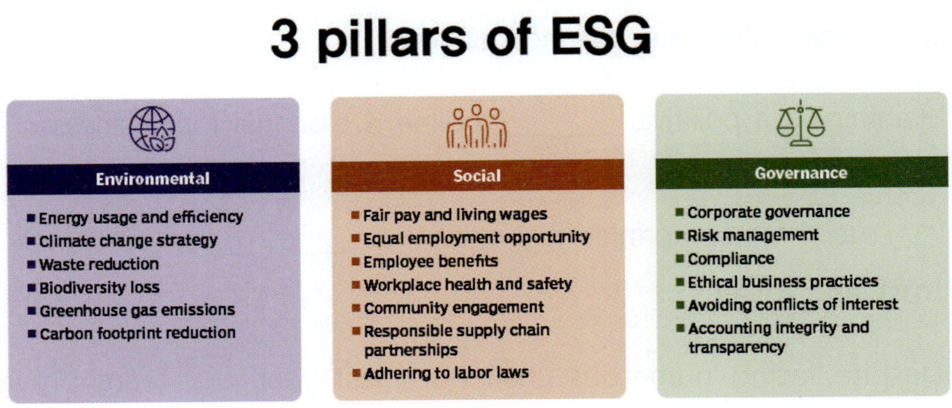

[S.S.] Additionally, ESG considerations, specifically the social and governance aspects, play a **pivotal** role in shaping a company's relationships with its **stakeholders**. It looks at the company's leadership, executive pay, and shareholder rights. Emphasizing these elements not only improves a company's **reputation** but also enhances trust among stakeholders. A survey conducted by ESG Today revealed that 70% of consumers are more likely to support brands that demonstrate strong ESG **commitments**. Thus, prioritizing ESG factors is not just an ethical choice but a strategic decision that can significantly influence consumer support and loyalty.

[C.S.] In conclusion [Transition], ESG is not merely a trend. It constructs a more **resilient** change in how businesses view their roles within broader society. Companies that prioritize ESG will likely be more **adaptable** and favored in our evolving global market.

Retrieved and modified from: https://www.techtarget.com/whatis/definition/environmental-social-and-governance-ESG

Topic Sentence Analysis Activity

Please refer to the resources about Topic Sentences and analyze the following Topic Sentence in the box according to the directions for each question.

An Example of a T.S.

For businesses, **prioritizing ESG** is not only ethically significant, but also crucial for a company's long-term prosperity.

1. Is the T.S. in the box a good topic sentence? Why or why not? Please explain your reasons and give details referring to the resources about T.S.

Step 1)

My Reasons (Write the reasons in complete sentences.)

2. If the T.S. in the box is a good topic sentence, please rephrase the T.S. in your own words using linking verbs that imply the same meaning.

Step 2)

My Topic Sentence First Draft (Paraphrase the example in the box.)

3. Please analyze the **first draft** of your topic sentence focusing on two parts: the **topic** and **controlling idea**. If your T.S. does not include a clear topic and C.I., it is recommended that you rewrite your T.S..

Step 3)

Analyze **Topic** and **Controlling Idea** in My Topic Sentence

[Chapter 3]
Academic Writing in Content Area

ACADEMIC WRITING SKILLS

Key Grammar & Expressions to Develop a Topic Sentence

Writers and speakers should use **clear linking verbs and phrases** that show the relationship between the topic and controlling idea on the basis of cause (topic, theme, what) and effect (what about, how and why it happened) relationships. Take a look at the sentence and think about **the relationship between a topic and a controlling idea**.

The two types of organizing T.S. are as follows:

(1) **TAC** version: **T**opic + **A**ctive verbs + **C**ontrolling idea
(2) **CPT** version: **C**ontrolling idea + **P**assive verbs + **T**opic

Here are some examples of **TAC** versions:

Topic	Active linking verbs or phrases that create your C.I.	Controlling Idea (C.I.): How, Why, What about & Reasons
Gene-editing technology	**helps somebody to +V** (have, has helped somebody to) **allows somebody to +V** (have, has allowed somebody to) **enables somebody to +V** (have, has enabled somebody to) **leads to (has led to) +N** causes (has caused) +N results in +N (has resulted in)	a new era in biotechnology with changes in life expectancy by altering human genes.

Writing Activity 1

Refer to the Topic Sentence you wrote on the previous page. Using the examples of **TAC** expressions, please **paraphrase your T.S.**. (*Double space if necessary*)

You may select appropriate expressions of **somebody**, **V (verbs)**, and **N (nouns)** referring to the examples of **TAC** versions. in the replacing or paraphrasing words box or you may create your own words and/or expressions.
Here are some examples of **replacing or paraphrasing words.**

Replacing or Paraphrasing Words		
Somebody	**V (verbs)**	**N (nouns)**
	start, begin	
	initiate, activate	
	implement	
human beings	open, develop	the invention of
the people of	facilitate	the development of
the scientists	introduce	the creation of
the researchers	announce	the innovation of
the research group	present	a new generation of
the workers in	make it available	the modern age
the bio science-laboratory	enable	a particular period
	allow	
	cause	
	report	

Writing Activity 2

Refer to the Topic Sentence you wrote on the previous page. Using the examples of **TAC** expressions (somebody + V + N), please **paraphrase your T.S.**. (*Double space if necessary*)

Here are the examples of **CPT** versions:

Controlling Idea(C. I.): How, Why, What about & Reasons	Passive linking verbs or phrases that create your C.I.	Topic
A new era in biotechnology with changes in life expectancy by altering human genes	**was allowed by +N** (have, has been allowed by + N) **was enabled by +N** (have, has been enabled by +N) **was caused by (has been caused) by +N** was due to +N was the result of +N	gene-editing technology.

Writing Activity 3

Refer to the Topic Sentence you wrote on the previous page. Using the examples of **CPT** expressions, please **paraphrase your T.S.**. (*Double space if necessary*)

LEARNING OBJECTIVES	IN THIS UNIT STUDENTS WILL ...
PERFORMANCE & TASK	produce impactful supporting sentences by introducing writing expressions with each type of evidence in order to strengthen the overall fluency of their paragraphs.
CRITICAL THINKING SKILLS 1	distinguish between types of evidence used to support reasons by examining the sample paragraphs in order to construct more persuasive arguments.
CRITICAL THINKING SKILLS 2	can enhance the cohesion of their supporting sentences by undergoing peer review in order to produce more unified and compelling paragraphs.
COMMUNICATION SKILLS	share ideas and feedback and communicate effectively in order to produce more unified and compelling paragraphs.
WRITING SKILLS	Conclude the supporting sentences with a succinct concluding sentence.

UNIT 05

Writing a Paragraph II: Supporting & Concluding Sentences

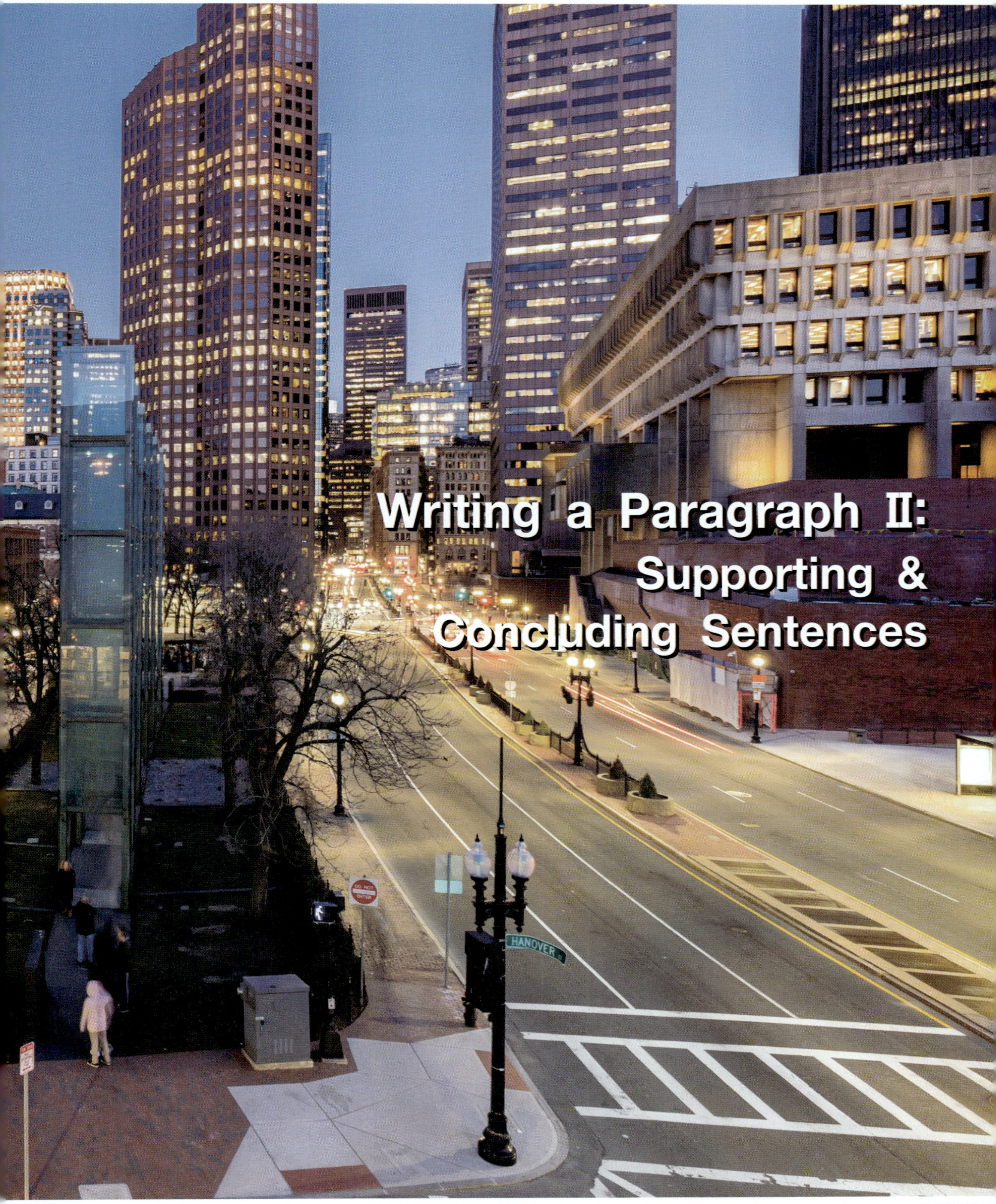

[Chapter 1]
Introduction to Supporting Sentences

ACADEMIC WRITING SKILLS

Supporting Sentences

What are Supporting Sentences?

1) They come after the Topic Sentence.
2) They are used to support (develop and explain) the topic sentence.
3) They should explain about the main idea in the topic sentence only without introducing any new ideas.
4) They consist of important points about the topic sentence and supporting details (e.g., facts, published works, statistical data, reasons, examples, personal experience).

Check-up Questions

Read the following paragraph examples and answer the questions.

Media Literacy

Media literacy, the ability to closely analyze what people read, see, and hear, is an essential skill that allows them to think critically about media in their lives. As the technologies have rapidly advanced in recent years, people are bombarded by numerous kinds of media which are intended to lead people to think in a particular way. Therefore, people need to be more active consumers of media by questioning what is its purpose and how it is presented. This can be a way for media consumers to evaluate whether it is a reliable source or not. For example, if a website is biased, it may not always present scientific and objective information, but instead, often uses different persuasive techniques to sell viewers a product, a political viewpoint, or a lifestyle. One must also carefully examine the design elements of a website, such as images, videos or sounds. If they are too striking or intrusive, the purpose of the website is likely to grab potential consumers' attention rather than providing credible information. To sum up, determining the purpose of the information and the credibility of the source is necessary for individuals to become wiser consumers of media in this digital age.

Retrieved and modified from: https://courses.lumenlearning.com/suny-massmedia/chapter/1-8-media-literacy/

1. Find the topic sentence and underline it.

2. What are the supporting sentences? Put brackets around the supporting sentences.

3. Do all the supporting sentences support the topic sentence? Explain your answer.

____

____

____

____

Gig Economy

The gig economy has emerged as a preferred career path for Millennials and Generation Z, or "MZ." In the gig economy, many people work on a part-time or freelance basis. While their parents' generations were guaranteed the stability of long-term jobs in their fields of expertise, the younger generations are well aware of employment insecurity. Therefore, they attempt to generate multiple sources of income in order to deal with uncertainty. In addition, experts attribute the trend to the MZ generation's unique characteristics. They tend to be individualistic valuing their freedom and self-fulfillment rather than showing loyalty to their employers. This is often considered one of the main causes of intergenerational conflicts. The easier access to multiple or side jobs has also contributed to the growth of the gig economy. As digital platforms for gig work are rapidly growing, various apps and services are providing workers with more opportunities to explore different jobs. Only time will tell, but diversifying income streams may continue into the future, and the gig economy could become the new norm.

Retrieved and modified from: https://www.koreatimes.co.kr/www/biz/2023/10/602_321283.html

1. Find the topic sentence and underline it.

2. What are the supporting sentences? Put brackets around the supporting sentences.

3. Do all the supporting sentences support the topic sentence? Explain your answer.

____

____

____

____

[Chapter 2]
Supporting Sentences: Building Strong Arguments

ACADEMIC WRITING SKILLS

Using Various Types of Evidence for Supporting Details

Various Types of Evidence for Supporting Details

1) Facts: Objective truth which can be proved
2) Published works: Information, research findings, or opinions published in academic journals, books, websites, newspapers, or magazines by experts or reputable organizations
3) Statistical data: Numerical data collected, organized, and analyzed from a sample or a population
4) Reasons: Explanation of what causes a fact or a situation to happen
5) Examples: Representative cases to show how the general statement is true
6) Personal experiences: Relevant individual stories

Check-up Questions

Check the following sentences and identify which type of evidence is used.

1. Approximately 65% of the adult students decided to further their education to gain promotion in their workplace or pursue a different career (Korea Statistics Association, 2023).

   ① Reason ② Example ③ Statistical data

2. Rapid technological advancements have caused a growing necessity for individuals to engage in lifelong education to stay relevant and competitive in their careers.

① Reason ② Example ③ Statistical data

3. In spite of all of the benefits of lifelong learning, many adult learners still encounter some barriers. For instance, investing time and money places a burden on their family as well as adult students themselves.

① Reason ② Example ③ Statistical data

Useful Expressions for Various Types of Evidence 1: Facts/Common Knowledge

Expressions for Facts/Common Knowledge

Industries are making efforts to develop hydrogen turbine technology that uses ammonia as fuel.

1) **In fact/As a matter of fact,** ammonia is one of the most eco-friendly energy sources as the usage of ammonia does not emit carbon dioxide.
2) **It is commonly/well known that** ammonia is one of the most eco-friendly energy sources as the usage of ammonia does not emit carbon dioxide.
3) **There is no doubt/question that** ammonia is one of the most eco-friendly energy sources as the usage of ammonia does not emit carbon dioxide.

TIPS

* Common knowledge is widely known and found in many sources, and does not need to be cited. Otherwise, any time facts are used, they should be cited properly as discussed in Unit 3.

Useful Expressions for Various Types of Evidence 2: Published Works

Expressions for Published Works

Implementing renewable energy technologies is hindered by various challenges, despite the potential benefits for economic and sustainable development.

1) **According to** Kuma and Majid (2020), challenges arising from technological and regulatory factors pose significant barriers to the widespread adoption of renewable energy in many parts of the world.
2) **In the research conducted by** Kuma and Majid (2020), challenges arising from technological and regulatory factors were found to pose significant barriers to the widespread adoption of renewable energy in many parts of the world.
3) **In their book, "Energy, Sustainability, and Society,"** Kuma and Majid (2020) discuss that challenges arising from technological and regulatory factors pose significant barriers to the widespread adoption of renewable energy in many parts of the world.

TIPS

* Any published works should be cited properly as discussed in Unit 3.

Check-up Questions

Write supporting details using the type of evidence in brackets.

1. Profound changes in climate demand international collaboration. (facts/common knowledge)

2. Electric vehicles (EV) batteries raise serious environmental concerns. (facts/common knowledge)

____

____

____

____

3. The adoption of vertical farming practices has the potential to revolutionize urban agriculture by optimizing space and resource use. (published work)

____

____

____

____

4. Digital marketing offers a myriad of advantages over traditional forms of advertising. (published work)

____

____

____

____

____

____

Useful Expressions for Various Types of Evidence 3: Statistical Data

Expressions for Data or Statistics

The VR industry as a whole is growing at a fast pace.

1) **A recent study suggests/finds/shows/concludes that** the VR market achieved global revenues of 1.8 billion USD during 2020 which was a 31.7% increase compared to 2019 (StatsUS, 2022).

2) **According to** StatsUS (2022), the VR market achieved global revenues of 1.8 billion USD during 2020 which was a 31.7% increase compared

to 2019.

TIPS

* When data or statistics are used, the source must be cited as discussed in Unit 3.

Useful Expressions for Various Types of Evidence 4: Reasons

Expressions for Reasons

Frequent use of social media can present certain risks to the mental health of teens.

1) Heavy social media use can **be linked to/lead to/cause/result in** depression and other mental disorders in teens.

2) Depression and other mental disorders in teens are **caused by/due to/the result of/because of** heavy social media use.

3) **Because** teens tend to use social media heavily, they are likely to suffer from depression and other mental disorders.
   = Teens are likely to suffer from depression and other mental disorders **because** they tend to use social media heavily.

Check-up Questions

Write supporting details using the type of evidence in brackets. For statistical data, you can refer to either Korea Statistics (https://kostat.go.kr) or other official sources.

1. One of the most serious social challenges faced by South Korea is the population decline. (statistical data)

2. FinTech, financial technology, is considered to be a key to the future of banking. (statistical data)

____

____

____

____

3. There are growing concerns regarding fashion-driven environmental damage. (reasons)

____

____

____

____

4. COVID-19 has accelerated the introduction of automation in industry. (reasons)

____

____

____

____

Useful Expressions for Various Types of Evidence 5: Examples

Expressions for Examples

Customers tend to support ethical green business practices.

1) **For example/For instance/To give a clear example/To illustrate,** profits of a toothpaste company called Toothie's have tripled within the last two years since it made its products organic and created fully recyclable packaging.

2) Profits of a toothpaste company called Toothie's, **for example,/for instance,** have tripled within the last two years since it made its products organic and created fully recyclable packaging.

3) Profits of many socially responsible companies**, such as** Toothie's have improved within the last two years.

Useful Expressions for Various Types of Evidence 6: Personal Experiences

Expressions for Personal Experience

The elderly generally have greater trouble participating in social activities in a society filled with digital technology.

1) **From my own experience, I can tell that** this is a very serious social problem. **I recently saw/experienced this first-hand when** I visited my favorite fast food restaurant. A lady in her 60s with her grandson was not familiar with an automated kiosk and ordered 20 hamburgers by mistakenly pushing different buttons on the screen.

Check-up Questions

Write supporting details using the type of evidence in brackets.

1. Previously, Hallyu was limited to popular culture, but it has been extended to various fields. (examples)

2. Non-Governmental Organizations (NGOs) perform a wide range of work across various sectors to address social, environmental, and humanitarian issues. (examples)

3. Robots are becoming increasingly integrated into our everyday lives, performing a variety of tasks. (personal experience)

4. Influencer marketing strategy is growing bigger than ever. (personal experience)

ACADEMIC READING

Reading Activity

Revisit the example paragraph you have read from Academic Reading & Writing in Content Area in Unit 4. Read the supporting sentences in the paragraph and answer the following questions.

1. Fill in the following table by identifying the supporting details used and their types.

Supporting Details	Type(s) of Supporting Details

2. In the space below, add another supporting detail of a different type than the ones used in the paragraph.

[Chapter 3]

Introduction to a Concluding Sentence

ACADEMIC WRITING SKILLS

Concluding Sentence

A Concluding Sentence...

1) Is the last sentence that wraps up a paragraph.
2) Often begins with transitional words/expressions, such as:
   – In conclusion/To conclude/Conclusively,
   – In summary/To summarize/To sum up,
   – In short/In brief
   – As mentioned/discussed above
3) Should accomplish one of the following:
   (1) Restate the Topic Sentence by paraphrasing it
   (2) Summarize the main arguments in the Supporting Sentences
   (3) Make a prediction based on the Supporting Sentences
   (4) Include the author's final thoughts or opinions on the topic

Check-up Questions

Answer the following questions to assess your understanding of a concluding sentence.

1. What are the four different methods to write a concluding sentence?

____

____

____

____

____

____

2. Reread the example paragraph, Media Literacy in Chapter 1 of this unit. What is the Concluding Sentence? What is the method used to create the Concluding Sentence? Write your answers in the space below.

____

____

____

____

____

3. Reread the example paragraph, Gig Economy in Chapter 1 of this unit. What is the Concluding Sentence? What is the method used to create the Concluding Sentence? Write your answers in the space below.

____

____

____

____

____

Reading Activity

Revisit the example paragraph, "K-Pop and Its Influence on the World: Culture & Business Report Change" in Unit 4. Referring to the reading passage, check the following sentences and identify which method of concluding sentence is used.

1. Even though the burgeoning genre's popularity may seem like a fad, the rise of K-pop has had greater cultural resonance through its reach, records, and aesthetics in Western society.
   ① Restate the Topic Sentence by paraphrasing it
   ② Summarize the main arguments in the Supporting Sentences
   ③ Make a prediction based on the Supporting Sentences
   ④ Include the author's final thoughts or opinions on the topic

2. The development of IT technology and media has enabled people all around the world to be connected through more globalized K-pop culture.
   ① Restate the Topic Sentence by paraphrasing it
   ② Summarize the main arguments in the Supporting Sentences
   ③ Make a prediction based on the Supporting Sentences
   ④ Include the author's final thoughts or opinions on the topic

3. The K-pop industry, artists, fans, and even Korean language play a crucial role in spreading K-pop in the global market which helps to remove cultural barriers of the world in genres and ethnicity.
   ① Restate the Topic Sentence by paraphrasing it
   ② Summarize the main arguments in the Supporting Sentences
   ③ Make a prediction based on the Supporting Sentences
   ④ Include the author's final thoughts or opinions on the topic

Writing Activity

Select one of the reading passages in Unit 4. In the space below, create your own concluding sentence using one of the four methods.

[Chapter 4]
Presenting Supporting & Concluding Sentences in a Logical Manner

ACADEMIC WRITING SKILLS

Cohesion in Paragraph Writing

Paragraph Cohesion

1) A cohesive paragraph means the sentences within a paragraph are connected and flow together.

2) There are several techniques to make a paragraph cohesive:
   (1) Transitional words/expressions between sentences
   (2) Synonyms to avoid using the same words
   (3) Pronouns to refer to nouns in previous sentences
   (4) this/that/these/those to refer to earlier nouns or ideas

Check-up Questions

Read the paragraph below and make it more cohesive by answering the following questions.

1. Put a number in brackets to arrange the supporting and concluding sentences in a logical order.

Topic Sentence: Virtual characters are emerging as a trend in the digital advertising market for many reasons.

(   ) Artificial characters can be made into any type of entertainer — be it an actor, fashion model or singer — and artificial characters' talents can be customized according to a brand's wishes.

( ) They can work all day throughout the year and there is very low chance of scandal.

(1) The biggest advantage of hiring a virtual character is that there is no time or space restriction on the virtual character's activities.

( ) Due to these advantages, more companies in the near future are expected to use virtual characters for their advertising instead of human celebrities.

(4) Finally, virtual characters, unlike humans, are a better choice in terms of cost and risk management.

(2) Companies can also optimize a digital model's image to suit the companies' promotional needs.

2. Rewrite the **Supporting** and **Concluding Sentences** in the correct order. Make sure to include the cohesive techniques discussed in this chapter as much as possible.

ENGAGED LEARNING PROJECT 3

FINAL SUBMISSION (IN-CLASS MIDTERM)

Class Day, Time: ________________

Student ID: ________________

Name: ________________

Read the **Topic Sentence** you have created in Unit 4. Come up with the **Supporting** and **Concluding sentences** for your **Topic Sentence**. Make sure to 1) include three key points, each supported with a different type of evidence, 2) finish with a statement that wraps up the paragraph, 3) apply cohesive techniques as much as possible, and 4) follow the formal academic writing mechanics discussed in **Unit 2**.

LEARNING OBJECTIVES	IN THIS UNIT STUDENTS WILL ...
PERFORMANCE & TASK	draft appropriate emails for selected scenarios in order to achieve greater professionalism.
CRITICAL THINKING SKILLS 1	recognize professional email formats and styles by reviewing real-world email examples.
CRITICAL THINKING SKILLS 2	distinguish professional emails by categorizing them as inquiries, responses, applications, notifications, complaints, or proposals.
COMMUNICATION SKILLS	critique their own and their peers' email drafts by participating in peer feedback sessions.
WRITING SKILLS	adapt writing styles and content for given scenarios in order to communicate effectively in various professional contexts.

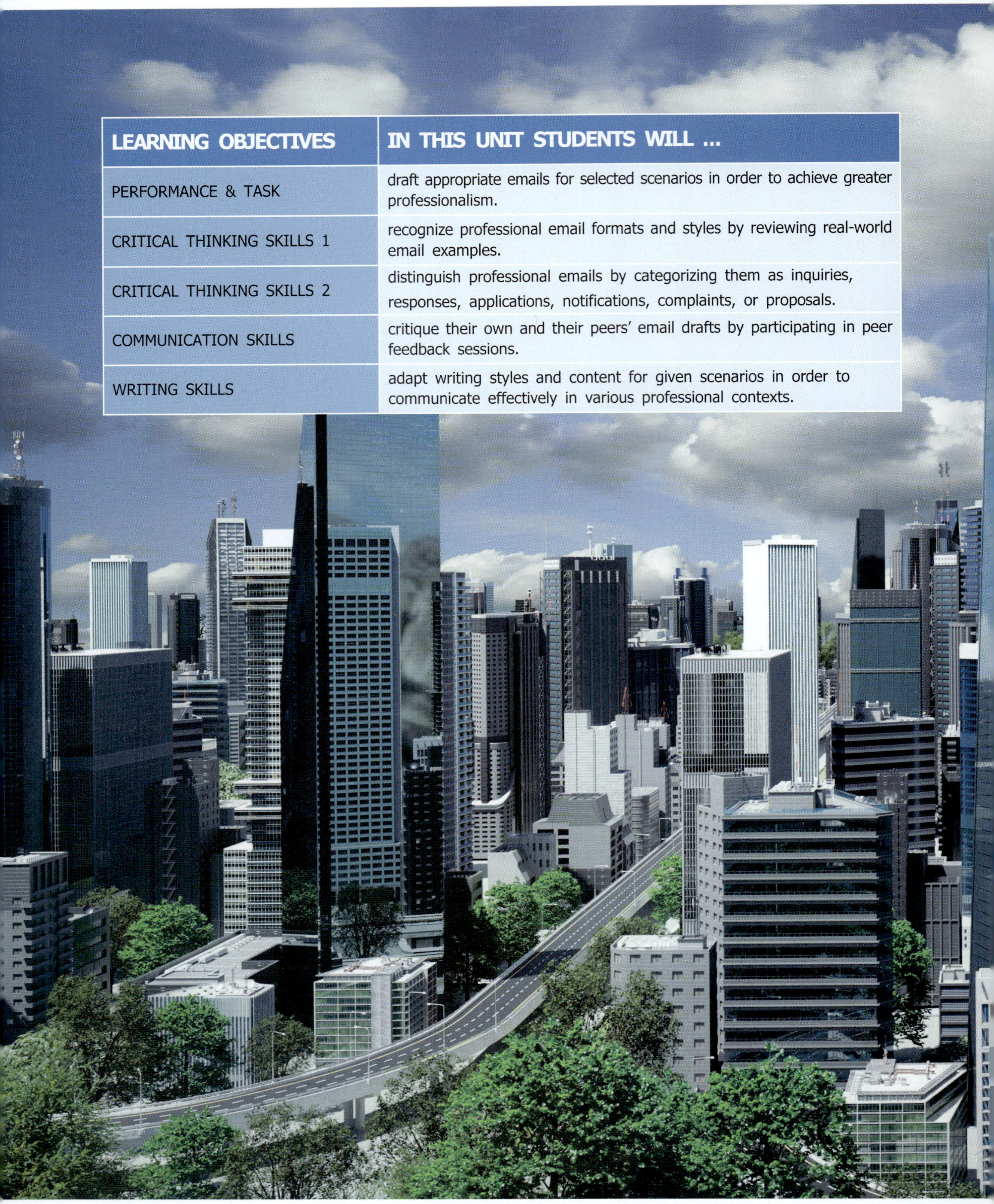

UNIT 06

Writing a Professional Email

[Chapter 1]
Introduction to Formal Email Writing

BRAINSTORMING

Discussion

This unit deals with how to write a formal email. Writing a formal email is required in business or professional settings when you want to be polite, when you don't know the recipient well, or when you don't want to be too casual. In many cases, work or academic emails use formal language. Answer the following questions with your partners.

1. Below are some examples of formal and informal emails. Find and circle the formal emails.

> – an invitation to a party celebrating a friend's promotion
> – a job application
> – an email to a professor
> – an email to a classmate
> – a complaint to a company

2. Come up with other examples of formal emails.

____

____

____

____

ACADEMIC WRITING SKILLS

Introduction to Writing a Formal Email

What is a formal email?

1) It is intended for professional, business or educational use.
2) It uses the professional language with a predefined structure.
3) It is written for an official purpose, such as:
   - an inquiry
   - a response
   - an application
   - a notification
   - a complaint
   - a proposal

Check-up Questions

Read the example of a formal email below. Answer the following questions.

Subject: Request for Further Information on Smart Materials

Dear Dr. Sophia Robinson,

My name is John Cook, and I am the project manager at Fashion Forward. I recently had the opportunity to attend the International Symposium on Innovations in Smart Materials conference, where you presented on the latest advancements in smart materials.

I am writing to ask you a few follow-up questions to gain a better understanding of the potential applications of smart materials in the clothing industry. I would greatly appreciate if you could provide further information on the following questions:

1. Could you provide more details on the properties and characteristics of smart materials that make them suitable for use in the clothing industry?

2. How does the process of incorporating smart materials into clothing design and production differ from traditional materials?

3. Are there any specific types of smart materials that you believe would be best suited for the clothing industry, and why?

Thank you in advance for your time and assistance. I look forward to hearing back from you at your earliest convenience.

Best regards,

John Cook

John Cook
Project Manager
Fashion Forward
(111)111-1111

1. Who is the intended recipient of this email message?

____

____

____

____

2. What is the purpose or the intention of this email message?

____

____

____

____

[Chapter 2]
Structuring Formal Emails: Techniques & Tips

ACADEMIC WRITING SKILLS

Writing a Formal Email: Structure (1)

Subject Line

1) This is the first piece of information that the recipient will see and may also affect whether it will be read or not.
2) It tells the recipient the main reason for your email.
3) It should be short but specific enough to reflect the main idea of the message as in the examples below:
   - Follow-up on the Previous Meeting on June 2nd
   - Immediate Action Required: Disconnection of Service

Salutation

1) This addresses the person you're writing to and serves as a greeting.
2) It varies depending on how well you know the recipient.
3) In business correspondence, it is preferable to use:
   - Dear Mr. Brown [last name] – When you address a particular man
   - Dear Ms. Brown – When you address a particular woman (No Miss or Mrs.)
   - Dear Project Manager [role]/Dear Human Resources Department [department] – When you cannot find an individual's name but only know the title of the person or the department
   - To Whom It May Concern: – When there is no single specific addressee or department (e.g., letters of recommendation)

TIPS

* When it comes to punctuating the salutation in business letters or professional emails, there may be a comma (,) or a colon (:).
* A colon is generally considered more formal.
* "To Whom It May Concern" should always be formatted with a capital letter at the beginning of each word and punctuated with a colon.

Opening Line

1) This starts by introducing yourself with your full name and job position if you're writing to someone for the first time.
2) It briefly describes the reason for your email using an expression, such as:
   - I am writing in regards to...
   - I am interested in.../I would like to know...
   - I am writing to inquire about...
   - I am writing in reference to...
   - I regret to inform you...
3) It expresses your thanks for the message if you're replying to a message you received, using an expression, such as:
   - Thank you for your email regarding...
   - Thank you for your prompt reply.
   - Thank you for contacting our company.

Body

1) This should be concise and to the point without unnecessary details.
2) It should explain the information you have already provided in the opening line.
3) It should be two to three paragraphs grouped with related information.

Check-up Questions

Below is the first part of a formal email which is divided into two parts. Based on the context and the formal email structure discussed above, fill in the blanks with appropriate phrases and sentences.

Subject: ______________________________

Dear Mr. Huck:

I am writing on behalf of Prime Engineering, a leading engineering company known for its innovative and sustainable solutions.

____

____

____

We believe that this partnership has the potential to revolutionize the energy industry by combining our engineering expertise of with the advanced green ammonia technology of your company. Our company is committed to developing sustainable solutions that have a positive impact on the environment and society, and we believe that your green ammonia technology can play a critical role in this.

Attached to this email, you will find a mutually beneficial contract that outlines the terms of our partnership. The contract will outline the roles and responsibilities of both companies as well as the revenue sharing arrangements and any other important details.

Writing a Formal Email: Structure (2)

Closing

1) This is meant for setting your expectations regarding the recipient's reply or further actions.
2) The different types of formal expressions include:
   - If you have any questions, please let me know.
   - Do not hesitate to contact me if you have any questions.
   - I appreciate your cooperation.
   - Thank you very much for your time regarding this matter.
   - Your response will be greatly appreciated.
   - I look forward to hearing from you at your earliest convenience.

Complimentary Close & Signature

1) Complimentary close goes right before your signature, using word(s) such as:
   - Sincerely,
   - Respectfully,
   - Yours sincerely,
   - Yours respectfully,
   - (With) [K]ind/[B]est/[W]arm regards,
2) You should identify yourself by full name, title, and contact information as seen below:

Sincerely,

Jennifer Brown

Jennifer Brown
Project Manager
New Gene Bio Company
(222) 222-2222

Check-up Questions

Below is the rest of the previous formal email example. Based on the context and the formal email structure discussed above, fill in the blanks with an appropriate closing and a signature.

> We are confident that this partnership would be a win-win for both companies and will lead to exciting new opportunities for growth and success. I would like to invite you to schedule a meeting to discuss the details of the proposal further.
>
> ____
>
> ____
>
> ____
>
> ____________________,
>
> *Sam green*
>
> Sam Green
> Vice President
> Prime Engineering
> (333) 333-3333

Writing a Formal Email: Style

Style for a Formal Email

1) Write a message in a predefined structure.

2) Don't use contractions (e.g., can't), abbreviations (e.g., BTW), slang or idioms.

3) Don't use all capital letters for emphasis.

4) Don't use emojis.

5) Remember that grammatical or typing mistakes can make you appear unprofessional and careless.

TIPS

* You can sound more polite when you write your questions or requests in an indirect, polite style as shown in the examples below:

Give me information on the progress made in the development of green hydrogen production technology.
→ Could you kindly provide information on the progress made in the development of green hydrogen production technology?
→ Would it be possible for you to provide...?
→ I would be grateful if you could provide...
→ I would appreciate it if you could provide...

Check-up Questions

Find and correct any parts which are not appropriate for a formal email.

Hi Lee,

Just wanted to reach out about the drone delivery I received yesterday. It was supposed to be a smooth sailing but turns out, it was more like a DISASTER!!

The drone crashed into a tree and my package was nowhere to be found. I was so excited to receive it, but my whole afternoon fell to pieces! It ain't a rocket science to make a successful drone delivery, don't you think?

Anyway, pls look into this and see what went wrong. If this happens again, I'm gonna have to stop using your drone delivery service. :(

Thanks,
David

[Chapter 3]
Writing Professional Emails: Types & Expressions

ACADEMIC WRITING SKILLS

Types of Formal Emails 1: Inquiry Emails

What is an Inquiry Email?

An inquiry email is a type of email that is used to request information or clarification from someone.

Useful Expressions for an Inquiry Email

1) Opening line examples:

- I am writing to inquire/ask...
- I am writing to ask for some clarification on...
- I am writing to seek your assistance regarding...
- I am writing in regards to...
- I am writing to request more information on...

2) Closing examples:

- I am looking forward to hearing from you.
- Thank you for your assistance in this matter.
- I would appreciate it if you could send me this information.
- I would greatly appreciate your response.

Types of Formal Emails 2: Response Emails

What is a Response Email?

A response email is a type of email that is written in response to a previous email or request.

Useful Expressions for a Reseponse Email

1) Opening line examples:

- I appreciate your email regarding...
- Thank you for your inquiry about...
- I am glad to respond to your email about...
- I am writing in regards to your recent email about...
- I am writing in regards to your request for...
- I am following up on your email regarding...

2) Closing examples:

- Let me know if there is anything else I can assist with.
- Please don't hesitate to reach out if you have any additional questions.
- If there is anything I can do to assist further, please let me know.

Check-up Questions

Answer the following questions to check your understanding of common expressions used in inquiry emails and response emails.

1. Among the following closing expressions, choose the one which has a different usage.

① Let me know if there is anything else I can assist with.
② Please don't hesitate to reach out if you have any additional questions.
③ Thank you for your assistance in this matter.
④ If there is anything I can do to assist further, please let me know.

2. Fill in the blank with an appropriate word or phrase.

① I am writing to ________________ information on quantum computing.

② I am writing ________________ your recent email about machine learning.

③ I am ________________ up your email regarding gene editing.

④ I would greatly ________________ your response.

Types of Formal Emails 3: Application Emails

What is an Application Email?

An application email is a type of email that is sent as part of the job application process.

Useful Expressions for an Application Email

1) Opening line examples:

- I am writing to express my interest in...
- I am writing to apply for the position of...
- I am writing to submit my candidacy for...
- I would like to apply for the job opening in...
- I am interested in the mechanical engineer position [position title] listed on your website on March 22nd [where and when you saw the ad] and would like to submit my application.

2) Closing examples:

- Thank you for considering my application.
- I am grateful for the opportunity to apply for this position.
- It would be great to have an opportunity to discuss my candidacy/ qualifications further.
- I would be grateful for the chance to interview for this position.
- Thank you for your time and consideration.

Types of Formal Emails 4: Notification Emails

What is a Notification Email?

A notification email is a type of email that is sent to inform someone about a specific event, change, or update.

Useful Expressions for a Notification Email

1) Opening line examples:

- I am writing to let you know that....
- This email is to inform you that...
- I am glad/pleased to let you know that...
- I am glad/pleased to inform you that...
- I regret to inform you that....

2) Closing examples:

- Please let me know if you need any further information.
- If you have any questions or concerns, please feel free to contact me.
- If there is anything else I can assist you with, please let me know.
- I appreciate your understanding and cooperation in this matter.
- Thank you for your consideration of this matter.

Check-up Questions

Answer the following questions to check your understanding of common expressions used in application emails and notification emails.

1. Below are different expressions used in the closing of application emails. Fill in the blank with an appropriate word or phrase.

   ① Thank you for considering my ________________.

   ② It would be great to have an opportunity to discuss my ____________ further.

   ③ I would be grateful for the chance to _____________ for this position.

   ④ Thank you for your ________________ and ________________.

2. Write the appropriate closing sentence for the opening line below.

I regret to inform you that our upcoming meeting regarding digital health care solutions must be rescheduled due to unforeseen circumstances.

____

____

____

____

Types of Formal Emails 5: Complaint Emails

What is a Complaint Email?

A complaint email is a type of email that is sent to express dissatisfaction or frustration with a product, service, or situation.

Useful Expressions for a Complaint Email

1) Opening line examples:

- The purpose of this email is to express my disappointment regarding...
- This email is to bring your attention to a problem with...
- With this email, I am complaining...
- I am writing to request immediate attention to...

2) Closing examples:

- It would be great to have a prompt resolution of this matter.
- A prompt response/Your attention to this issue would be desirable.
- I hope to hear back from you soon with a satisfactory solution.
- I hope to receive a resolution in a timely manner.
- Any steps that can be taken to correct this situation would be useful/helpful.

Types of Formal Emails 6: Proposal Emails

What is a Proposal Email?

A proposal email is a type of email that is sent to present an idea, concept, or solution to someone.

Useful Expressions for a Proposal Email

1) Opening line examples:

– This email is to propose a solution for...
– I am reaching out to offer my services for...
– With this email, I am submitting a proposal for the project of...
– I would like to propose a plan for...

2) Closing examples:

– I look forward to the opportunity to discuss this proposal further.
– I appreciate your consideration of my proposal.
– Please let me know if you need any additional information.
– I am available to answer any questions you may have.
– I am confident that this proposal will meet your needs.

TIPS

* An effective proposal email often includes an attachment with the important information a client or customer needs.
* Examples of some expressions to indicate that there is an attached file:

– Please find the attached...
– I have included... as an attachment for you to review.
– Attached to this email, you will find...
– For your reference, I have attached...
– More detailed information can be found in the file attached to this email.

Check-up Questions

Answer the following questions to check your understanding of common expressions used in complaint emails and proposal emails.

1. Among the following closing expressions, choose the one which has a different usage.

① I hope to hear back from you soon with a satisfactory solution. ② I am available to answer any questions you may have. ③ Your attention to this issue would be desirable. ④ It would be great to have a prompt resolution of this matter.

2. Correct the mistakes in the following sentences.

① For your reference, I attached the summaries of research studies on the use of Extended Reality in education.

______________________ → ______________________

② Any steps that can be taken to correct this situation is helpful.

______________________ → ______________________

③ This email is to bring your attention a problem with your humanoid robot product.

______________________ → ______________________

[Chapter 4]
Email Writing in Practice

ACADEMIC WRITING

Pre-writing Activity

Below are a list of different scenarios to write a formal email. Based on the scenario, identify the type of email needed in the blank.

1. ______________________________

From: Jason Miller, Intellectual Property Manager at Canvas, a graphic designing company
To: PromoFusion Advertising Company

The copyrighted images and graphics that were created and are owned exclusively by Canvas have been found on PromoFusion Advertising's website.

2. ______________________________

From: Jennifer Rodriguez, graduate student
To: Steve Li, Recruiting Manager

Jennifer is interested in working for the NGO, World Wildlife Fund (WWF) as an intern in the communication department to help with creating content for social media, websites, newsletters, and press releases to raise awareness about environmental issues and WWF's initiatives.

3. ______________________________

From: Jack Powell, CEO of IntelliBot
To: Steve Rogers, Red Pepper Executive

Jack would like to introduce humanoid robots for use in restaurant chains and to arrange a demonstration.

4. ______________________________

From: Lea Smith, project manager at Volt Drive
To: Research & Development (R&D) Department at ElectraCell

Lea requests a meeting with the R&D team at ElectraCell to seek consultation on the latest developments in solid-state battery technology and how they apply to Volt Drive's electric vehicles.

Writing Activity

Choose one of the scenarios from above and write your first draft of the formal email. Remember to use the proper format, expressions and styles discussed in this unit so far.

Subject: ______________________________

Feedback Activity

Receive feedback on your first draft of the formal email from your group members. Based on their feedback, create the second draft. Then, seek feedback on your second draft from your professor.

1.

Peer Feedback 1:

Done by: ______________

Peer Feedback 2:

____

____

____

____

____

____

Done by: ____________________

2.

The second draft of your formal email based on the peer feedback:

Subject:____

3.

Professor Feedback:

Rewriting Activity

Based on the professor's feedback, complete the final email on the following page for submission.

FINAL SUBMISSION

Class Day, Time: ________________

Student ID: ________________

Name: ________________

LEARNING OBJECTIVES	IN THIS UNIT STUDENTS WILL ...
PERFORMANCE & TASK	demonstrate the ability to grasp and articulate the meaning of **Liberal Arts & Humanities** content in English, showcasing comprehension of subject-specific terminology and concepts.
CRITICAL THINKING SKILLS 1	examine the organizational framework and substantive content of texts within the domains of **Liberal Arts & Humanities** through the application of diverse reading techniques.
CRITICAL THINKING SKILLS 2	extract key information from reading passages for a nuanced understanding and facilitate clear understanding of complex concepts.
COMMUNICATION SKILLS	discuss **Liberal Arts & Humanities** major related complex concepts clearly.
WRITING SKILLS	write summarization of reading passages by identifying key information of **Liberal Arts & Humanities** major related content.

UNIT 07

Content Readings for Final Presentation Project I: Liberal Arts & Humanities

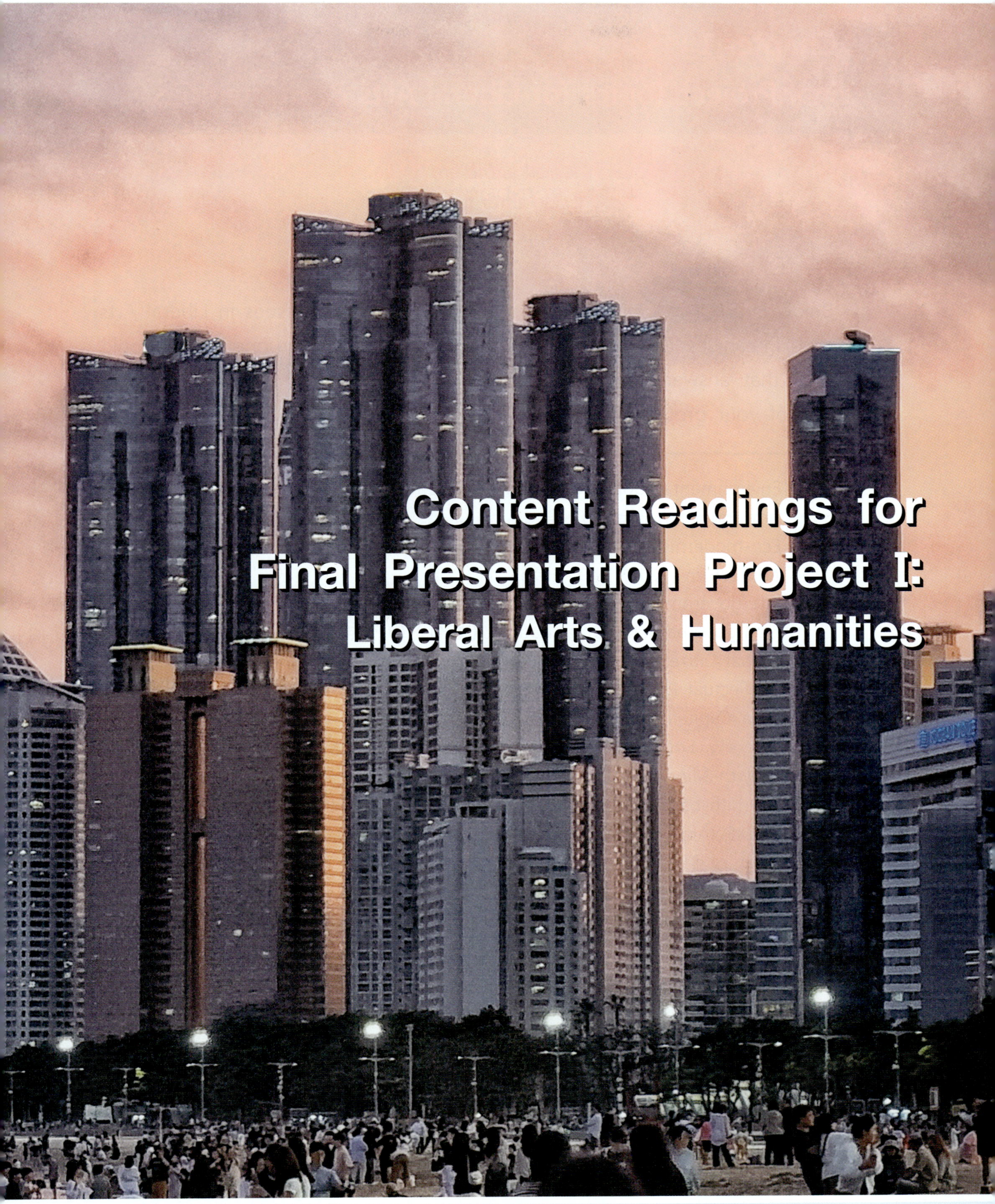

[Chapter 1]
Final Project Topics for Liberal Arts & Humanities

BRAINSTORMING

Discussion

Below is a list of 15 reading resource titles related to issues in Liberal Arts and Humanities. Each group member is required to choose one reading topic. After that, answer the following questions and share your responses with the rest of your group members.

- Environmental, Social, & Governance (ESG) (환경, 사회, & 지배 구조)
- Anthropocene Epoch (인류세)
- Eco-modernism (에코모더니즘)
- Agritecture (자연친화적 건축)
- Intergovernmental Organizations (IGOs) (정부간기구)
- Non-governmental Organizations (NGOs) (비정부기구)
- Global Citizenship (세계시민의식)
- Intellectual Property (지적 재산권)
- Data Capitalism (데이타 자본주의)
- Diversity, Equity, & Inclusion (DEI) (다양성, 형평성, & 포용성)
- Growth Mindset (성장 마인드셋)
- Strength-based Helping Strategies (강점 중심 지원 전략)
- ADDIE (Analysis Design Development Implementation Evaluation) Model (분석 설계 개발 실행 평가 모델)
- Digital Storytelling (디지털 스토리텔링)
- Glocalization (세방화)

1. What made you select the reading topic?

____

____

____

____

2. What do you already know about the selected reading topic?

ACADEMIC READING & WRITING SKILLS

You are going to read an article about the topic you have selected. Complete Pre-reading Activity, Reading Activity, and Writing Activity.

CONTENT READING RESOURCE 1

Pre-reading Activity

Read the definitions of the key vocabulary found in the article, Environmental, Social, & Governance (ESG). Fill in the blanks with the correct form of the words in bold.

dedication (n) the quality of being dedicated or committed to a task or purpose
sustainability (n) the ability to maintain or improve standards of living without damaging or using up available resources for the present and the future
inclusivity (n) the practice or policy of including people who might otherwise be excluded or marginalized
invest (v) to put money into different financial services like start-ups or mutual funds with the hope of gaining a profit
encompass (v) to include or cover a wide range of things
stewardship (n) taking responsibility to use and care for something that is valuable or important
compliance (n) the act of obeying an order, rule, or request
adapt (v) to change or adjust to new conditions or environments
ethical (adj) determining actions by following moral principles and using ideas of what is right and proper
evaluate (v) to judge or determine the significance, worth, or quality of something

1. The company is focusing on ___________ to ensure they do not deplete natural resources for future generations.
2. Many individuals choose to ___________ in companies that are committed to good environmental and social practices.
3. Her ___________ to the job ensured the project's success.
4. Some critics have doubts about the CEO's ___________ of the company.
5. It is crucial for companies to operate in an ___________ manner, ensuring that they adhere to moral principles.
6. Businesses must ___________ to new market trends and technologies to remain competitive.
7. The organization promotes ___________, ensuring that all individuals, regardless of background, have equal opportunities within the company.
8. To avoid legal issues, the firm ensures ___________ with all relevant laws and regulations.
9. Before launching a new program, it's important to ___________ its potential impacts and benefits.
10. The new policy aims to ___________ diverse perspectives and address the complex issues surrounding immigration reform.

Reading Activity

Please underline or highlight the parts containing key information as you read.

Environmental, Social, & Governance (ESG)

ESG, which stands for Environmental, Social, and Corporate Governance, serves as a strategic framework used to identify, assess, and address various aspects of an organization's objectives and operations. These aspects span from the company's impact on the environment and **dedication** to **sustainability**, to its workplace culture and **inclusivity**, as well as its overall approach to corporate risks and practices. This organizational structure has gained significant importance, particularly among socially responsible investors who seek to **invest** in companies with high ESG ratings or scores.

The three primary pillars of ESG are as follows:

Environmental Responsibility: This pertains to a company's commitment to sustainability and its effects on the environment. It **encompasses** factors such as carbon emissions, energy consumption, waste management, and overall environmental **stewardship**.

Social Engagement: This focuses on a company's internal workplace environment and how it treats its employees. It includes aspects such as employee satisfaction, retention, diversity, workplace conditions, and health and safety measures. Companies with content and healthy employees tend to perform better and are considered more attractive investments.

Corporate Governance: This pillar involves a company's dedication to good governance practices, which includes **compliance** with laws and regulations, fostering a positive corporate culture, fair pay ratios, transparent and accountable leadership, and a commitment to equity and equality in the workplace. Investors are interested in companies that can **adapt** to changing legal landscapes and demonstrate a strong commitment to **ethical** and responsible conduct.

In summary, ESG is a comprehensive framework that **evaluates** an organization's impact on the environment, its treatment of employees, and the quality of its corporate governance. As awareness of sustainable and socially responsible practices grows, ESG has become a critical factor in investment decision-making for investors who prioritize ethical and responsible business practices.

Retrieved and modified from: https://www.cio.com/article/409892/what-is-esg-environmental-social-and-governance-commitment-explained.html

Writing Activity

Using the key information you have underlined or highlighted, summarize the article in 3-5 sentences.

____

____

____

____

____

____

____

CONTENT READING RESOURCE 2

Pre-reading Activity

Read the definitions of the key vocabulary found in the article, The Anthropocene Epoch. Fill in the blanks with the correct form of the words in bold.

epoch (n) a period of time marked by an important change or development
geology (n) the study of the Earth's rocks, minerals, and processes that shape its surface
coincide (v) to occur at the same time or correspond in nature
profound (adj) having deep insight, significance, or understanding
industrialization (n) the development of industries in a country or region on a wide scale
urbanization (n) the process by which towns and cities are formed and become larger as more and more people begin living and working in central areas
deforestation (n) the action of clearing a wide area of trees
biodiversity (n) the variety of plant and animal life in the world or in a particular habitat
recognize (v) to acknowledge the existence, validity, or legality of something
shape (v) to influence, mold, or determine the course or development of something

1. The proposal to officially ____________ the Anthropocene Epoch as a new geological epoch is still under debate.
2. Mechanized methods of mass production are an essential component of ____________.
3. The extensive ____________ in the region has led to loss of habitat for many animal species.
4. The ____________ of different species in the rainforest is astounding, with new species still being discovered.
5. The two events seemed to ____________ perfectly, happening at the exact same time.
6. The Pleistocene ____________, known for its ice ages, saw the evolution of early humans and the megafauna that roamed the Earth.
7. One effect of ____________ is the rise of the megacity, which is a city that has more than 10 million inhabitants.
8. The term "Anthropocene" is used to describe a time when human activity has had a significant impact on Earth's ____________ and ecosystems.
9. The documentary provided a ____________ look into the societal challenges faced by marginalized communities.
10. Precedent-setting cases often ____________ the interpretation of legal principles for years to come.

Reading Activity

Please underline or highlight the parts containing key information as you read.

The Anthropocene Epoch

The Anthropocene is a proposed geological **epoch** that signifies a period in Earth's history when human activity has become a dominant influence on the planet's **geology** and ecosystems. The proposed start date for the Anthropocene Epoch is typically placed in the mid-20th century, **coinciding** with the rapid acceleration of human impacts on the Earth's systems. It is a concept that suggests that human actions have had a **profound** and lasting impact on the Earth's natural systems, to the extent that they have become a geological force.

The term "Anthropocene" combines the Greek word "anthropo," meaning human, with "-cene," a suffix used in geology to denote a specific time period. The idea behind the Anthropocene Epoch is that human activities, such as **industrialization**, **urbanization**, **deforestation**, agriculture, and the burning of fossil fuels, have altered the Earth's climate, landscapes, **biodiversity**, and natural processes in significant ways.

The Anthropocene Epoch is still a debated concept among geologists and scientists, and it is not yet formally **recognized** as an official epoch by the International Commission on Stratigraphy. Nevertheless, it has gained considerable attention in discussions about environmental issues and the recognition of humanity's role in **shaping** the planet's future.

Retrieved and modified from: https://www.washingtonpost.com/climate-environment/2023/07/12/anthropocene-epoch-meaning-crawford-lake/

Writing Activity

Using the key information you have underlined or highlighted, summarize the article in 3-5 sentences.

CONTENT READING RESOURCE 3

Pre-reading Activity

Read the definitions of the key vocabulary found in the article, Eco-modernism. Fill in the blanks with the correct form of the words in bold.

preserve (v) to maintain something in its original or existing state
address (v) to deal with or tackle a specific issue or problem
degradation (n) the process of getting worse or breaking down
convert (v) to change something into a different form or use
genetically modified (adj phr.) altered by manipulation of an organism's genetic material
resist (v) to oppose or withstand something
skepticism (n) an attitude of doubting or distrusting the truth of something
advocate (v) to publicly recommend or support
conservation (n) the prevention of wasteful use of a resource
restore (v) to bring something back to its original or proper condition

1. Many people view the widespread use of ____________ crops with concern, questioning their impact on health and the environment.
2. The organization ____________ for the use of renewable energy to replace fossil fuels.
3. Despite initial ____________, the new technology proved to be efficient and environmentally friendly.
4. The national park was established to ____________ the area's natural beauty and biodiversity.
5. Wildlife ____________ is of utmost importance for maintaining the balance of our ecosystems.
6. The skilled artisan worked diligently to ____________ the faded paintings in the museum, bringing out their vivid colors once more.
7. The deforestation caused severe ____________ of the local environment, including soil erosion and loss of biodiversity.
8. The engineer needed to ____________ the analog signal from the sensor into a digital format for processing by the microcontroller.

9. Some plants have developed the ability to ____________ harsh environmental conditions, allowing them to thrive in extreme climates.
10. The government implemented policies to ____________ the rising inflation rates and stabilize the economy.

Reading Activity

Please underline or highlight the parts containing key information as you read.

Eco-modernism

Eco-modernism argues that advanced technology can help **preserve** nature and **address** environmental challenges. This movement recognizes that while industrialization and urbanization have caused environmental **degradation**, the answer does not lie in **rejecting** modernity. Instead, it suggests that we can use technology to find sustainable solutions.

For instance, modern agricultural practices can reduce the need to **convert** natural habitats into farmlands. By using **genetically modified** crops that **resist** pests or require less water, farmers can produce more food on less land. This approach not only helps in preserving natural habitats but also addresses food security issues.

Another aspect of eco-modernism is the push for cleaner energy sources. For example, eco-modernists often **advocate** for nuclear energy, though it is met with **skepticism** from other groups. It produces electricity without emitting greenhouse gases, a leading cause of climate change. According to a report by Dr. James Hansen, former director of NASA's Goddard Institute for Space Studies, nuclear power has prevented nearly 1.8 million deaths worldwide between 1971 and 2009 by reducing air pollution.

Critics argue that technology alone can't save the environment and that we need a broader change in human values and lifestyles. However, eco-modernism believes in a balanced approach, where we don't have to choose between technological progress and environmental **conservation**.

In conclusion, eco-modernism presents a compelling vision of the future. It invites us to see technology not as a threat to the environment but as a tool to **restore** and sustain it.

Retrieved and modified from: https://link.springer.com/chapter/10.1007/978-3-030-63523-7_10

Writing Activity

Using the key information you have underlined or highlighted, summarize the article in 3-5 sentences.

CONTENT READING RESOURCE 4

Pre-reading Activity

Read the definitions of the key vocabulary found in the article, Agritecture. Fill in the blanks with the correct form of the words in bold.

groundbreaking (adj) introducing new and innovative ideas or methods that significantly revolutionize a particular field
merge (v) to combine two or more organizations, groups, or systems
premise (n) a key idea that supports an argument, an opinion, or a decision
produce (n) agricultural products, especially fruits and vegetables
pressing (adj) urgent or important
vertical (adj) positioned or oriented in an upright direction
aesthetic (adj) related to beauty, art, and taste
overarching (adj) comprehensive or including everything
swell (v) to increase in size, volume, or intensity
fleeting (adj) temporary or lasting for a very short period of time

1. The lawyer built her case on the ____________ that the defendant had a valid alibi for the time of the alleged crime.
2. The stock market experienced a ____________ surge in trading activity, driven by the announcement of a new product release.
3. The ____________ aim of the curriculum is to promote well-rounded growth in students.
4. The scientist's ____________ research in genetic engineering opened up new possibilities for treating genetic diseases.
5. The ____________ matter of income inequality has sparked widespread debates and calls for policy reforms in recent years.
6. As demand for the product grew, the company's profits began to ____________.
7. The pillars in the cathedral's architecture added a strong ____________ element, drawing the eye upward toward the ceiling.
8. The two major banks decided to ____________ in order to create a stronger financial institution with a larger market share.

9. The poet's use of vivid imagery and carefully chosen words created an ____________ experience that resonated deeply with the readers.
10. The ____________ from the agricultural sector significantly impacts the economy, encompassing cereals, fruits, and livestock.

Reading Activity

Please underline or highlight the parts containing key information as you read.

Agritecture

Agritecture offers a **groundbreaking** approach to urban sustainability by **merging** agriculture with modern architectural design. The central **premise** is the incorporation of agricultural systems within urban environments, reshaping the traditional view of where and how we grow our food. By adapting practices to fit unconventional settings like rooftops, vertical walls, and even underground spaces, agritecture seeks to provide fresh, local **produce** while addressing **pressing** issues of food security and urban planning.

A notable example of this is **vertical** farming. According to Dr. Dickson Despommier, author of "The Vertical Farm," this agritectural method could significantly reduce transportation costs, as food is produced where it's consumed. This cuts down on carbon emissions linked to transportation and the associated environmental impact. Additionally, agritecture promotes urban greenery, which brings more **aesthetic** appeal to cityscapes once dominated by grey concrete. In this way, it offers not only food but also a more pleasant city setting.

The **overarching** goal of agritecture is twofold. First, it's about resource conservation, utilizing limited urban space and water more efficiently than traditional farming. Second, it's a solution for sustainable urban development, especially vital as urban populations **swell** and the demand for locally sourced food increases.

In conclusion, agritecture isn't just a **fleeting** trend; it's a necessary evolution. As cities continue to expand, finding innovative ways to integrate agriculture with urban spaces ensures not just aesthetic appeal but also food security and sustainability.

Retrieved and modified from: https://www.da.gov.ph/agritecture-transforming-cities-into-green-food-producing-hubs/

Writing Activity

Using the key information you have underlined or highlighted, summarize the article in 3-5 sentences.

CONTENT READING RESOURCE 5

Pre-reading Activity

Read the definitions of the key vocabulary found in the article, Intergovernmental Organizations (IGOs). Fill in the blanks with the correct form of the words in bold.

entity (n) something that exists as a distinct and separate unit
sovereign (adj) relating to the supreme authority or power held by a government or ruling body over a specific territory or domain
treaty (n) a formal written agreement or contract between two or more countries or entities
interdependence (n) the mutual reliance and connection between different individuals, groups, or systems
assume (v) to take on a particular position, responsibility, or identity
collective (adj) made or shared by every member of a group
prosperous (adj) successful, thriving, and rich
indispensable (adj) absolutely necessary or essential
enduring (adj) long-lasting, or continuing for a long time
trajectory (n) a path, course, or direction

1. The global economy demonstrates the ____________ of nations, as changes in one country's economy can have ripple effects worldwide.
2. The ____________ appeal of classic literature continues to captivate readers across generations.
3. Public schools are not independent ____________ as they are influenced by broader educational policies and societal needs.
4. The ____________ efforts of the research team led to significant breakthroughs in renewable energy technology.
5. Innovative educational policies are crucial for shaping the ____________ of student success and learning outcomes.
6. After the retirement of the previous CEO, an experienced executive ____________ the role of leading the company.

7. The ____________ nation declared its independence from colonial rule and established its own government.
8. Access to clean water is ____________ for sustaining life and promoting public health.
9. After months of negotiations, the two countries finally decided to sign a ____________ to formalize their trade partnership.
10. The region experienced a period of ____________ growth after the implementation of strategic economic policies.

Reading Activity

Please underline or highlight the parts containing key information as you read.

Intergovernmental Organizations (IGOs)

IGOs are **entities** formed by **sovereign** states through international agreements or **treaties** to address common issues and promote cooperation on various matters. The primary purposes of IGOs are twofold: to facilitate global collaboration in the pursuit of peace, security, and stability, and to address pressing economic and social challenges.

In a world characterized by increasing globalization and **interdependence** among nations, IGOs have **assumed** a central role in international political systems and global governance. By providing a structured mechanism for nations to work together, IGOs contribute significantly to the **collective** efforts aimed at achieving a more secure and **prosperous** global community.

IGOs cover a diverse array of issues, encompassing governments from every corner of the world. This inclusivity underscores the universal reach and influence of these organizations. Some important IGOs include the United Nations (UN), which focuses on global peace and development, the World Trade Organization (WTO), which deals with international trade rules, and the World Health Organization (WHO), which works to improve global health.

Since the establishment of IGOs like the UN, these organizations have evolved into **indispensable** actors within the international community. Their ability to formulate rules and exert influence within their member countries underscores their growing global impact. IGOs provide a forum for collective decision-making, allowing nations to address complex global challenges more effectively. This evolution signifies the **enduring** relevance and importance of IGOs in shaping the **trajectory** of international relations.

Retrieved and modified from: https://hls.harvard.edu/bernard-koteen-office-of-public-interest-advising/about-opia/what-is-public-interest-law/public-service-practice-settings/international-public-interest-law-practice-setting/intergovernmental-organizations-igos/

Writing Activity

Using the key information you have underlined or highlighted, summarize the article in 3-5 sentences.

CONTENT READING RESOURCE 6

Pre-reading Activity

Read the definitions of the key vocabulary found in the article, Non-governmental Organizations (NGOs). Fill in the blanks with the correct form of the words in bold.

autonomous (adj) able to operate or function independently without direct control or intervention
tackle (v) to deal with a problem, task, or situation
endeavor (n) determined effort towards achieving a goal or undertaking a task
stakeholder (n) a person or organization that has an interest or investment in a particular project, organization, or system
pivotal (adj) crucial, essential, or of critical importance
advocacy (n) the act of supporting, promoting, or speaking in favor of a particular cause, idea, or policy
contravene (v) to go against a rule, law, or principle
tangible (adj) real, concrete, and can be clearly seen or understood
relief (n) assistance or support provided to alleviate a problem or suffering
foster (v) to nurture, support, or encourage the growth and development of something

1. The government's ____________ package provided much-needed financial assistance to the struggling businesses during the economic downturn.
2. ____________ for clean energy rules grew stronger as more people talked about protecting nature in politics.
3. The discovery of penicillin was ____________ in revolutionizing modern medicine, drastically reducing mortality rates from bacterial infections.
4. The company's decision to dump hazardous waste directly into the river ____________ numerous environmental regulations.
5. His ____________ to create a masterpiece required hours of meticulous brushwork and unwavering dedication.

6. In the proposed urban redevelopment project, the ____________ include residents, local businesses, and city officials, all of whom have a significant interest in the outcome.
7. To address the issue of declining sales, the company decided to ____________ it by implementing a new marketing strategy.
8. The ____________ region was granted the authority to manage its own economic policies and cultural affairs.
9. The university's mentorship program aims to ____________ a supportive environment for students to explore their academic interests.
10. In the experiment, the scientist observed ____________ results when the chemical reaction produced a distinct change in color.

Reading Activity

Please underline or highlight the parts containing key information as you read.

Non-governmental Organizations (NGOs)

NGOs, or Non-Governmental Organizations, are **autonomous** bodies free from direct governmental control. They are essentially non-profit entities that **tackle** a broad spectrum of social, environmental, and humanitarian issues. Such organizations lobby for specific causes, deliver essential services, and engage in fundraising **endeavors** to sustain their operations. Collaborating with a range of **stakeholders**, NGOs often undertake research initiatives aimed at shaping policies. Well-known examples include Amnesty International, Greenpeace, and Doctors Without Borders. NGOs serve as crucial agents in driving sustainable change and tackling global challenges.

To substantiate the controlling idea that NGOs are **pivotal** in creating sustainable change, one can look at their impact on social issues. For example, Amnesty International has long been a voice against human rights abuses, and their **advocacy** work has led to changes in legal frameworks. According to Susan Akram, in her publication "International Human Rights Clinic," Amnesty's campaigns have influenced the repeal of certain laws that **contravened** human rights. This exemplifies the power of NGOs in inciting **tangible** change on a legislative level.

Additionally, NGOs often collaborate with local communities, thus ensuring that changes are sustainable and context-appropriate. Doctors Without Borders, for instance, not only provides emergency medical services but also engages with local healthcare providers to build long-term solutions. Their work is a testament to how NGOs can collaborate for sustainable improvements, rather than offering temporary fixes.

In conclusion, NGOs contribute significantly to addressing various global challenges by influencing laws and collaborating with local communities. Their role is not just to provide immediate **relief** but to **foster** lasting, sustainable change, raising the question: What would our global landscape look like without the enduring efforts of NGOs?

Retrieved and modified from: https://www.britannica.com/topic/nongovernmental-organization

Writing Activity

Using the key information you have underlined or highlighted, summarize the article in 3-5 sentences.

CONTENT READING RESOURCE 7

Pre-reading Activity

Read the definitions of the key vocabulary found in the article, Global Citizenship. Fill in the blanks with the correct form of the words in bold.

embrace (v) to accept or adopt a new idea or opinion willingly
inhabitant (n) a person or animal that resides or occupies a particular place
appreciate (v) to recognize the value, significance, or beauty of something
concrete (adj) specific or tangible
eradication (n) getting rid of something
solidarity (n) unity or mutual support within a group
transcend (v) to go beyond, surpass or exceed
nationalism (n) a strong sense of loyalty and devotion to one's nation
vulnerable (adj) easily harmed or hurt
just (adj) fair and morally right

1. There are no ____________ plans to revitalize the downtown area despite the community's expressed desire for urban renewal and development.
2. Understanding the behavior of urban ____________ is crucial for effective city planning.
3. There was a feeling of ____________ between the team members as they worked together to achieve a common goal.
4. Political science scholars study the impact of ____________ on international relations and policymaking.
5. These regions will ____________ sustainable energy practices to address environmental concerns and promote a greener future.
6. After careful consideration, the judge reached a ____________ settlement that seemed fair to everyone involved in the case.
7. Bioengineering researchers aim for the ____________ of harmful germs through advanced medical interventions.
8. Certain NGOs have a mission or goal to protect ____________ populations and advocate for equal rights for everyone.

9. A powerful melody has the ability to ____________ words and languages, creating a universal connection among listeners worldwide.
10. Readers often ____________ the nuanced character development that contributes to the depth and richness of a novel.

Reading Activity

Please underline or highlight the parts containing key information as you read.

Global Citizenship

Global citizenship encompasses the idea that individuals and communities share social, environmental, and economic responsibilities on a global scale. In today's interconnected world, where transportation and communication have made the Earth a "global village," the consequences of decisions in one region can affect people worldwide. As our world faces challenges like climate change, pandemics, and refugee crises, the need for international cooperation becomes crucial. Global citizenship involves recognizing oneself as part of a global community and actively contributing to solving shared problems for the well-being of all individuals.

Being a global citizen means understanding and actively participating in the broader world. It goes beyond national identity to **embrace** a sense of responsibility for the planet and its **inhabitants**. Embracing this concept requires accepting and **appreciating** diverse identities, cultures, and perspectives. Global citizens reject discrimination based on religion, race, or nationality and actively engage in addressing challenges faced by the global community.

Global citizens possess important values such as human rights, recognizing the interdependence of all people, embracing diversity, and promoting sustainability. They empathize with those whose human rights are violated, respect differences, and adopt critical and creative thinking to analyze and solve global issues. Action-oriented, global citizens actively participate in addressing challenges by staying informed, forming opinions, and taking **concrete** actions.

The call for global citizenship becomes more urgent when considering the Sustainable Development Goals set by the UN. These goals encompass areas such as poverty **eradication**, zero hunger, environmental protection, and peace. Global citizens acknowledge the interconnectedness of these challenges and work collectively to achieve these goals for the benefit of humanity.

In times of crises, such as the COVID-19 pandemic, global citizens recognize the importance of international cooperation and **solidarity**. Overcoming global challenges requires collective efforts, **transcending nationalism**, and addressing the needs of **vulnerable** populations. Global citizenship is not just a concept; it is a practical call to action for individuals to contribute to a world that is interconnected, **just**, and harmonious for everyone.

Retrieved and modified from: http://sunhakpeaceprize.org/en/news/issue.php?bgu=view&idx=429

Writing Activity

Using the key information you have underlined or highlighted, summarize the article in 3-5 sentences.

CONTENT READING RESOURCE 8

Pre-reading Activity

Read the definitions of the key vocabulary found in the article, Intellectual Property. Fill in the blanks with the correct form of the words in bold.

output (n) the amount of something that a process, machine, or person produces
bestow (v) to give or grant something to someone
exclusivity (n) something is limited to a specific person, group, or situation, and not available to everyone
patent (n) a legal document that gives the person or company who invents something the exclusive right to make and sell it for a certain period of time
boost (v) to help something increase or improve, often by adding energy, support, or strength
elaborate (v) to give more details or information about something
formality (n) following established rules, customs, or protocols, especially in social or official situations
driving force (n phr.) the main factor or motivation that pushes or guides something forward or causes it to progress
incentivize (v) to provide a reward, benefit, or encouragement to motivate someone to do a particular action
landscape (n) the characteristic features of a particular situation or an area of activity

1. Diplomatic ____________ is crucial in establishing respectful relationships between nations during international negotiations.
2. The new policy aimed to ____________ voting participation by implementing measures to make the voting process more accessible and convenient.
3. The recent election result has changed the ____________ of the nation's politics.
4. The ____________ of the luxury brand contributed to its high pricing strategy, attracting a niche market of affluent consumers.
5. After presenting the initial findings, the researcher was asked to ____________ on the methodology used in the experiment.

6. The company decided to ____________ employees by offering performance-based bonuses to encourage higher levels of productivity.
7. The inventor applied for a ____________ to protect the intellectual property rights of their groundbreaking technology.
8. Technological innovation has been identified as a ____________ behind economic growth and development in many countries.
9. Prestigious awards are often ____________ upon scholars who have made significant contributions to their respective fields of study.
10. The engineer measured the daily ____________ of the solar panels to evaluate their efficiency in converting sunlight into electricity.

Reading Activity

Please underline or highlight the parts containing key information as you read.

Intellectual Property

Intellectual property encompasses legal rights that safeguard intangible creations, be they inventions, artistic **outputs**, or commercial trademarks. These rights **bestow exclusivity** upon creators, allowing them to manage and profit from their innovations. They come in various forms, such as **patents** for technological advancements, copyrights for literature and art, trademarks for branding, and trade secrets for proprietary information. Intellectual property rights are vital instruments for fostering innovation, **boosting** the economy, and ensuring market equity.

To **elaborate** on the controlling idea that intellectual property rights are key to innovation and economic growth, one only needs to look at the statistics. According to a study by the U.S. Chamber of Commerce's Global Innovation Policy Center, intellectual property-intensive industries contributed over $6 trillion to the U.S. economy in a single year. The report, authored by David Hirschmann, illustrates that intellectual property isn't just a legal **formality** but a **driving force** for economic vitality.

Furthermore, intellectual property rights also ensure that creators can compete fairly in the marketplace. For example, trademarks prevent confusion among consumers and protect the reputation of companies. This not only helps consumers make informed choices but also **incentivizes** companies to maintain quality, thus contributing to market equity.

In conclusion, intellectual property rights serve as essential mechanisms for stimulating innovation and sustaining economic well-being. Their impact goes beyond the individual creator, shaping the **landscape** of economies and marketplaces—prompting us to consider what a world without such protections would resemble.

Retrieved and modified from: https://www.investopedia.com/terms/i/intellectualproperty.asp
https://www.theglobalipcenter.com/resources/why-is-ip-important/

Writing Activity

Using the key information you have underlined or highlighted, summarize the article in 3-5 sentences.

CONTENT READING RESOURCE 9

Pre-reading Activity

Read the definitions of the key vocabulary found in the article, Data Capitalism. Fill in the blanks with the correct form of the words in bold.

transaction (n) an act of buying or selling goods or services, typically involving an exchange of money
scrutinize (v) to examine or inspect something closely and thoroughly, often with careful attention to detail
revenue (n) the total income generated by an organization or government from its normal business activities
exert (v) to apply force, effort, or influence in a determined or vigorous manner
reconcile (v) to bring into agreement or harmony, especially when dealing with conflicting ideas, beliefs, or data
imperative (n) something that is of vital importance or a crucial requirement
lag (v) to fall behind or fail to keep pace with others
extensive (adj) covering a large area or involving a wide range of details or elements
formidable (adj) difficult to deal with and requiring a lot of effort or skill
compromise (v) to settle a dispute or reach an agreement by finding a middle ground

1. In political negotiations, it is often necessary to ____________ on certain policy details in order to pass legislation that benefits the greater population.
2. There is no possibility of ____________ the two theories.
3. The government's ____________ from taxes is a key source of funding for public services and infrastructure projects.
4. The ____________ research conducted in the field of biology led to groundbreaking discoveries about genetic diversity.
5. In economics, a ____________ between a buyer and a seller forms the basis of market activity, influencing prices and overall economic performance.
6. It is ____________ to understand the historical context of a policy to assess its potential impact on society.

7 Creating machines that can replicate human decision-making skills has been a ____________ challenge.

8. Scientists must ____________ a great deal of precision and control when conducting experiments to ensure the validity of their research findings.

9. When conducting legal research, it is crucial to ____________ the case law to identify relevant precedents.

10. Failure to invest in the latest technologies can cause some countries to ____________ behind in terms of economic development.

Reading Activity

Please underline or highlight the parts containing key information as you read.

Data Capitalism

Data capitalism refers to an economic model in which data is a high-value asset that influences both economic **transactions** and power structures. Corporations gather, **scrutinize**, and commercialize personal and user-generated data to boost their **revenues** and **exert** societal impact. These practices raise urgent questions about privacy, mass surveillance, and the concentration of power. In the age of data capitalism, a pressing challenge is to **reconcile** technological innovation and economic growth with the **imperative** of safeguarding individual freedoms.

One of the challenges in balancing innovation with personal rights involves considering regulatory hurdles. According to Frank Pasquale, author of "The Black Box Society," current regulations are often reactive and **lag** behind rapid technological advancements, making them inadequate for today's data-centric landscape. This lag contributes to power imbalances, as companies like Facebook and Google amass enormous amounts of data, thus increasing their economic and social leverage.

Additionally, the issue of consent in data collection highlights the clash between individual rights and corporate interests. Many people unknowingly agree to **extensive** data collection when they accept user agreements, sacrificing their privacy for the use of "free" services. This practice places individuals at a significant disadvantage in the data capitalist system, reinforcing the urgent need for more transparent and equitable policies.

In conclusion, the complexities of data capitalism present a **formidable** challenge for society: how to encourage technological progress while also ensuring individual freedoms are not **compromised**. The time is ripe for a collective conversation and action on updating regulations that can address this pressing issue.

Retrieved and modified from: https://www.demos.org/research/data-capitalism-and-algorithmic-racism

Writing Activity

Using the key information you have underlined or highlighted, summarize the article in 3-5 sentences.

CONTENT READING RESOURCE 10

Pre-reading Activity

Read the definitions of the key vocabulary found in the article, Diversity, Equity, & Inclusion (DEI). Fill in the blanks with the correct form of the words in bold.

promote (v) to actively support or encourage growth or development of someone or something
represent (v) to act or speak on behalf of someone or something
compensation (n) the payment, benefits, or rewards given to an individual in return for their work, services, or losses
initiative (n) a new plan or action introduced to address a particular issue or achieve a specific goal
disparity (n) a significant difference or inequality between two or more things
marginalized (adj) pushed to the edges of society, often experiencing discrimination, exclusion, or limited access to resources
confront (v) to face or address a problem, challenge, or difficult situation directly
relinquish (v) to voluntarily give up or release control, possession, or a claim to something
dominance (n) having power, authority, or control over others
redistribution (n) the process of reallocating resources, wealth, or opportunities to create a more equitable distribution

1. Understanding the experiences of ____________ communities is a key focus in sociology and social justice studies.
2. The government's new education policy includes a plan for the ____________ of funding to ensure that schools in poorer communities have access to the same quality of resources.
3. Elected officials in political science are chosen to ____________ the concerns and needs of the residents.
4. Researchers are studying the ____________ in income levels between various socioeconomic groups to propose policies to reduce economic inequality.

5. It is essential to ____________ inclusive teaching practices that cater to diverse learning styles and abilities.
6. Lawyers must often ____________ complex legal issues and develop effective strategies for their clients.
7. Environmental ____________ aim to mitigate negative impacts of human activities on the natural world.
8. Achieving ____________ in the 100-meter sprint requires years of dedicated training, strategic planning, and unwavering determination.
9. The issue of fair ____________ for labor is a central topic of discussion within the field of labor economics.
10. Managers sometimes ____________ certain powers to improve employees' independence.

Reading Activity

Please underline or highlight the parts containing key information as you read.

Diversity, Equity, & Inclusion (DEI)

DEI refers to a set of principles and practices that **promote** equal opportunities and fair treatment for individuals from diverse backgrounds. Diversity refers to **representing** individuals from various backgrounds, including races, genders, sexual orientations, disabilities, and religions, at all organizational levels. "Equity" emphasizes fairness in **compensation** and treatment. "Inclusion" focuses on fostering a sense of belonging and valuing voices within the organization. DEI **initiatives** encompass training, policies, and culture to promote inclusivity and address **disparities**.

DEI traces its roots to 1960s anti-discrimination laws like the Equal Pay Act and Civil Rights Act. These laws prompted ongoing efforts to create equitable workplaces and schools. Beyond non-discrimination, the goal of DEI became also to promote inclusivity in these places.

While DEI initiatives may have different names, their shared aim is to prompt reflection on how **marginalized** groups are treated. DEI **confronts** power dynamics, questioning whether certain groups are inherently better suited to lead. Resistance to DEI can arise from discomfort in **relinquishing dominance** and privilege.

Critiques of DEI often paint it as an unfair **redistribution** of opportunities, framing it as giving unearned advantages to marginalized individuals while taking them away from others. Supporters of DEI argue that relinquishing dominance and privilege can be uncomfortable, but it's a necessary step for the greater good of the workplace, the nation, and its democracy. They further contend that some critiques view diversity as a problem belonging to "them" rather than an issue that encompasses all of society.

Retrieved and modified from: https://abcnews.go.com/US/dei-programs/story?id=97004455

Writing Activity

Using the key information you have underlined or highlighted, summarize the article in 3-5 sentences.

CONTENT READING RESOURCE 11

Pre-reading Activity

Read the definitions of the key vocabulary found in the article, Growth Mindset. Fill in the blanks with the correct form of the words in bold.

pioneer (n) a person or group who is among the first to explore or settle in a new area, or who takes a lead in developing or introducing new ideas
embrace (v) to accept or adopt a new idea, method, or concept, often with enthusiasm or openness
setback (n) a temporary or minor obstacle or delay that hinders progress or achievement of a goal
restrict (v) to limit, control, or regulate something
pinpoint (v) to identify or locate something precisely
extend (v) to make something longer, broader, or more comprehensive
realm (n) a specific area, domain, or field of study or activity
resilience (n) the ability to bounce back or recover quickly from difficulties or challenges
adversity (n) difficult or unfavorable circumstances or events
unlock (v) to open or release something that was previously inaccessible or restricted

1. Firewalls are implemented to ____________ unauthorized access to a network.
2. Ada Lovelace is considered a ____________ in computer science, being one of the first individuals to recognize the potential for using machines for purposes beyond mere calculation.
3. The ____________ of political science encompasses the study of governance structures, policies, and their impact on societies.
4. Scholars increasingly ____________ interdisciplinary approaches to foster innovation.
5. Throughout history, the ____________ of human societies has been evident in their ability to recover and rebuild after natural disasters and other significant challenges.
6. Innovative teaching methods aim to ____________ students' full potential, fostering creativity and critical thinking.

7. The law was ___________ to cover new forms of online privacy breaches in response to rapid technological advancements.
8. How individuals cope with and adapt to ___________ shapes their mental well-being.
9. Researchers use advanced imaging techniques to ___________ the exact location of specific proteins within a cell.
10. Despite facing a ___________ in the form of budget cuts, the engineering team persevered and completed the project ahead of schedule.

Reading Activity

Please underline or highlight the parts containing key information as you read.

Growth Mindset

The concept of a growth mindset is a mental framework that inserts significant influence over our thoughts, decisions, and behaviors. The positive implications of adopting a growth mindset are numerous. The **pioneer** of growth mindset, Carol Dweck, pointed out that it empowers athletes to **embrace** learning and to welcome challenges, mistakes, and feedback.

A growth mindset fundamentally shapes how we respond to challenges and **setbacks**, as well as our capacity for self-reflection. In contrast, a fixed mindset, characterized by perceiving situations as unchangeable, **restricts** personal agency.

Is the ball too fast to catch, or does it require focus and quick reflexes? Is the opposing team too skilled to beat? In these situations, the initial response often stems from a fixed mindset, possibly driven by fear of falling short. If one claims the task is impossible, they may not give their all, leading to minimal self-assessment.

Now, consider adopting a growth mindset. Recognizing that even though the challenge is significant, with full commitment, it can be tackled. This perspective turns the experience into a learning opportunity. Success or failure becomes a source of valuable feedback, enabling the athlete to **pinpoint** areas for improvement or make adjustments in their approach.

The application of a growth mindset **extends** far beyond the **realm** of sports. In everyday life, adopting this outlook empowers individuals to approach challenges with a constructive mindset. Whether it's tackling a difficult work project, navigating personal relationships, or pursuing personal goals, a growth mindset encourages continuous learning and improvement. It fosters **resilience**, adaptability, and a willingness to invest effort even in the face of **adversity**. By embracing the belief that abilities can be developed through dedication and hard work, individuals can **unlock** their full potential in various aspects of their lives.

Retrieved and modified from: https://appliedsportpsych.org/blog/2021/04/revisiting-growth-mindset-as-a-core-capacity-of-sport-psychology/

Writing Activity

Using the key information you have underlined or highlighted, summarize the article in 3-5 sentences.

CONTENT READING RESOURCE 12

Pre-reading Activity

Read the definitions of the key vocabulary found in the article, Strength-based Helping Strategies. Fill in the blanks with the correct form of the words in bold.

diverge (v) to go in different directions or to develop in separate ways
unearth (v) to discover or reveal something that was previously hidden or unknown
innate (adj) existing naturally within a person or organism, rather than learned or acquired
leverage (v) to use something to gain an advantage or achieve a desired result
pivotal (adj) of crucial importance or central to the development or outcome of a situation
evolve (v) to develop or change gradually over time, often involving improvements or adaptations
facilitator (n) a person or thing that helps make a process or task easier or smoother
amplify (v) to make something stronger, more pronounced, or more significant
foster (v) to encourage or promote the development or growth of something
self-efficacy (n) the belief in one's own ability to successfully accomplish tasks, solve problems, or achieve goals

1. The Supreme Court's ____________ decision in the case set a legal precedent that would impact future interpretations of constitutional rights.
2. Government policies aimed at ____________ competition in the telecommunications industry have led to greater innovation and lower prices for consumers.
3. The researcher argued that the ____________ ability for language acquisition is a fundamental aspect of human cognitive development.
4. The archaeologists ____________ ancient artifacts that provided valuable insights into the daily life of the civilization that once thrived in the region.
5. The natural disaster made changes on the land, and they will be ____________ as time goes on.
6. High ____________ is associated with increased academic performance, as students with strong beliefs in their abilities tend to persist in the face of challenges.

7. The workshop ____________ guided participants through interactive exercises to enhance their teamwork and problem-solving skills.
8. The research findings began to ____________ from the initially hypothesized outcomes, leading to a reevaluation of the experimental design.
9. The theory of natural selection explains how species ____________ to better adapt to their environments through successive generations.
10. The company ____________ its strong brand reputation to secure partnerships with influential stakeholders in the industry.

Reading Activity

Please underline or highlight the parts containing key information as you read.

Strength-based Helping Strategies

Strength-based helping strategies, rooted in positive psychotherapy, **diverge** from conventional approaches by prioritizing internal strengths and abilities over weaknesses and shortcomings. This change in focus helps create a positive way of thinking, giving individuals the power to use their best qualities, become stronger, and see the world in a brighter light. The underlying principle is that discussing a client's challenges serves as a means to **unearth** the **innate** strengths they can **leverage** to construct solutions. This approach traces its origins back to the 1950s and was further refined by the influential psychologist Donald Clifton, known as the pioneer of strength-based therapy and a **pivotal** figure in the realm of positive psychology.

Over time, strength-based therapy has grown and **evolved** thanks to the work of many professionals from different fields like social work and counseling. What sets it apart is that it believes a person should be a big part of their own healing process. While the therapist should know a lot about different ways to help, they think the person should take the lead in finding the answers, with their support.

Critics of strength-based therapy have contended that it assumes individuals possess all the necessary resources within themselves to tackle any problem. Advocates, however, assert that while certain issues may be exceptionally complex, therapists still bring their unique expertise to the table. They serve as guides and **facilitators**, helping clients navigate their strengths and providing insights that augment the client's own abilities. In this way, strength-based therapy offers a balanced approach that acknowledges both the inherent capabilities of individuals and the valuable contributions of skilled therapists.

In practice, strength-based therapy encourages a shift away from focusing solely on problems towards highlighting an individual's capacities. By recognizing and **amplifying** these internal assets, clients are better equipped to face challenges with confidence and determination. This approach not only promotes personal growth but also **fosters** a sense of agency and **self-efficacy**, ultimately leading to more sustainable and positive outcomes in the client's life journey.

Retrieved and modified from: https://www.psychologytoday.com/intl/therapy-types/strength-based-therapy

Writing Activity

Using the key information you have underlined or highlighted, summarize the article in 3-5 sentences.

CONTENT READING RESOURCE 13

Pre-reading Activity

Read the definitions of the key vocabulary found in the article, ADDIE Model. Fill in the blanks with the correct form of the words in bold.

comprise (v) to consist of or be made up of
comprehensive (adj) covering or including all aspects of a subject or topic
scrutinize (v) to examine or inspect closely and thoroughly for details or accuracy
refinement (n) the process of making improvements or enhancements to something, often to increase its quality or effectiveness
corroborate (v) to provide evidence or support for a claim or statement
align (v) to bring elements or components into proper or coordinated arrangement or agreement
cyclical (adj) recurring in a regular pattern or sequence, typically with a defined cycle or rhythm
linear (adj) following a straight line or a sequential, step-by-step progression
iteration (n) the process of repeating or reworking a set of steps or procedures to achieve a desired outcome
indispensable (adj) absolutely necessary or essential, without which something cannot function or succeed

1. The engineers focused on the ____________ of the algorithm to optimize its performance in processing large datasets.
2. The educational curriculum was ____________ with national standards to ensure consistency in learning outcomes across schools.
3. The committee ____________ the proposed legislation to ensure it complied with existing legal frameworks.
4. The software engineer conducted multiple ____________ of code testing to identify and fix any bugs or errors.
5. Through careful analysis of the experimental data, the researchers observed a clear ____________ relationship between the independent variable and the dependent variable.

6. The laboratory equipment was ____________ for conducting experiments and generating reliable data for the scientific study.
7. The research project ____________ a team of scientists from different disciplines working together to achieve a common goal.
8. The study's findings were ____________ by independent research conducted by a separate team of scientists.
9. The ____________ report on economic trends analyzed various indicators, including inflation rates, employment data, and GDP growth.
10. The economist's analysis showed that economic recessions tend to be part of a ____________ pattern, alternating with periods of growth.

Reading Activity

Please underline or highlight the parts containing key information as you read.

ADDIE Model

The ADDIE model **comprises** five critical stages: Analysis, Design, Development, Implementation, and Evaluation. These stages collectively serve as a **comprehensive** guide for instructors to plan, execute, and assess educational programs. In the Analysis stage, the learning environment and the needs of the students are carefully **scrutinized**. During the Design phase, educators lay out the instructional techniques, organize the course content, and decide on assessment strategies. The Development phase is centered on crafting the instructional content, while the Implementation stage focuses on the actual teaching process using these materials. Finally, the Evaluation stage measures how effective the educational program is and gathers feedback for further **refinements**. Understanding and applying the ADDIE model is pivotal for devising education and training programs that are not only effective but also adaptable.

Numerous studies **corroborate** the effectiveness of the ADDIE model in instructional design. According to Branch in his book "Instructional Design: The ADDIE Approach," the model leads to superior learning outcomes compared to other non-structured methods. This comprehensive framework allows educators to identify gaps in both content and delivery, thereby **aligning** the instructional goals more closely with learner needs.

The Evaluation stage in the ADDIE model has a dual role: it not only assesses the program's current effectiveness but also informs future **iterations**. This feature makes the model **cyclical** rather than **linear**, facilitating continual adjustments and improvements in instructional design.

In summary, the ADDIE model provides a systematic, research-backed approach for designing and improving educational programs. Its cyclical nature allows for continual adaptations to better meet learner needs. The model's inherent flexibility and focus on continuous improvement make it an **indispensable** tool in the ever-evolving landscape of education.

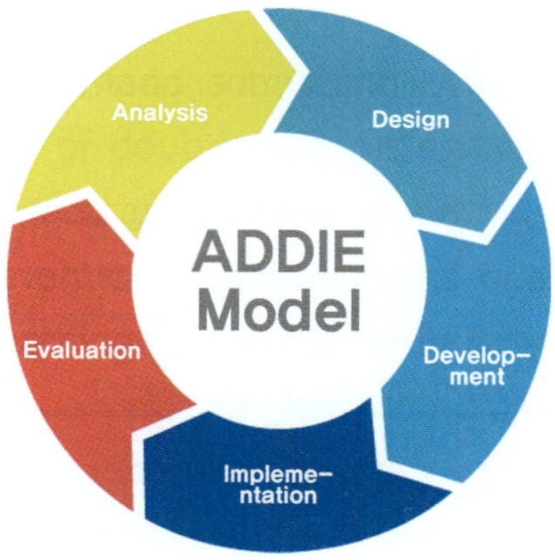

Retrieved and modified from: https://educationaltechnology.net/the-addie-model-instructional-design/

Writing Activity

Using the key information you have underlined or highlighted, summarize the article in 3-5 sentences.

CONTENT READING RESOURCE 14

Pre-reading Activity

Read the definitions of the key vocabulary found in the article, Digital Storytelling. Fill in the blanks with the correct form of the words in bold.

prominence (n) the state of being important, well-known, or standing out in a particular context
encompass (v) to include, cover, or surround a wide range of ideas, topics, or elements
medium (n) a means or method of communication, such as books, films, or digital platforms
immersive (adj) deeply involving and engaging participants, often providing a sense of absorption
ubiquity (n) the state of being everywhere or widely present
empower (v) to give authority, confidence, or rights to individuals or groups, enabling them to take control of their own circumstances
marginalized (adj) being pushed to the edge or excluded from the mainstream, often due to social, economic, or political factors
evoke (v) to bring forth or elicit a specific emotion, memory, or response in someone
discern (v) to perceive or recognize something with clarity, often involving the ability to distinguish details or nuances
fabricated (adj) created or constructed, often with the implication that it is not genuine or has been artificially produced

1. The professor emphasized the importance of choosing the appropriate ____________ for presenting research findings.
2. Education plays a vital role in ____________ individuals to make informed decisions about their financial well-being.
3. The study of environmental science ____________ various disciplines, including biology, chemistry, and geology.
4. The artist's use of color and composition in the painting ____________ a sense of nostalgia among viewers.
5. The virtual reality simulation offered an ____________ learning environment for engineering students.

6. The reviewer discovered ____________ data in the paper, violating the integrity of the research.
7. The ____________ of smartphones has revolutionized the way information is accessed and shared in today's society.
8. In the field of economics, the ____________ of certain theories has shaped policy decisions for decades.
9. The sociological study focused on the experiences of ____________ communities in urban settings.
10. The biologist was able to ____________ subtle genetic variations that were crucial to the research findings.

Reading Activity

Please underline or highlight the parts containing key information as you read.

Digital Storytelling

Digital storytelling is a dynamic and evolving form of narrative expression that has gained **prominence** in the digital age. It **encompasses** the creation and sharing of stories through various digital **mediums**, such as videos, podcasts, interactive websites, and social media platforms. Unlike traditional storytelling, which primarily relied on verbal or written communication, digital storytelling leverages multimedia elements like images, audio, and video to engage and captivate audiences. This innovative approach to storytelling has transformed how individuals, communities, and organizations communicate, allowing for more **immersive** and interactive storytelling experiences.

One of the key advantages of digital storytelling lies in its accessibility and inclusivity. With the **ubiquity** of smartphones and internet connectivity, people from diverse backgrounds and geographical locations can participate in the creation and consumption of digital stories. This democratization of storytelling **empowers** individuals to share their unique perspectives, experiences, and voices with a global audience. It breaks down barriers of entry traditionally associated with traditional publishing or media platforms, providing a platform for **marginalized** or underrepresented communities to be heard.

Moreover, digital storytelling enables a multidimensional narrative experience.

Through the integration of various media formats, storytellers can **evoke** emotions, convey information, and create atmospheres in ways that traditional text alone may struggle to achieve. For example, a combination of visuals, music, and spoken word can convey a depth of meaning and emotion that surpasses what can be achieved through written words alone. This richness of expression allows for more nuanced and impactful storytelling, fostering a deeper connection between the storyteller and the audience.

However, it is essential to acknowledge that, like any form of communication, digital storytelling is not without its challenges. The proliferation of digital content demands critical thinking skills from audiences to **discern** between authentic, credible narratives and misleading or **fabricated** stories. Moreover, privacy concerns and ethical considerations must be carefully navigated when sharing personal stories in the digital realm.

Retrieved and modified from: https://www.ala.org/acrl/publications/keeping_up_with/storytelling

Writing Activity

Using the key information you have underlined or highlighted, summarize the article in 3-5 sentences.

CONTENT READING RESOURCE 15

Pre-reading Activity

Read the definitions of the key vocabulary found in the article, Glocalization. Fill in the blanks with the correct form of the words in bold.

adaptation (n) the process of adjusting or modifying something to suit a particular environment or circumstance
tailor (v) to customize or modify something to suit specific needs or preferences
norm (n) standard or rule that is widely accepted and followed in a particular society or group
homogenization (n) the process of making something uniform or standardized, often at the expense of diversity or variation
multinational (adj) involving multiple nations or countries
resonate (v) to evoke a strong or sympathetic response, often due to a deep connection or relevance to one's experiences or beliefs
sensitivity (n) the capacity to detect or respond to subtle changes or differences often with care and consideration for others' feelings
commerce (n) the exchange of goods and services, typically involving buying and selling on a large scale
preserve (v) to protect or maintain something in its original state or condition
landscape (n) the overall visual or sensory impression of an area

1. The ____________ of products can sometimes lead to a lack of consumer choice, as similar items flood the market.
2. In the field of biology, ____________ refers to the evolutionary process by which organisms develop traits that help them survive and thrive in their habitats.
3. The artist's portrayal of social injustice in their painting ____________ deeply with viewers, sparking important discussions about inequality.
4. The ____________ of citing sources ensures accuracy and credibility in academic research.
5. The rapidly evolving technological ____________ has transformed the way we communicate and conduct business in the 21st century.

6. The establishment of national parks aims to ____________ natural habitats and biodiversity for future generations.
7. Excellent teachers often ____________ their lesson plans to accommodate different learning styles and abilities within a diverse classroom.
8. The study of international ____________ explores the complex networks and regulations that govern trade between nations.
9. The ____________ of consumer spending to changes in prices can greatly impact a country's economy.
10. The ____________ corporation's operations spanned several continents, making it a major player in the global economy.

Reading Activity

Please underline or highlight the parts containing key information as you read.

Glocalization

Glocalization is a term that combines "globalization" and "localization." It refers to the **adaptation** and blending of global influences with local cultures and contexts. In essence, it is the process by which global products, ideas, and practices are **tailored** to suit the preferences, values, and **norms** of specific local communities or regions.

This concept recognizes that while globalization has led to the spread of common ideas and products worldwide, it doesn't mean a complete **homogenization** of cultures. Instead, glocalization emphasizes the importance of recognizing and respecting the unique characteristics and needs of local communities.

For example, **multinational** corporations may adjust their marketing strategies, product features, or even brand names to **resonate** better with specific regional audiences. This could involve modifying product flavors, packaging, or advertising campaigns to align with local tastes and cultural **sensitivities**.

Glocalization can also extend to areas beyond **commerce**, influencing politics, education, and even language. It acknowledges that even in our increasingly interconnected world, there remains a strong desire for people to **preserve** and celebrate their cultural identities.

Ultimately, glocalization represents a dynamic interaction between the global and the local, highlighting the importance of understanding and appreciating diverse perspectives and traditions in today's interconnected world. It plays a crucial role in shaping the evolving **landscape** of our global society.

Retrieved and modified from: https://www.britannica.com/money/topic/globalization

Writing Activity

Using the key information you have underlined or highlighted, summarize the article in 3-5 sentences.

[Chapter 2]
Outlining a Final Group Project

DISCUSSION

1. Introduce the topic you have read to the rest of the group members by providing a summary of the key points from the article.

2. Determine a topic for the final group project from the readings shared by group members considering the following questions.

- Does the topic capture the interest of the audience, including your group members?
- Does the topic match the knowledge level and needs of your audience?
- Does the topic bring a fresh idea, new research findings, or unique insights?
- Is the topic current and up-to-date? Does it address issues or trends that are currently relevant?
- Can your topic be used in the real world, or does it have practical implications?
- Are there enough sources (e.g., articles or data) to support your presentation?
- Can you create an engaging presentation on this topic using interactive elements, visuals, or demonstrations?

3. Once the group project topic is selected, fill in the blanks with the main argument and three supporting arguments.

Topic: ______________________________

Main Argument for Your Final Group Project

Topic Sentence for Supporting Argument 1:

Topic Sentence for Supporting Argument 2:

Topic Sentence for Supporting Argument 3:

LEARNING OBJECTIVES	IN THIS UNIT STUDENTS WILL ...
PERFORMANCE & TASK	demonstrate the ability to grasp and articulate the meaning of **Social Science & Business** content in English, showcasing comprehension of subject-specific terminology and concepts.
CRITICAL THINKING SKILLS 1	examine the organizational framework and substantive content of texts within the domains of Social **Science & Business** through the application of diverse reading techniques.
CRITICAL THINKING SKILLS 2	extract key information from reading passages for a nuanced understanding and facilitate clear understanding of complex concepts.
COMMUNICATION SKILLS	discuss **Social Science & Business** major related complex concepts clearly.
WRITING SKILLS	write summarization of reading passages by identifying key information of Social **Science and Business** major related content.

UNIT 08

Content Readings for Final Presentation Project II: Social Science & Business

[Chapter 1]
Final Project Topics for Social Science & Business

BRAINSTORMING

This unit focuses on the study of Social Science and Business issues. Before reading the article in depth, as a group, predict the content of the article by matching topics with definitions and write the correct terms in the blanks. Refer to the readings in the unit as needed.

Topic Set A

1) Douglas McGregor's Theory X and Theory Y
2) Enterprise Resource Planning (ERP)
3) Framing Theory (or Framing Effect)
4) Window Dressing in Finance
5) Call Money Rate

__________ 1. The act of making something appear more attractive or favorable than it truly is, often seen in financial reporting.

__________ 2. A full software solution that brings together different business processes and functions into a single, unified system.

__________ 3. The idea that how information is presented can influence people's opinions or decisions by emphasizing certain aspects.

__________ 4. These influence how people work and suggest flexible leadership based on Maslow's ideas. Recognizing that work can be complicated, they help everyone keep learning and understanding.

__________ 5. The interest rate at which banks lend money to each other for short-term financing needs.

Topic Set B

6) Double-dip Recession
7) Lorenz Curve and Gini Coefficient
8) The Four Points of SWOT Analysis
9) The Five Levels of Maslow's Hierarchy of Needs
10) Big Mac Index

__________ 6. Tools used in economics to illustrate income or wealth distribution within a population, helping to assess inequality and disparities.

__________ 7. An economic situation where an economy recovers from a recession but then falls back into a second downturn, leading to extended economic difficulties.

__________ 8. A strategic planning tool that assesses an organization's Strengths, Weaknesses, Opportunities, and Threats, aiding in decision-making and planning.

__________ 9. A playful way to compare purchasing power and currency values by looking at the cost of a Big Mac in different countries.

__________ 10. A psychological theory that categorizes human needs from basic necessities like food and shelter to higher-level needs such as love and self-fulfillment.

Topic Set C

11) Leverage Effect
12) Spillover Effects
13) The Market for Lemons
14) Bandwagon Effect
15) Red - Blue - Purple Ocean Strategy

__________ 11. Describe a situation where determining product quality poses challenges, leading to issues in buying and selling.

__________ 12. Unintended impacts of one event or decision on something else, often causing a chain reaction in related areas.

__________ 13. The phenomenon where a small change in one factor results in a larger change in another, often used in finance to amplify gains or losses.

__________ 14. When people follow a trend or make decisions because many others are doing the same, often influenced by social pressure.

__________ 15. Explore varied business competition strategies through colors: red for intensity, blue for tranquility, and purple for a balanced approach.

Discussion

Below is a list of 15 reading resource titles related to issues in Social Science & Business. Each group member is to choose one reading topic. Then respond to the following questions and share answers with group members.

Major-related Topics
1. Douglas McGregor's Theory X and Theory Y 2. Enterprise Resource Planning (ERP) 3. Framing Theory (or Framing Effect) 4. Window Dressing in Finance 5. Call Money Rate
6. Double-dip Recession 7. Lorenz Curve and Gini Coefficient 8. The Four Points of SWOT Analysis 9. The Five Levels of Maslow's Hierarchy of Needs 10. Big Mac Index
11. Leverage Effect 12. Spillover Effects 13. The Market for Lemons 14. Bandwagon Effect 15. Red - Blue - Purple Ocean Strategy

1. What topic did you select? Why did you select the topic?

____

2. What do you already know about the topic?

____

3. What do you want to learn about the topic?

____

ACADEMIC READING & WRITING SKILLS

Read an article about the topic you have selected and complete Pre-reading Activity, Reading Activity, and Writing Activity.

CONTENT READING RESOURCE 1

Pre-reading Activity

Read the definitions of the key vocabulary found in the article, **Douglas McGregor's Theory X and Theory Y**. Fill in the blanks with the correct form of the words in bold.

hierarchy (n) a system or organization in which people or groups are ranked one above the other according to status or authority
proposition (n) a statement or assertion expressing a judgment or opinion
intertwined (adj) twisted or woven together; closely connected or related
self-actualization (n) the realization or fulfillment of one's talents, potentialities, or capabilities
aligns (v) to bring into line or alignment; to adjust or arrange in a straight line
advocates (n) persons who publicly support or recommend a particular cause or policy
traits (n) distinguishing qualities or characteristics, especially of one's personal nature
divergence (n) the act of moving, extending, or branching off in different directions
contingency (n) a future event or circumstance that is possible but cannot be predicted with certainty; a provision for an unforeseen event or circumstance
legacy (n) something handed down or received from an ancestor or predecessor; anything received from the past, as from an ancestor or predecessor

1. The project manager worked to ______________ the team's goals with the company's overall objectives.
2. In the workplace, the ______________ dictates the order of authority, with managers at the top and employees below.
3. Companies often have ______________ plans in place to address unexpected

challenges or disruptions.

4. The politician presented a bold ____________ during the debate, outlining his stance on economic reforms.
5. Pursuing education and personal development can lead to a sense of ____________, as individuals realize their full potential.
6. Environmental ____________ rallied for the protection of endangered species.
7. Positive ____________ like honesty and perseverance contribute to an individual's overall character.
8. The history of the two countries is ____________, with shared traditions and cultural influences.
9. The ____________ in opinions among team members led to a creative discussion on new approaches.
10. The historic building stood as a ____________ of the city's architectural and cultural heritage.

Reading Activity

Reading the following article. Underline or highlight the parts containing key information as you read.

Douglas McGregor's Theory X and Theory Y

Douglas McGregor's Theory X and Theory Y, emerging in the 1950s at MIT Sloan School of Management, shape workforce motivation models. Rooted in motivation theory and Maslow's **hierarchy**, they influence diverse managerial approaches. The following explores McGregor's theories, their impact on employee motivation and productivity, and the innovative **proposition** of combining Theory X and Theory Y.

McGregor's Dual Framework and Motivation Theory

McGregor's theories are deeply **intertwined** with motivation theory, notably influenced by Abraham Maslow's hierarchy of needs. Maslow's hierarchy, ranging from physiological needs to **self-actualization**, forms the backdrop for

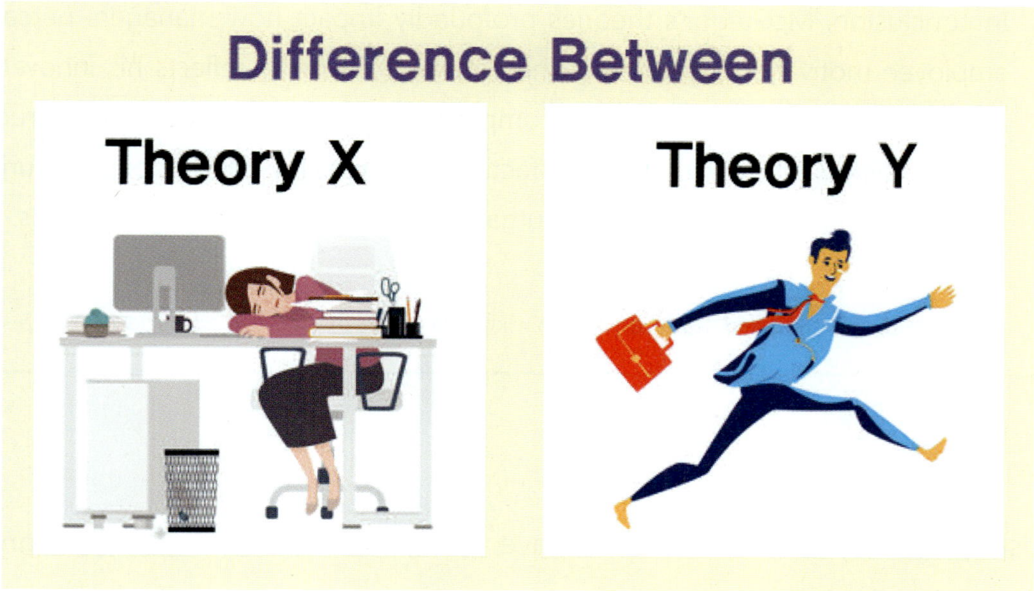

McGregor's contrasting theories. Theory Y **aligns** with higher-level needs, emphasizing esteem and self-actualization, signaling a paradigm shift towards a focus on employee fulfillment and potential realization.

Theory X and Theory Y - Contrasting Management Assumptions

Theory X and Theory Y represent opposing paradigms of management. Theory X, rooted in negative assumptions about employees, **advocates** for a hands-on approach, assuming workers lack ambition and motivation. Conversely, Theory Y assumes positive **traits**, viewing employees as internally motivated individuals. This **divergence** in assumptions leads to different management styles, impacting workplace dynamics and employee performance.

Integrating Theory X and Theory Y

McGregor proposes that Theory X and Theory Y are not mutually exclusive; instead, they exist on different continua. The **contingency** approach, influenced by Fred Fiedler's research, suggests that managers should evaluate internal and external conditions when choosing a leadership style. This approach acknowledges that both Theory X and Theory Y may be necessary, with managers adopting an authoritarian or hands-off style based on the evolving circumstances and the internal and external locus of control within the workplace.

In conclusion, McGregor's theories profoundly impact how managers perceive employee motivation. Combining Theory X and Theory Y reflects his innovative approach, recognizing workplace complexity. This adaptive strategy is crucial for achieving efficiency and satisfaction, showcasing McGregor's enduring **legacy** in understanding diverse human motivations within organizations.

Retrieved and modified from: https://en.wikipedia.org/wiki/Theory_X_and_Theory_Y

Writing Activity

Using the key information you have underlined or highlighted, summarize the article in 3-5 sentences.

____

____

____

____

____

____

____

CONTENT READING RESOURCE 2

Pre-reading Activity

Read the definitions of the key vocabulary found in the article, **Enterprise Resource Planning (ERP)**. Fill in the blanks with the correct form of the words in bold.

streamline (v) to optimize or make a process more efficient by eliminating unnecessary steps, complexities, or redundancies
cohesive (adj) united or connected in a way that forms a comprehensive and harmonious whole, often applied to a group or system
implementation (n) the process of putting a plan, system, or decision into effect, often involving practical application or execution

tailored (adj) customized or specially designed to fit specific needs or requirements
seamless (adj) smooth and continuous, without interruptions or visible seams, creating a unified and unbroken flow
evolved (v) gradually developed or changed over time, often indicating a progression towards a more advanced or complex state
synergistically (adv) working together in a way that enhances each other's effectiveness, creating a combined effect greater than the sum of individual efforts
reluctance (n) hesitation or unwillingness to do something, often due to doubt, indecision, or opposition
overrun(s) (n) exceeding a set budget, time frame, or expected limits, typically associated with costs or schedules going beyond the initially planned amount
mitigate (v) to lessen the severity or impact of something, such as risks, challenges, or negative consequences

1. The different departments worked ___________, combining their efforts to achieve a more significant impact.
2. The team implemented strategies to ___________ the risks associated with the new business venture.
3. The successful ___________ of the new software enhanced the company's overall productivity.
4. The company decided to ___________ its production process to reduce costs and improve efficiency.
5. The transition between the two phases of the project was ___________, with no disruptions or delays.
6. Over the years, technology has ___________, bringing about advanced and sophisticated solutions.
7. The fashion designer created a ___________ dress for the client, incorporating specific preferences and measurements.
8. Despite initial ___________, she eventually agreed to take on the leadership role.
9. The construction project experienced a cost ___________, requiring additional funds to complete.

10. The team demonstrated __________ collaboration, ensuring that everyone's contributions aligned seamlessly.

Reading Activity

Read the following article, and as you read, underline or highlight the parts containing key information.

Enterprise Resource Planning (ERP)

Enterprise Resource Planning (ERP) is a powerful platform that companies utilize to **streamline** and integrate essential components of their operations. ERP is explained as a **cohesive** force in binding diverse systems, outlining its benefits such as enhanced accuracy, and addressing crucial considerations for successful **implementation**."

ERP Functionality and Evolution

ERP serves as a cohesive force, binding diverse computer systems within a large organization. In the absence of ERP, each department operates with optimized systems **tailored** to its specific needs. ERP applications facilitate **seamless** communication and information sharing among departments, promoting a more interconnected and efficient organization. Over the years, ERP has **evolved** from traditional models to web-based applications, offering remote access and efficient data management.

Benefits of ERP Implementation

The adoption of ERP brings numerous advantages to businesses. Firstly, it enhances accuracy and productivity by automating processes and eliminating redundancies. Secondly, ERP improves reporting through real-time data, aiding in better planning, budgeting, and communication. Thirdly, ERP increases efficiency by providing quick access to information, contributing to enhanced customer and employee satisfaction. Additionally, ERP fosters collaboration, allowing departments to work **synergistically**, reducing manual tasks, and enabling employees to focus on meaningful work.

ERP Weaknesses and Key Considerations

Despite its benefits, ERP does not guarantee the elimination of all inefficiencies within a business. Companies may need to rethink their organizational structure and overcome **reluctance** to abandon old processes or software. ERP projects may fail if split into smaller components, leading to cost **overruns**. Change management principles throughout the ERP lifecycle are crucial to prevent or **mitigate** failures and ensure successful implementation.

In conclusion, ERP is pivotal in modern business, enhancing accuracy, efficiency, and collaboration. While evolution and functionality bring benefits, recognizing weaknesses and implementing change management are imperative for successful adoption.

Retrieved and modified from: www.investopedia.com/terms/e/erp.asp

Writing Activity

Using the key information you have underlined or highlighted, summarize the article in 3-5 sentences.

CONTENT READING RESOURCE 3

Pre-reading Activity

Read the definitions of the key vocabulary found in the article, **Framing Theory (or Framing Effect)**. Fill in the blanks with the correct term of the words in bold.

framing (n) the way in which information or situations are presented, influencing perceptions and interpretations
intricate (adj) very detailed, complex, and complicated
pivotal (adj) of crucial importance; central to the development or success of something
cognitive (adj) relating to the processes of perception, thought, and understanding
illuminate (v) to clarify or make something easier to understand; to provide light.
exert (v) applies force, influence, or control over something
underscore (v) emphasizes the importance or value of something
entices (v) attracts or tempts someone, usually by offering something desirable
instill (v) gradually but firmly establish an idea or attitude in a person's mind
signage (n) visual symbols or graphics used for conveying information in signs

1. The alarming statistics __________ the need for urgent action to address the environmental challenges facing our planet.
2. The politician's clever use of __________ in her speech influenced public opinion and shaped the way voters perceived the issue.
3. The success of the project hinged on the __________ decision to secure funding from the major investor.
4. The __________ design of the antique clock revealed the craftsmanship and attention to detail of its maker.
5. The study aimed to explore the __________ processes involved in decision-making and problem-solving.
6. The professor used vivid examples to __________ complex theories, making the subject more accessible to students.

7. The researcher sought to _______ a passion for inquiry and discovery in his team by fostering a collaborative and intellectually stimulating research environment.
8. The coach encouraged the team to _________ maximum effort during the crucial moments of the game.
9. The enticing aroma from the high-end perfumery _________ passersby, drawing them inside to experience the exquisite fragrance collections.
10. In urban planning, well-placed ____________ enhances community engagement and fosters inclusive public spaces.

Reading Activity

Read the following article, and as you read, underline or highlight the parts containing key information.

Framing Theory (or Framing Effect)

The theory of **framing**, as proposed by George Lakoff, introduces the concept of frames shaping our reactions and decisions. This **intricate** thought system, interconnected with language, plays a **pivotal** role in our **cognitive** processes. This facet also **illuminates** the profound influence framing **exerts** on human cognition and its practical application in strategic communication and marketing strategies. The framing effect is explored, highlighting how people perceive information, how it influences decisions, and how it is applied in digital signage engagement (gain framing) and impactful marketing (loss framing).

Understanding the Framing Effect
The framing effect is a psychological phenomenon that molds how humans perceive information. Illustrated by the example of the moon appearing different based on its context, this effect **underscores** the importance of framing in shaping reactions. The moon's perceived size varies depending on whether it is on the horizon or in the sky, emphasizing the role of context in decision-making processes.

Gain Framing for Positive Engagement
Digital signage can strategically utilize gain framing by emphasizing the

positive aspects of a product or service. This approach **entices** consumers by highlighting benefits through words or images evoking positive emotions. For instance, makeup companies leverage flawless faces to convey a message of youthfulness and blemish-free results. By encouraging customers to envision themselves positively, businesses can effectively engage their audience.

Loss Framing for Impactful Messaging

In contrast, loss framing proves effective when businesses aim to **instill** urgency or fear in consumers. Employing this strategy in digital **signage** taps into the fear of missing out (FOMO), convincing consumers that they cannot live without a specific product or service. Commonly observed in limited-time sales or promotions, loss framing leverages negative consequences to drive consumer engagement.

In conclusion, the framing effect, as outlined by George Lakoff, significantly influences decision-making processes. Businesses, particularly in digital signage, can harness this psychological phenomenon through gain framing for positive engagement and loss framing for impactful messaging. Understanding the framing effect empowers businesses to tailor their marketing messages, effectively influencing consumer perceptions and choices within the dynamic and competitive realm of marketing.

Retrieved and modified from: https://www.kuusoft.com/blogs/digital-signage-framing-effect-generalanx/

Writing Activity

Using the key information you have underlined or highlighted, summarize the article in 3-5 sentences.

____

____

____

____

____

____

____

CONTENT READING RESOURCE 4

Pre-reading Activity

Read the definitions of the key vocabulary found in the article, **Window Dressing in Finance**. Fill in the blanks with the correct term of the words in bold.

realm (n) a domain or field of activity or influence; a kingdom or sphere
manipulating (v) controlling or influencing skillfully, often in a deceptive manner
stakeholder (n) a person, group, or organization that has an interest or concern in an enterprise, project, or system
intricate (adj) very detailed, complex, and complicated; having many interconnected parts
facade (n) an outward appearance that conceals the true nature of something; a false or superficial appearance
deploy (v) to strategically use or arrange resources or methods; to bring into effective action
misaligned (adj) not properly aligned or positioned; not in the correct or desired arrangement
scrutinizing (v) examining or inspecting closely and thoroughly; analyzing with great attention to detail

pervade (v) spreads throughout and is evident in every part; exists in or permeates every aspect
vigilant (adj) watchful and alert, especially to avoid danger; keenly attentive and aware

1. Inequality arises when economic policies are _____ with the fundamental principles of social justice.
2. In the dynamic _____ of corporate finance, understanding market trends is crucial for making strategic investment decisions.
3. Social scientists must remain _____ in critically analyzing data to avoid bias and ensure objective research outcomes.
4. Engaging with every _____ is essential during project planning to ensure alignment with organizational goals.
5. A transparent corporate culture is built on honesty and openness, avoiding the creation of a false _____ to investors.
6. The IT department plans to _____ the latest software to enhance operational efficiency across all departments.
7. The _____ web of social relationships within a community shapes the collective identity and cultural dynamics.
8. Ethical leaders avoid _____ data to present a false image of the company's financial health in annual reports.
9. Researchers are _____ historical documents to gain insights into the societal impacts of economic policies.
10. Cultural influence _____ every aspect of human behavior, impacting societal norms and individual choices.

Reading Activity

Read the following article, and as you read, underline or highlight the parts containing key information.

Window Dressing in Finance

Window dressing, a term initially associated with attracting customers through visually appealing displays, has found an unethical application in the financial **realm**. In finance, window dressing refers to the practice of **manipulating** financial data to create a more favorable image for investors. This deceptive strategy is employed by both mutual funds and publicly-owned companies, aiming to present a rosier financial picture than reality. By understanding the methods and implications of window dressing, investors and **stakeholders** can better navigate the **intricate** context of financial reporting. The following explores the concept of window dressing, its workings in mutual funds, and its manifestation in accounting practices.

Window Dressing in Mutual Funds

Window dressing in mutual funds involves strategic portfolio adjustments to enhance reported performance before publishing required reports. Fund managers engage in tactical buying and selling of securities, particularly towards the end of reporting periods, to project improved returns. This practice, while not illegal in itself, raises ethical concerns as it aims to mislead investors about the fund's actual performance. Techniques such as selling underperforming stocks and acquiring high-performing ones create a **facade** of consistent success.

Methods for Window Dressing in Funds

Fund managers **deploy** various methods to execute window dressing, manipulating the composition of their portfolios. By selling stocks with losses and replacing them with high-performing ones, managers create the illusion of sustained success. Additionally, purchasing stocks **misaligned** with the fund's strategy is another deceptive tactic. Investors can identify window dressing by **scrutinizing** the fund's holdings, comparing returns, and examining turnover patterns.

Window Dressing in Accounting

In the realm of accounting, window dressing involves altering financial reports to present a more favorable financial position. Publicly-owned companies, bound by accounting guidelines, may resort to adjusting accounts or methods to avoid investor disinterest. Techniques such as cash window dressing and capitalization window dressing subtly manipulate cash balances and profits, respectively, to create a more positive perception.

In conclusion, window dressing remains a deceitful practice that **pervades** both mutual funds and accounting practices. While it may not always be illegal, it undermines the trust between investors and financial institutions. By being **vigilant** and employing methods to identify window dressing, stakeholders can make informed decisions in a financial context often clouded by misleading maneuvers. Recognizing the signs of window dressing is crucial for safeguarding the integrity of financial reporting and ensuring transparency in investment decisions.

Retrieved and modified from: https://www.investopedia.com/terms/w/windowdressing.asp

Writing Activity

Using the key information you have underlined or highlighted, summarize the article in 3-5 sentences.

CONTENT READING RESOURCE 5

Pre-reading Activity

Read the definitions of the key vocabulary found in the article, **Call Money Rate**. Fill in the blanks with the correct term of the words in bold.

pivotal (adj) of crucial importance; central or essential
realm (n) a field or domain of activity or experience; a kingdom or domain
immediacy (n) the quality of being immediate; the state of being present or felt without delay
judicious (adj) having, showing, or done with good judgment or sense; wise and careful
surplus (n) an amount of something left over when requirements have been met; an excess
liquidity (n) the availability of liquid assets to a market or company; the ability to convert assets into cash quickly
transaction (n) an instance of buying or selling something; a business deal
repayment (n) the action of paying back a loan, debt, or amount borrowed
indispensable (adj) absolutely necessary or essential; crucial
terrain (n) a stretch of land, especially with regard to its physical features; an area of land; ground

1. After streamlining operations, the company found itself with a ___________ of resources that could be allocated to future investments.
2. The customer service team prioritized the ___________ of addressing client concerns with immediacy, ensuring satisfaction and loyalty.
3. The successful implementation of the new strategy was ___________ to the company's growth, marking a pivotal shift in its operations.
4. In the competitive ___________ of e-commerce, companies vie for dominance in the online shopping realm.
5. Human interactions form the basis of social ___________, reflecting the exchange of ideas, goods, and services within a community.
6. The CEO's ___________ decision to diversify the product line was seen as judicious, leading to increased market share.
7. In the study of sociology, diverse perspectives are ___________, providing a comprehensive understanding of societal structures.

8. The cultural ___________ of a society influences its ability to adapt to change and respond to external influences.
9. Mutual respect and understanding are essential for the ___________ of relationships within a community, fostering harmony.
10. The geographical ___________ of a region shapes the development of communities, affecting their social, economic, and cultural dynamics.

Reading Activity

Read the following article, and as you read, underline or highlight the parts containing key information.

Call Money

Call money, also known as money at call, plays a **pivotal** role in the financial **realm**. It serves as a short-term, interest-earning loan that demands immediate repayment upon the lender's request. Call money, characterized by its flexibility and **immediacy**, serves as a critical component in money markets, offering a unique set of advantages, and crucial **judicious** use despite inherent risks and dynamics.

The Essence of Call Money
Call money, a short-term financial instrument, involves immediate repayment upon the lender's demand, differentiating it from traditional term loans. This financial tool allows banks to earn interest, known as the call loan rate, on **surplus** funds. Brokerages, seeking short-term funding for margin accounts, leverage call money to meet the dynamic needs of their clients. The **liquidity** and quick transferability of funds make call money a crucial element on balance sheets.

Advantages of Call Money
The utilization of call money provides various advantages for financial institutions. Its low **transaction** cost, conducted directly between banks, enhances efficiency. Call money aids in managing balance sheets, contributing to liquidity and regulatory compliance. Furthermore, it empowers banks to hold a higher reserve-to-deposit ratio, fostering greater profitability. Despite its benefits, the inherent risk is acknowledged, prompting brokerages to use call money judiciously for swiftly resolved transactions.

Highlighting Call Money's Crucial Role
Distinguishing call money from short-notice money, the former demands immediate **repayment**, while the latter allows up to 14 days after notice. Both serve as highly liquid assets, crucial in managing short-term financial requirements. Understanding the dynamics of call money and its comparison with short-notice money is vital for financial institutions navigating the complex terrain of money markets.

In conclusion, call money stands as a versatile and **indispensable** financial tool, providing short-term liquidity for institutions engaged in dynamic financial transactions. Understanding its essence, advantages, and distinctions from similar instruments is crucial for financial entities seeking efficient fund management in the ever-evolving **terrain** of money markets.

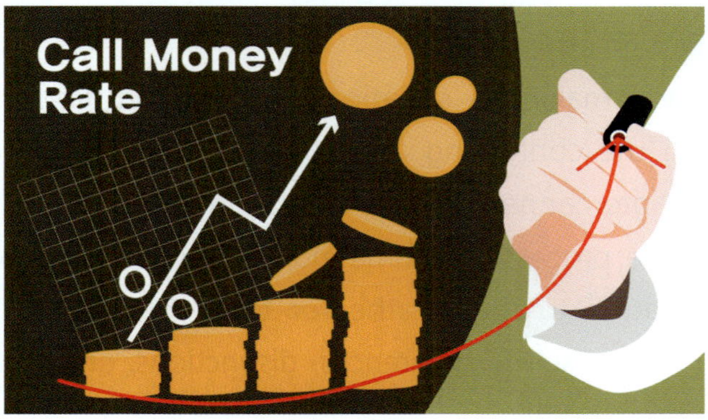

Retrieved and modified from: https://www.investopedia.com/terms/c/call-money-rate.asp & https://en.wikipedia.org/wiki/Call_money

Writing Activity

Using the key information you have underlined or highlighted, summarize the article in 3-5 sentences.

CONTENT READING RESOURCE 6

Pre-reading Activity

Read the definitions of the key vocabulary found in the article, **Double-dip Recession**. Fill in the blanks with the correct term of the words in bold.

colloquially (adv) in a conversational or informal style; used in everyday language
downturns (n) a decline or reduction, especially in economic or financial activity
sustain (v) to support, uphold, or maintain over a period of time; to endure or continue
navigating (v) the act of finding one's way or directing a course, especially through complex or challenging situations
determinant (n) something that decisively influences or determines the nature or outcome of something else
exacerbating (adj) making a situation or condition worse or more severe
ripple effect (n) the continuing and spreading results of an event or action, often affecting interconnected or related elements
forecasting (n) the process of estimating or predicting future events or trends, especially in relation to the weather or the economy
nuanced (adj) having subtle differences, distinctions, or variations; characterized by nuanced understanding
corporate (adj) relating to a corporation or a group of businesses authorized to act as a single entity

1. The availability of natural resources is a key ___________ in determining the success of the agricultural sector.
2. The organization works hard to ___________ its commitment to environmental conservation over the years.
3. His careless actions ended up ___________ the already tense situation, making it even more difficult to resolve.
4. The recent economic ___________ have led to job losses and reduced consumer spending.
5. The diplomat's ___________ understanding of cultural differences allowed for successful negotiations.

6. The policy change had a __________, impacting various sectors of the economy.
7. Meteorologists use advanced technology for accurate weather __________, helping people plan accordingly.
8. The __________ restructuring led to improved efficiency within the business conglomerate.
9. In the rapidly changing business environment, skilled leaders are adept at __________ challenges and uncertainties.
10. During the informal discussion, they spoke __________, using everyday language that everyone could easily understand.

Reading Activity

Read the following article, and as you read, underline or highlight the parts containing key information.

Double-dip Recession

A double-dip recession, characterized by economic decline, partial recovery, and subsequent stagnation, is **colloquially** known as a "W-shaped economic recovery" due to its dual **downturns** resembling the letter 'W.' This phenomenon unfolds when the economy fails to **sustain** growth after initial recovery, creating challenges in understanding and **navigating** economic cycles. The following investigates a double-dip recession, highlighting consumer confidence, the impact of reduced corporate investments on jobs, and key economic indicators.

Consumer Confidence and Spending
One **determinant** of a double-dip recession is the lack of consumer confidence, impacting spending habits. When people hesitate to spend money, it leads to reduced buying activities, contributing to a smaller economy and **exacerbating** the downturn.

Corporate Investments and Job Creation
Another factor influencing a double-dip recession is reduced corporate investments, resulting in decreased production and fewer job opportunities.

As companies cut back on spending, the **ripple effect** is felt across various sectors, contributing to the economic downturn.

Economic Indicators and **Forecasting**
Predicting economic shifts, particularly a double-dip recession, involves analyzing key indicators. The inverted yield curve, signaling investor concern, and real-time metrics like a rising unemployment rate serve as reliable predictors. While monitoring the stock market is crucial, low interest rates can alter traditional recessionary signals, making forecasting a **nuanced** challenge.

In conclusion, understanding a double-dip recession involves exploring its phases and contributors, from consumer confidence affecting spending to **corporate** investments influencing job creation. Experts analyze economic indicators for early warnings, considering the fluctuating stock market and revealing GDP reports. This complex context necessitates a comprehensive understanding for effective navigation.

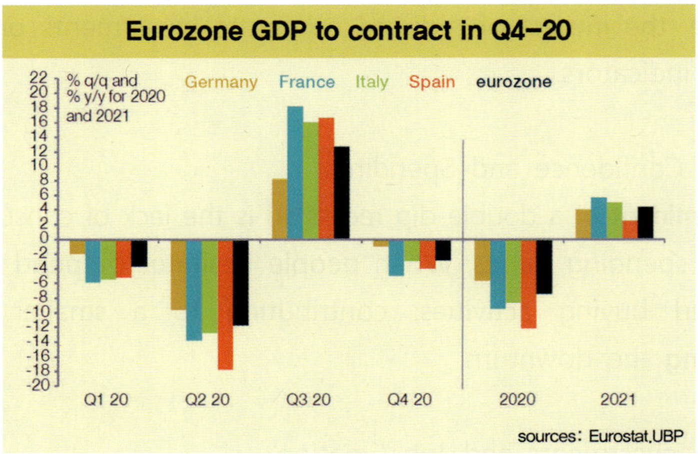

Retrieved and modified from: https://www.forbes.com/advisor/ca/investing/what-is-a-double-dip-recession/

Writing Activity

Using the key information you have underlined or highlighted, summarize the article in 3-5 sentences.

____

____

____

____

____

____

____

CONTENT READING RESOURCE 7

Pre-reading Activity

Read the definitions of the key vocabulary found in the article, **Lorenz Curve and Gini Coefficient**. Fill in the blanks with the correct term of the words in bold.

focal (adj) having a central or main focus; relating to or situated at the point of origin
coefficient (n) a numerical or constant factor placed before and multiplying the variable in an algebraic expression (e.g., in 3x, 3 is the coefficient of x)
nuanced (adj) characterized by subtle and precise distinctions; exhibiting fine shades of meaning or detail
quantifiable (adj) capable of being measured, counted, or expressed in numerical terms; able to be quantified
disparities (n, pl) inequalities or differences, especially in terms of age, rank, wages, or conditions; contrasts between things
cumulative (adj) increasing or growing by accumulation or successive additions; formed by the addition of successive parts or elements
distribution (n) the act of distributing or the state of being distributed; the arrangement or location of a set of things
quantitatively (adv) in a manner related to quantity; involving or expressible in terms of quantity

metric (n) a system or standard of measurement; a quantifiable unit used to gauge or evaluate something
illuminate (v) to provide light; to make clear or bright; to clarify or explain something

1. When analyzing economic models, understanding the role and significance of the __________ in equations such as 4x + 2y = 10 is crucial for accurate predictions and policy formulation.
2. Social scientists investigate the root causes of educational and healthcare __________ to propose policy interventions that address systemic inequalities and promote equitable access.
3. In the field of cultural anthropology, researchers employ a ________ analysis to unveil intricate societal structures and highlight subtle cultural shifts over time.
4. Project managers rely on __________ success metrics to assess the efficacy of initiatives, ensuring alignment with predetermined quantitative targets.
5. Economists often employ Gross Domestic Product (GDP) as a fundamental ________ to evaluate the overall economic health and performance of a nation.
6. The ______ point of the strategic meeting revolved around the implementation of sustainable practices to enhance the long-term viability of the business.
7. Economic policymakers grapple with challenges related to the ________ of resources, striving to rectify regional imbalances and promote inclusive economic development.
8. Assessing the _________ profits over several fiscal periods provides a comprehensive understanding of the company's financial trajectory and overall performance.
9. Social science researchers utilize statistical methods to analyze data __________, unveiling trends and patterns that contribute to a deeper understanding of societal phenomena.
10. The new sociological findings ________ the intricate interplay of factors contributing to societal issues, providing valuable insights for policymakers and advocates working to address complex challenges.

Reading Activity

Read the following article, and as you read, underline or highlight the parts containing key information.

Lorenz Curve and Gini Coefficient

Income distribution's societal impact is a **focal** point in economic studies. The Lorenz curve, crafted by American statistician Lorentz in 1905, visually captures a nation's income distribution. However, it falls short in quantifying inequality. Corrado Gini's Gini **coefficient** steps in, offering a **nuanced**, **quantifiable** measure to explore income **disparities**. The following explains the Lorentz curve and Gini coefficient in detail.

The Lorentz curve was proposed by American statistician Lorentz in 1905 to measure the degree of inequality in income. The **cumulative** proportion of the population is placed on the horizontal axis and the cumulative share of income is placed on the vertical axis, and their relationship is plotted in a figure. The Lorentz curve has the advantage of being able to see a country's income **distribution** status in a figure,/ but it has the disadvantage of not being able to **quantitatively** display the degree.

The Gini coefficient is a complement of the shortcomings of the Lorentz curve by Italian statistician Corrado Gini to strategically grasp the status of income distribution. The Gini coefficient is usually an indirect **metric** of inequality such as income distribution. It is a coefficient used to calculate the degree of income inequality through the ratio of low-income and high-income groups by collecting the entire income class. The higher the Gini coefficient, the more severe the degree of income inequality. The closer to zero, the more equal it is, and the closer to one, the greater the gap between the rich and the poor.

In conclusion, the Lorentz curve and Gini coefficient jointly **illuminate** the intricate context of income distribution. While the Lorentz curve provides a visual snapshot, the Gini coefficient quantifies disparities. Together, they form a comprehensive toolkit for policymakers and researchers, offering insights crucial for navigating the complexities of societal inequality.

Retrieved and modified from: https://ubp.com.tw/en/eurozone-facing-a-double-dip-recession-in-q4-20/

1) Retrieved and modified from:

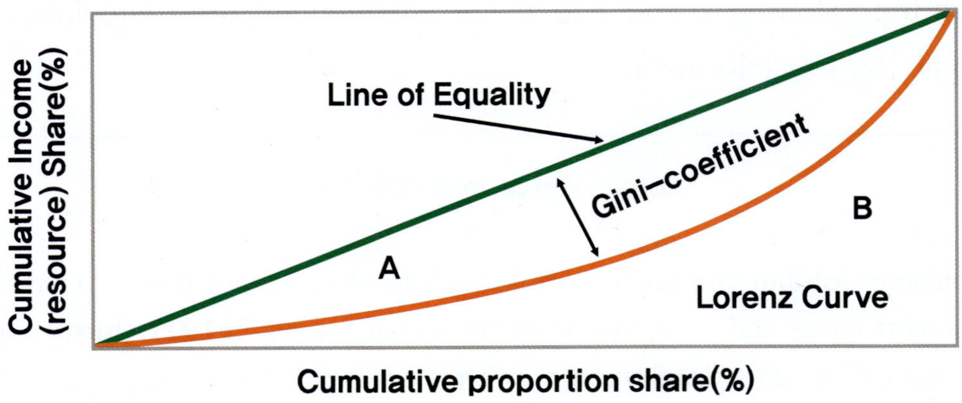

Retrieved and modified from: https://www.researchgate.net/publication/292606776_Is_Inequality_threat_to_Small-Scale_Agriculture_in_GamoGofa_Zone_of_Ethiopia

2) Retrieved and modified from:

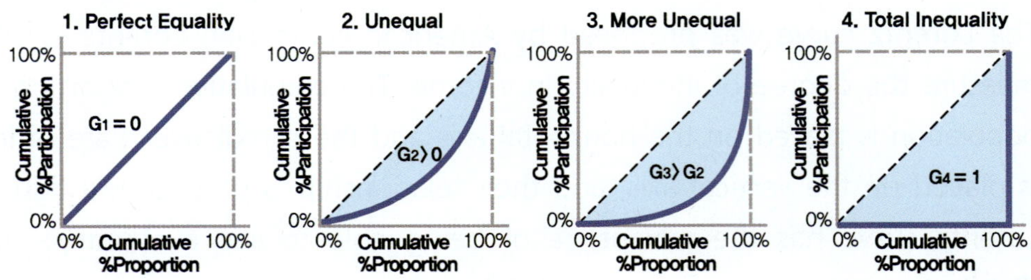

Retrieved and modified from: https://towardsdatascience.com/clearly-explained-gini-coefficient-and-lorenz-curve-fe6f5dcdc07

Writing Activity

Using the key information you have underlined or highlighted, summarize the article in 3-5 sentences.

CONTENT READING RESOURCE 8

Pre-reading Activity

Read the definitions of the key vocabulary found in the article, **The Four Points of SWOT Analysis**. Fill in the blanks with the correct term of the words in bold.

embody (v) to represent or exemplify in tangible form
affirmative (adj) positive or confirming; expressing agreement
encompass (v) to include or contain a wide range or variety of elements
facet (n) different aspects or features of something
fiscal (adj) relating to financial matters, especially those concerning government revenue, expenditures, and policies related to taxation and public finances
constraints (n) limitations or restrictions that shape or restrict actions and decisions
myriad (n) a vast number or multitude; a large and indefinite number
detrimental (adj) causing harm or damage; disadvantageous
proliferation (n) rapid growth or spread, especially of something undesirable
groundwork (n) initial essential steps or foundation laid for further development or action

1. Our marketing strategy should ____________ a variety of platforms to reach a wider audience.
2. The ____________ effects of the economic downturn forced the company to reassess its budget.
3. The __________ feedback from clients boosted the team's morale and confidence.
4. In sociology, researchers study a __________ of things like cultures, money, and how people relate to each other to learn more about why people behave the way they do in different social situations.
5. The ____________ of information on social media contributes to the spread of various perspectives.
6. The project manager sought to ________ the company's values in every client interaction.
7. The gemstone had many __________, each reflecting light in a unique and beautiful way.

8. In the government's annual budget, the ____________ policies guide decisions on taxes, spending, and overall financial strategies.
9. In planning a project, budgetary ____________ shape what you can do and how you use resources, guiding the overall approach to implementation.
10. Before starting something new, it's important to do some ____________ by researching and planning to make sure everything gets off to a good and successful start.

Reading Activity

Read the following article, and as you read, underline or highlight the parts containing key information.

The Four Points of SWOT Analysis

A proper SWOT analysis involves considering four important aspects: Strengths, Weaknesses, Opportunities, and Threats. Strengths and Weaknesses focus on your company's internal factors, while Opportunities and Threats look at external factors and competition. The following explores four aspects in more detail to understand how to evaluate each one correctly.

Strengths

Strengths **embody** the **affirmative** aspects within your company that you control and that give you an advantage over others. These might **encompass facets** such as possessing a superlative product, efficient processes, valuable team members, or other advantageous benefits.

Weaknesses

Weaknesses are negative aspects within your company that counteract your strengths. These might include gaps in your team's knowledge, a product of lower quality, **fiscal constraints**, lack of tangible assets, unfavorable locations, and a **myriad** of other **detrimental** elements.

Opportunities

Opportunities are external factors that offer potential or could contribute to your success. These may encompass the **proliferation** of the industry, beneficial laws or policies, positive feedback from customers, or advancements in technology that could help your business.

Threats
Threats are external factors beyond your control that could harm your success. Identifying these helps you plan to overcome them. Examples include future competitors, rising supply costs, changing market trends, negative technology shifts, or upcoming regulations.

In summary, an effective SWOT analysis is like a guide for businesses, helping them navigate through the internal and external factors. Strengths and Weaknesses analyze internally within the company to identify what's good and what needs improvement. Opportunities and Threats focus on outside factors, showing chances for growth and possible challenges. Doing thorough research is crucial for a strong SWOT analysis, providing the **groundwork** for smart strategies and a strong business plan. Presenting this analysis well ensures that everyone in the company, investors, and those who can benefit understand the strategic plan easily.

Retrieved and modified from: https://www.econposts.com/business-management/swot-analysis/

Writing Activity

Using the key information you have underlined or highlighted, summarize the article in 3-5 sentences.

CONTENT READING RESOURCE 9

Pre-reading Activity

Read the definitions of the key vocabulary found in the article, **The Five Levels of Maslow's Hierarchy of Needs**. Fill in the blanks with the correct term of the words in bold.

groundbreaking (adj) innovative or pioneering; introducing new methods, ideas, or techniques that significantly advance a field
delineate(s) (v) clearly describes or outlines; presents in a detailed and specific manner
hierarchical (adj) arranged in a hierarchy or graded series; organized in levels or ranks
prerequisite(s) (n) necessary conditions or requirements that must be fulfilled beforehand; essential elements needed for a particular purpose
instinctively (adv) acting on instinct, without conscious thought; behaving in a natural, unlearned manner
encompassing (adj) inclusive or comprehensive; covering a wide range of elements or ideas
sustenance (n) the act of sustaining or providing the necessities for life; nourishment or support
physiological (adj) relating to the functions and processes of living organisms and their parts, especially as it pertains to the body's physical and chemical aspects
denote(s) (v) indicates, signifies, or represents a particular meaning or concept
esteem (n) high regard or respect for someone or something; the value or reputation attributed to a person or an idea

1. Teams ___________ collaborate when faced with challenges, demonstrating the company's commitment to adaptability and teamwork.
2. In times of economic downturn, societies depend on governmental policies for ________, such as unemployment benefits and public assistance programs.
3. The community leader received high ________ for promoting inclusivity and social cohesion.
4. ______________ initiatives in product development have positioned our company as an industry leader, setting new standards for innovation.

5. The strategic plan clearly ___________ the key performance indicators that will drive our organizational success over the next fiscal year.
6. Our __________ structure emphasizes effective communication channels, ensuring seamless coordination between teams at different levels.
7. Meeting the ___________ for the project includes acquiring the necessary certifications and skills to ensure a successful implementation.
8. The sociological study provides an ________ overview of the community's socio-economic dynamics.
9. Socio-cultural practices have numerous ________ impacts, influencing mental health and community well-being.
10. The change in political leadership ________ a shift in national priorities and policies.

Reading Activity

Read the following article, and as you read, underline or highlight the parts containing key information.

The Five Levels of Maslow's Hierarchy of Needs

Abraham Maslow's **groundbreaking** theory, introduced in 1943, **delineates** the fundamental psychological needs that drive human behavior. Through a **hierarchical** pyramid, Maslow categorizes these needs into five distinct levels, each building upon the other. The theory suggests that individuals instinctively prioritize these needs in a sequential manner, seeking fulfillment and progression through the hierarchy.

1. Physiological Needs

Physiological needs are considered the most important need, so they are at the bottom of the pyramid. They are the needs we humans seek out first. These are the **prerequisites** that humanity **instinctively** pursues initially, **encompassing** fundamental elements essential for survival, such as oxygen, **sustenance**, hydration, and the like.

2. Safety Needs

Safety needs are considered the second most important, so they are one step above **physiological** needs on the pyramid. If we are secure in our physiological needs, we seek out safety needs. Safety needs are the ideas that humans like to feel safe at what they do. For example, a child feels safe when they are with parents, or an adult at work feels safe when they are given tenure.

3. Love Needs

Love needs are considered the third most important, ranking one step above safety needs on the pyramid. When we feel safe, the pursuit of love needs ensues. This concept relates to the inherent human desire to both receive love and extend affection to others. Furthermore, it **denotes** the inclination of individuals to perceive a sense of belongingness within a collective entity.

4. Esteem Needs

Esteem needs are considered the fourth most important, so they are one step above love needs on the pyramid. If we feel loved, then we seek out esteem needs. Esteem needs refer to the idea that humans like to feel confident, achieve things, and find independence and freedom. Also, it refers to the idea that humans desire to have a good reputation, find prestige and recognition for the things we do, and feel as if people pay attention and appreciate us.

5. Self-actualization Needs

Self-actualization needs are considered the fifth most important, so they are one step above esteem needs on the pyramid. When all other needs are satisfied, humans may still feel dissatisfied with their lives. This will get worse unless a person starts to do what they believe is their calling, or what they think they should be doing with their lives, like a writer who must write a novel to feel happy.

In summary, Maslow's hierarchy of needs describes the various layers that affect human motivation, ranging from basic needs to self-actualization. It stresses the importance of acknowledging and addressing these needs for well-being and personal growth. This model highlights the inherent human pursuit of purpose and fulfillment as individuals progress through these layers.

Retrieved and modified from: https://www.thoughtco.com/maslows-hierarchy-of-needs-4582571

Writing Activity

Using the key information you have underlined or highlighted, summarize the article in 3-5 sentences.

____

____

____

____

____

____

____

CONTENT READING RESOURCE 10

Pre-reading Activity

Read the definitions of the key vocabulary found in the article, **Big Mac Index**. Fill in the blanks with the correct term of the words in bold.

benchmark (n) a standard for comparison and measurement
discrepancies (n) differences or inconsistencies between things
overvaluation (n) assessing something as more valuable than its true worth
intricacies (n) complex and detailed aspects within a system
juxtapose (v) to position contrasting elements side by side for comparison

comprehend (v) to grasp or understand fully
limitations (n) restrictions or shortcomings defining boundaries
influenced (v) to have an effect on or alter
non-traded (adj) describing goods or services not exchanged in markets
purchasing power (n) the ability of currency or wealth to buy goods and services

1. Inflation can erode the ______________ of a currency, reducing the ability of consumers to buy goods and services.
2. Auditors discovered _____________ in the financial reports that raised concerns about the company's accuracy.
3. The stock's __________ became evident when its market value plummeted despite positive industry trends.
4. The success of the previous marketing campaign served as a ________ for future promotional strategies.
5. It may take time to ____________ the complexities of quantum physics, even for those with a strong scientific background.
6. The artist decided to _________ vibrant colors with muted tones to create a visually striking masterpiece.
7. Lawyers are trained to navigate the __________ of legal documents to provide accurate advice to their clients.
8. Researchers should acknowledge the __________ of their study to ensure the findings are interpreted appropriately.
9. Social media has greatly __________ public opinion, shaping perspectives on various societal issues.
10. Local artisans often create unique, __________ goods that are not readily available in global markets.

Reading Activity

Read the following article, and as you read, underline or highlight the parts containing key information.

Big Mac Index

The Big Mac Index, created by The Economist in 1986, uniquely uses the globally recognized McDonald's Big Mac as a **benchmark** for straightforward price comparison. Highlighting **discrepancies** in currency values when prices vary between nations, it suggests potential **overvaluation**. This index, utilizing a familiar fast-food item, simplifies currency assessment and unveils the **intricacies** of global economics. The following explains the methodology behind the index, critically examining limitations, and dissecting economic disparities revealed by the Big Mac Index.

Understanding the Big Mac Index
To interpret the Big Mac Index, one need only **juxtapose** the prices of Big Macs in different countries and convert them to a common currency, usually US dollars. The resulting exchange rates reveal insights into the relative strength or weakness of currencies. Published annually by The Economist and accessible for free on their website, the index covers approximately 50 countries, providing a fascinating and accessible lens through which to **comprehend** global economics.

Limitations of the Big Mac Index
While the Big Mac Index offers an entertaining approach to grasp international economics, it is not without its **limitations**. **Influenced** by factors such as local labor costs, rent, and taxes, Big Mac prices may not solely reflect currency values. Additionally, the index overlooks **non-traded** goods like housing, which can significantly impact the overall cost of living. Despite these limitations, the Big Mac Index remains a valuable tool for gaining insights into the economic disparities among nations.

Big Mac Index by Country
Examining the differences in the Big Mac Index across countries reveals substantial disparities. In India, the price of a Big Mac is 53.6% lower than in the United States, highlighting the higher **purchasing power** of the US dollar. Conversely, Switzerland boasts a Big Mac Index over 30% higher than the US, indicative of a weaker purchasing power. The top five countries with the highest Big Mac Index - Switzerland, Norway, Uruguay, Sweden, and Canada - accentuate the varied economic conditions globally.

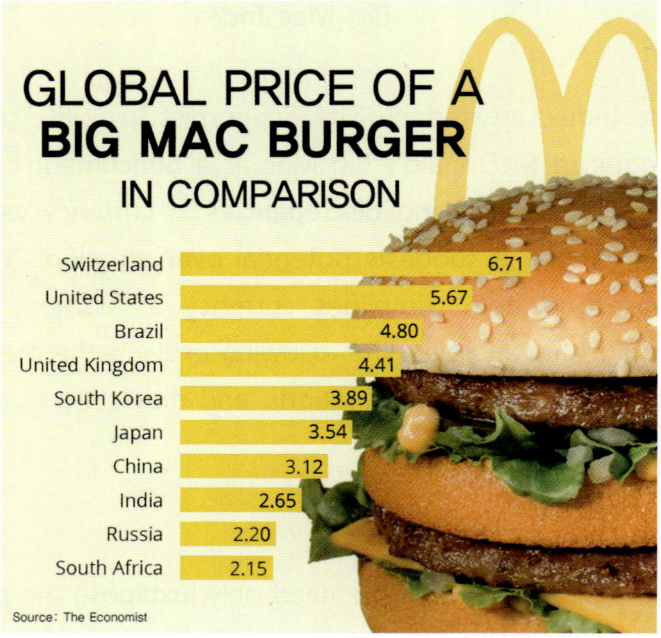

In summary, the Big Mac Index, crafted by The Economist, captivates with its simplicity, using a fast-food staple to reveal complex economic realities. Unveiling the complexities of currency evaluation, it offers a unique perspective on global economic dynamics. Despite its shortcomings, the index stands as a valuable tool, providing a lens into the intricate dance of currencies and economies worldwide.

Retrieved and modified from: https://wisevoter.com/country-rankings/big-mac-index-by-country/

Writing Activity

Using the key information you have underlined or highlighted, summarize the article in 3-5 sentences.

CONTENT READING RESOURCE 11

Pre-reading Activity

Read the definitions of the key vocabulary found in the article, **Leverage Effect**. Fill in the blanks with the correct form of the words in bold.

leverage (n) strategic use of borrowed capital to amplify returns
manifestations (n) observable outcomes or expressions of a phenomenon
optimize (v) make the most effective use, maximizing desired outcomes
counterproductive (adj) hindering achievement of a goal, having a contrary effect
diminishing (adj) referring to the process of decreasing or reducing
anticipated (adj) expected or predicted; foreseen based on informed expectations
profiting (v) gaining financial benefits, achieving positive returns
prudently (adv) acting with wisdom, care, and sound judgment
mitigate (v) lessen the severity or impact of something
potent (adj) having great power, influence, or effectiveness

1. The __________ growth in the market prompted the company to expand its production capacity to meet the expected increase in demand.
2. The _________ of the leverage effect on return on equity are observable in both positive and negative manifestations.
3. A well-informed understanding of the dynamics of positive and negative leverage effects is crucial to ___________ financial outcomes.
4. The company decided to ________ its resources by strategically borrowing capital to maximize returns on equity.
5. Excessive debt can be ___________, leading to a decline in returns and hindering the achievement of financial goals.
6. It is crucial to ________ potential risks associated with financial decisions to avoid unexpected setbacks.
7. ____________ from borrowed capital requires individuals and companies to borrow wisely and invest strategically.
8. As the company continued to invest heavily, they experienced ___________ returns, emphasizing the importance of strategic financial planning.

9. The company __________ allocated resources to ensure a stable cash flow, anticipating potential challenges in the market.
10. The new marketing strategy proved to be _______, significantly boosting the company's sales and market presence.

Reading Activity

Read the following article, and as you read, underline or highlight the parts containing key information.

Leverage Effect

The **leverage** effect, a key concept in finance, unveils the impact of debt on return on equity, offering strategic insights into financial decision-making. This could be explained focusing on its positive and negative **manifestations** and its role as a strategic tool for profit through borrowed capital. By understanding these dynamics, individuals and companies can make informed decisions to **optimize** financial outcomes.

Positive Leverage Effect

A positive leverage effect arises when additional debt enhances return on equity. For instance, if a project yields a 5% return and incurs a 3% interest on debt, leveraging becomes beneficial. With lower interest payments, the project requires less equity capital, leading to enhanced economic efficiency and, consequently, a higher return on equity. This scenario exemplifies how strategic debt utilization can elevate financial returns.

Negative Leverage Effect

Conversely, a negative leverage effect occurs when debt interest surpasses the project's total return. In a situation where the total return is 5% and debt interest is 6%, leveraging becomes **counterproductive**, **diminishing** return on equity. This underscores the importance of aligning debt utilization with **anticipated** returns to avoid financial setbacks.

Strategic Implications and Risk Considerations

Beyond individual projects, the leverage effect serves as a strategic tool for **profiting** from borrowed capital. By borrowing wisely and investing **prudently**, individuals and companies can potentially achieve significant profits even with modest investments. However, it is crucial to note that leveraging is advantageous only when the anticipated return on investment exceeds the interest rate cost of borrowing. During economic downturns, careful consideration and risk assessment become essential to **mitigate** potential investment losses and interest rate burdens.

In conclusion, the leverage effect offers a roadmap to financial success through strategic borrowing. By grasping the dynamics of positive and negative leverage effects and approaching strategic borrowing with caution, individuals and companies can optimize financial outcomes, transforming borrowed capital into a **potent** tool for financial prosperity.

Retrieved and modified from: https://www.greenmatch.ch/en/knowledge-center/what-is-the-leverage-effect/

Writing Activity

Using the key information you have underlined or highlighted, summarize the article in 3-5 sentences.

CONTENT READING RESOURCE 12

Pre-reading Activity

Read the definitions of the key vocabulary found in the article, **Spillover Effects**. Fill in the blanks with the correct form of the words in bold.

phenomenon (n) a fact or event that can be observed and studied
resonate (v) to produce or be filled with a deep, full, reverberating sound; in a figurative sense, to evoke a strong emotion or reaction
interconnected (adj) mutually joined or related, often in a complex way, forming a network
dynamics (n) the forces or properties that stimulate growth, development, or change within a system; in this context, the patterns and interactions involved in spillover effects
amplifies (v) increases the volume, extent, or effect of something
repercussions (n) unintended and usually negative effects or results that follow from an action, decision, or event
sophisticated (a) highly developed, complex, or refined, often implying a high level of skill or complexity in management or systems
intensify (v) to become or make something more intense, stronger, or more extreme
reliance (n) the state of depending on or trusting in something or someone
pronounced (adj) clearly and strongly indicated or evident

1. The new computer software is highly _______, offering advanced features for professional users.
2. The solar eclipse was a rare _______ that captured the attention of people around the world.
3. In the modern world, technology and communication networks are highly _______, allowing information to flow seamlessly.
4. The speaker's words seemed to _______ with the audience, leaving a lasting impact on their thoughts.
5. The team studied the group _______ to understand how different factors influenced their performance.
6. The use of a megaphone _______ the speaker's voice, making it audible even in a large crowd.

7. As the storm approached, the winds began to _______, signaling the impending danger.
8. The company's success was built on the strong _______ it had on its loyal customer base.
9. The hasty decision had serious _______, affecting not only the individual but also the entire team.
10. The scientist made a _______ statement about the potential impact of climate change on global ecosystems.

Reading Activity

Read the following article, and as you read, underline or highlight the parts containing key information.

Spillover Effects

The spillover effect, a **phenomenon** wherein events in one nation **resonate** globally, is critical in our **interconnected** world. The following explores the **dynamics** of spillover effects in an era of heightened globalization, investigating how a U.S. economic slowdown **amplifies** effects on Canada and examining the global **repercussions** of economic shifts in the United States and China. Through these examples, it emphasizes the need for **sophisticated** management in our interconnected global sphere.

The Cascading Effect of Globalization

Spillover effects **intensify** with the deepening financial connections between economies. Examining the Canada-U.S. trade relationship reveals that even a minor U.S. slowdown can lead to amplified effects due to Canada's heavy **reliance** on the U.S. market. This highlights how interconnectedness can transform a localized event into a global economic challenge.

The Dominance of Economic Leaders

The bigger the country's economy, the more significant the spillover effects. The United States, being a powerful global economic leader, has a lot of influence, making other countries more likely to be affected by problems within the United States. This can lead to issues and troubles within those countries. This is evident in the significant spillover effects experienced worldwide during

downturns or macro events in the world's two largest economies: the United States and China.

China's Global Impact

China has emerged as a major source of spillover effects since 2009. As the world's second-largest economy, China's impact on global commodity demand, driven by its manufacturing sector, is substantial. A slowdown in China triggers palpable effects on worldwide trade, causing economic repercussions, especially in regions like Eastern Europe, the Middle East, and Africa, where reliance on China for revenue is **pronounced**.

In conclusion, spillover effects show how connected the world's economies are. Whether it's the trade between Canada and the U.S. or how changes in the U.S. and China affect the world, it's crucial to recognize and handle these effects for long-term economic stability in our interconnected global world.

Retrieved and modified from: https://www.investopedia.com/terms/s/spillover-effect.asp

Writing Activity

Using the key information you have underlined or highlighted, summarize the article in 3-5 sentences.

CONTENT READING RESOURCE 13

Pre-reading Activity

Read the definitions of the key vocabulary found in the article, **The Market for Lemons**. Fill in the blanks with the correct form of the words in bold.

uneven (adj) not level, flat, or smooth; having variations or irregularities in height or surface
significant (adj) sufficiently great or important to be worthy of attention; having meaning or influence
perceived (v) to become aware of, know, or identify by means of the senses; to recognize or understand
inefficiencies (n) the state or quality of lacking efficiency; the presence of factors that hinder the optimal performance of a system or process
robust (adj) strong and healthy; vigorous; able to withstand or overcome adverse conditions
innovations (n) the introduction of something new, such as a method, idea, or product; the act or process of innovating
looms (v) appears as a large or threatening shadow; emerges as a significant and imminent presence
hindering (adj) acting as an obstacle or impediment; causing delay or difficulty
alleviate (v) to make (a problem, suffering, or difficulty) more bearable or less severe; to ease or reduce
intricate (adj) complicated, detailed, and complex; having many interconnected parts or elements

1. The company conducted a thorough review to identify and address ______________ in its production process.
2. The diligent researcher keenly _______ the subtle patterns emerging in the data, prompting a more in-depth investigation.
3. In social science research, the __________ impact of community engagement programs on youth development cannot be overstated.
4. Social workers aim to _________ the economic disparities in the community through targeted intervention programs.
5. The distribution of educational resources in underprivileged areas is ________, perpetuating inequalities in the social fabric.

6. A ________ social policy framework is essential to address the complex challenges faced by diverse populations.
7. In the realm of social science, the impending demographic shift _______ large, necessitating proactive policy measures.
8. In the fast-paced world of business, continuous _________ in technology are vital for staying competitive in the market.
9. Outdated regulations can be _________ factors for businesses seeking to adopt new and efficient practices.
10. Developing an ________ business strategy requires a comprehensive understanding of market dynamics and consumer behavior.

Reading Activity

Read the following article, and as you read, underline or highlight the parts containing key information.

The Market for Lemons

The lemons problem, coined by Nobel laureate George Akerlof, addresses the challenges arising from asymmetric information between buyers and sellers, disrupting the value assessment of products or investments. In his seminal work, "The Market for 'Lemons': Quality Uncertainty and the Market Mechanism," Akerlof explores how this issue, initially observed in the used car market, permeates various sectors, hindering profitable exchanges. This essay delves into the lemons problem, examining its manifestation, impact, and potential solutions across different markets.

The lemons problem, named by Nobel laureate George Akerlof, addresses the challenges caused by **uneven** information between buyers and sellers, disrupting the evaluation of product or investment value. Akerlof, in his **significant** work, "The Market for 'Lemons': Quality Uncertainty and the Market Mechanism," examines how this problem, first noticed in the used car market, spreads to different areas, making profitable exchanges difficult. The following explores the lemons problem, looking at how it appears, its effects, and potential solutions across various markets.

The Used Car Market Problem

Akerlof's study of the used car market reveals the built-in gap in information between sellers and buyers, causing a breakdown in opportunities for profitable exchanges. The problem arises because sellers know a lot about a product's true value, while buyers lack this crucial information. As a result, buyers become cautious, hesitant to pay more than an average price, worried they might unknowingly buy a "lemon" – a product with hidden defects.

Information Imbalance Across Markets

The lemons problem goes beyond the used car market, affecting consumer and business product markets, as well as the world of investing. In these areas, **perceived** differences in product or investment values between buyers and sellers lead to market **inefficiencies**. Akerlof suggested **robust** warranties as a potential solution, providing protection to buyers against the consequences of buying a lemon. Additionally, the rise of the internet has made information more accessible, reducing the information gap and helping buyers make more informed choices.

The Lemons Principle and Beyond Tangible Goods

The lemons principle, based on the lemons problem, suggests that low-value products dominate the market, pushing high-value ones out due to information imbalances. This phenomenon not only impacts the used car market but also influences other industries. Akerlof's insights extend to situations beyond tangible goods, such as **innovations** challenging to patent. The lemons problem becomes clear when inventors struggle to sell their ideas without revealing critical details, hindering their ability to negotiate fair prices.

To sum up, the lemons problem, stemming from information imbalances, **looms** over various markets, **hindering** fair exchanges. While Akerlof proposed solutions like warranties, the digital age has brought new tools to **alleviate** the problem. Navigating the **intricate** context of uneven information requires understanding and implementing effective solutions to foster transparent and efficient markets.

Retrieved and modified from: https://www.investopedia.com/terms/l/lemons-problem.asp & https://saylordotorg.github.io/text_introduction-to-economic-analysis/s19-01-market-for-lemons.html

Writing Activity

Using the key information you have underlined or highlighted, summarize the article in 3-5 sentences.

____

____

____

____

____

____

____

CONTENT READING RESOURCE 14

Pre-reading Activity

Read the definitions of the key vocabulary found in the article, **Bandwagon Effect**. Fill in the blanks with the correct form of the words in bold.

intricacies (n) detailed and complex features or aspects of a particular subject
allure (n) the irresistible quality of being attractive or enticing, exerting a powerful and captivating attraction
conformity (n) compliance with established customs, attitudes, or rules prevalent in a society or group
dictating (v) giving authoritative orders or commands, essentially guiding or determining a course of action
affordability (n) the quality of being within one's financial means, ensuring

accessibility or manageability
mitigate (v) taking actions that make a situation less severe or harmful, alleviating its impact
reverberate (v) events or decisions that reverberate have a lasting effect, echoing or resounding over time
manifests (v) visibly showing or demonstrating, bringing forth tangible evidence or clear indications
vigilant (adj) being watchful, alert, and attentive to potential dangers or problems, maintaining constant awareness
impulsive (adj) actions done without forethought, characterized by sudden desires or unpremeditated decisions

1. Societal expectations often demand ____________ to prevailing norms, shaping collective behavior and identity.
2. Understanding the ____________ of international trade agreements is vital for economists analyzing global markets.
3. Analyzing the ____________ of welfare programs is crucial for understanding their impact on vulnerable populations.
4. Anthropologists are tasked with ____________ the evolution of cultural practices within indigenous communities.
5. Governments may face challenges when making ____________ decisions during economic crises.
6. Social policies aim to ____________ inequalities by addressing the root causes of economic disparity.
7. The decisions of central banks often ____________ through financial markets, influencing investor behavior.
8. Maintaining a ____________ stance in economic research is essential for accurate policy recommendations.
9. The ________ of urban environments in migration studies often manifests by examining socio-economic opportunities.
10. Economic analyses reveal how positive fiscal policies ____________ in sustainable economic growth and development.

Reading Activity

Read the following article, and as you read, underline or highlight the parts containing key information.

Bandwagon Effect

The bandwagon effect, a phenomenon deeply rooted in behavioral psychology, exerts a powerful influence on our decisions, shaping everything from our product choices to major financial moves. The following explains the **intricacies** of the bandwagon effect in terms of examining its origins, exploring its impact on household finances, and finally long-term financial decisions and investments, that provides practical strategies to safeguard our financial health.

The Bandwagon Effect in Everyday Purchases and Behavioral Psychology
The bandwagon effect is an inherent human tendency to align our actions with those of the majority. Stemming from the need to belong, this behavioral phenomenon often steers our decisions without a thorough evaluation of their merit. As people succumb to the **allure** of **conformity**, our choices in everyday scenarios, such as supermarket purchases and restaurant selections, are frequently dictated by what is popular rather than what is practical. Recognizing and limiting the bandwagon effect is essential to curbing unnecessary expenditures and fostering smarter financial habits.

Impact on Household Finances
The bandwagon effect extends its influence into our households, **dictating** the products we buy and the places we frequent. The pull effect, a consequence of the bandwagon effect, can lead us to choose popular brands and restaurants, potentially neglecting considerations of **affordability** and proximity. To **mitigate** this impact on our finances, adopting savings simulators and budgeting tools, such as those recommended by Santander Consumer Spain and Tuiio, becomes crucial. Learning to balance popularity with fiscal responsibility ensures that our spending aligns with our true needs and financial goals.

Long-term Financial Consequences and Investing
While the bandwagon effect may sway minor purchases, its implications can **reverberate** into major life decisions, such as homeownership and property location. In the realm of investments, the bandwagon effect often **manifests**

in the popularity-driven choices of financial products, like cryptocurrencies. To safeguard long-term financial health, it is imperative to resist the allure of trends, focusing instead on the profitability and maturity dates of chosen financial instruments. By remaining **vigilant**, investors can protect themselves from **impulsive** decisions prompted by the bandwagon effect.

In conclusion, the bandwagon effect is a powerful force that shapes our consumer behavior and financial decisions. Whether influencing everyday purchases, household choices, or long-term investments, its impact can be profound. However, with an awareness of its existence and practical strategies such as financial planning and thoughtful consideration of discounts, individuals can navigate the bandwagon effect, ensuring that their financial health remains intact amidst the ever-changing trends of the consumer landscape.

Retrieved and modified from: https://www.santander.com/en/stories/the-bandwagon-effect-why-we-spend-money-on-fads

Writing Activity

Using the key information you have underlined or highlighted, summarize the article in 3-5 sentences.

CONTENT READING RESOURCE 15

Pre-reading Activity

Read the definitions of the key vocabulary found in the article, **Red, Blue, and Purple Ocean Market Strategies**. Fill in the blanks with the correct form of the words in bold.

facilitate (v) to make a process or action easier or more efficient; to assist or enable the occurrence or realization of something
well-established (adj) existing and recognized for a long time
direct competition (n phrase) head-to-head rivalry between businesses
outperform (v) do better than others
rivalry (n) competition between groups
licensing agreements (n) official permissions to do something
recognizable (adj) easily identified or known
boundaries (n) limits or borders
innovative (adj) introducing new ideas
trajectory (n) the path followed by an object or entity in motion, or figuratively, the course of development indicating progress or change

1. Using AI for customer support is an ______ approach in the tech industry.
2. The use of technology in the classroom can _________ student engagement and interaction during collaborative learning activities in a social science setting.
3. The study of historical events allows us to trace the _______ of societal changes over time, revealing patterns and influences that shape the course of human development.
4. To win in the market, a company must ______ its competitors.
5. The ______ between Apple and Samsung in the smartphone market is well-known.
6. Movie studios make ______ with toy manufacturers to produce toys based on their movies.
7. McDonald's is a ______ brand in the fast-food industry.
8. A company's logo should be ______ so that people instantly know the brand.

9. Local shops often face ______ from big chain stores.
10. Companies exploring new markets should not limit themselves by existing _______.

Reading Activity

Read the following article, and as you read, underline or highlight the parts containing key information.

Red, Blue, and Purple Ocean Market Strategies

In the world of business, success depends on strategic choices that **facilitate** navigation through tough competition. The ideas of red and blue ocean strategies, along with the new concept called Purple Ocean, show how businesses try to be the best in the market. Whether facing strong competition or exploring new ideas, these strategies play a big role in deciding how businesses grow. The following explains distinct marketing strategies—red, blue, and purple oceans—revealing their unique approaches and impacts.

Red Ocean Strategy

A red ocean strategy involves businesses competing in industries that are already **well-established**. This is a common approach in various sectors like fast-food restaurants, clothing stores, and car dealerships. To succeed in a red ocean, you need to overcome strong and **direct competition** where companies are mainly trying to offer the best prices. The main goals are to **outperform** competitors and take advantage of the existing demand.

For instance, look at the soft drink industry. When you think of soda, you probably think of the **rivalry** between Pepsi and Coke. Coca-Cola started in 1886, and Pepsi followed in 1893. The soft drink industry is well-established, and it is not easy for new companies to join. Even though some smaller companies try to compete for a share of the market, there are limitations like limited space on store shelves. Also, things like **licensing agreements**, **recognizable** brands, and advertising costs make it hard for new companies to succeed in the soft drink industry.

Blue Ocean Strategy

On the opposite side of things, there is a strategy called the blue ocean strategy. Instead of directly competing with big established companies, a blue ocean strategy aims to create a demand for something that has not been made yet. This often involves expanding the **boundaries** of existing industries that are already competitive.

The key to succeeding with this strategy is to find a space in the market that has not been filled yet and taking advantage of it before any other businesses even think about it. Because there is no competition yet, companies using a blue ocean strategy do not have to worry as much about prices compared to other businesses.

Blue ocean strategists do not necessarily have to invent completely new industries. They are more about finding new opportunities that no one has explored before, allowing new ideas to become successful in industries that might have seemed too tough to compete in before.

Purple Ocean Strategy

Purple Ocean is a recent term that merges the ideas of red ocean and blue ocean. It describes a market formed in a unique way, using technology advancements, new ideas, and **innovative** services. The red ocean represents a market with limited growth potential due to intense competition, while the blue ocean stands for a market that can be a leader because it lacks competitors. Just like how blue and red create purple when mixed, Purple Ocean combines the benefits of both these market types.

To sum up, in business, deciding between red and blue oceans or combining them in the Purple Ocean significantly impact a company's **trajectory**. Red oceans need strength in established markets, blue oceans promote innovation in new areas. The Purple Ocean strategy uses technology and creative services, combining old and new ways, influencing future success stories.

Retrieved and modified from: https://ibimapublishing.com/articles/JEERBE/2021/165416/ & https://www.linkedin.com/pulse/red-ocean-vs-blue-how-tap-new-market-space-tim-vogel

Writing Activity

Using the key information you have underlined or highlighted, summarize the article in 3-5 sentences.

[Chapter 2]
Outlining a Final Group Project

DISCUSSION

1. Introduce the topic you have read to the group by delivering a spoken summary of the key points from the article. As listeners, the rest of the group members write down the key points.

2. Determine a topic for the final group project from the readings shared by group members considering the following questions.

1) How is the topic being applied or can be applied to improve our actual lives or any industrial site?

2) How could a start-up company be created using the information from the reading, and what are the possible obstacles and concerns that people might have in this start-up company?

3) What are the advantages and disadvantages of the topic?

4) Where can it be contrasted with the topic?

5) What are the possible causes and effects, problems and solutions, evaluations and predictions, etc., related to the topic?

3. Once the group project topic is selected, discuss and select three most important ideas you want to develop for your final group project. Then fill in the blanks with the main argument and three supporting arguments.

Topic: ______________________________

Main Argument for Your Final Group Project

Topic Sentence for Supporting Argument 1:

Topic Sentence for Supporting Argument 2:

Topic Sentence for Supporting Argument 3:

LEARNING OBJECTIVES	IN THIS UNIT STUDENTS WILL ...
PERFORMANCE & TASK	demonstrate the ability to grasp and articulate the meaning of **IT, Engineering & Natural Science** content in English, showcasing comprehension of subject-specific terminology and concepts.
CRITICAL THINKING SKILLS 1	examine the organizational framework and substantive content of texts within the domains of **IT, Engineering & Natural Science** through the application of diverse reading techniques.
CRITICAL THINKING SKILLS 2	extract key information from reading passages for a nuanced understanding and facilitate clear understanding of complex concepts.
COMMUNICATION SKILLS	discuss **IT, Engineering & Natural Science** major related complex concepts clearly,
WRITING SKILLS	write summarization of reading passages by identifying key information of **IT, Engineering & Natural Science** major related content.

UNIT 09

Content Readings for Final Presentation Project III: IT, Engineering & Natural Science

[Chapter 1]

Brainstorming & Discussion for Group Presentation Topics: IT, Engineering & Natural Science

BRAINSTORMING

As a group, take a look at the 12 reading topics and select one as your **preferred topic. After reading** that passage carefully, discuss **and answer** the following questions.

1. In your chosen passage, underline the Topic Sentence in each paragraph, circle the controlling idea, and summarize the main arguments below.

____

____

____

____

2. How could this technology you chose improve our lives?

____

____

____

____

3. What start-up company could be created using the information from this reading? What are the obstacles and concerns you might have in this start-up company?

____

____

____

____

4. What questions do you have after reading this passage?

____

____

____

____

5. Please fill in the blanks in the box with the following questions. (1) What do you **know about** and what do you **want to learn about** this subject? (2) After reading and doing some research, what did you **learn about** this subject?

K **(What I Know)**	**W** **(What I Want to Learn)**	**L** **(What I Learned)**
Write about what you already know.	Write about what you want to know.	After the completion of the reading, researching, and discussion, write about what you learned.

ACADEMIC READING

CONTENT READING RESOURCE 1

Pre-reading Activity

The Ten Most Important Developments in IT Technology

Read the definitions of the key vocabulary found in the example paragraph. Fill in the blanks with the correct form of the words in bold.

virtualization (n) – creating virtual versions of resources
connectivity (n) – state of being connected
infrastructure (n) – basic systems and facilities
diffusion (n) – spreading of an innovation
redouble (v) – double one's efforts
expenditure (n) – spending of funds
associated (adj) – connected or related
sequencing (n) – arranging in order
as-yet-untouched (adj) – not yet explored
disruption (n) – radical change or interruption

1. The ________ of blockchain technology into various industries is still in its early stages.
2. ________ allows multiple operating systems to run on a single physical server, optimizing hardware use.
3. Good ________ is crucial for cloud services to function optimally.
4. The ________ risks of implementing new software must be carefully evaluated.
5. After identifying vulnerabilities in the system, we must ________ our efforts on cybersecurity.
6. The rapid advance of AI technology is causing significant ________ in the job market.
7. Any tech company requires a solid ________ to handle large amounts of data.
8. ________ the installation of updates is crucial to ensure system stability.

9. The ________ regions of the internet present both opportunities and challenges.
10. The IT department needs to keep track of ________ to ensure the budget is well-managed.

Reading Activity

The Ten Most Important Developments in IT Technology in the next 10 Years

Developments in the following 10 technological fields are likely to bring about fundamental changes in the modern workplace and organizations over the next decade: (1) process automation and **virtualization**, (2) **connectivity**, (3) distributed IT **infrastructure**, (4) next-generation computing, (5) applied artificial intelligence (AI), (6) the future of programming with new software, (7) trust architectures, (8) the bio revolution, (9) next-generation materials, and (10) clean tech trends (McKinsey, 2023).

Top Tech Trends

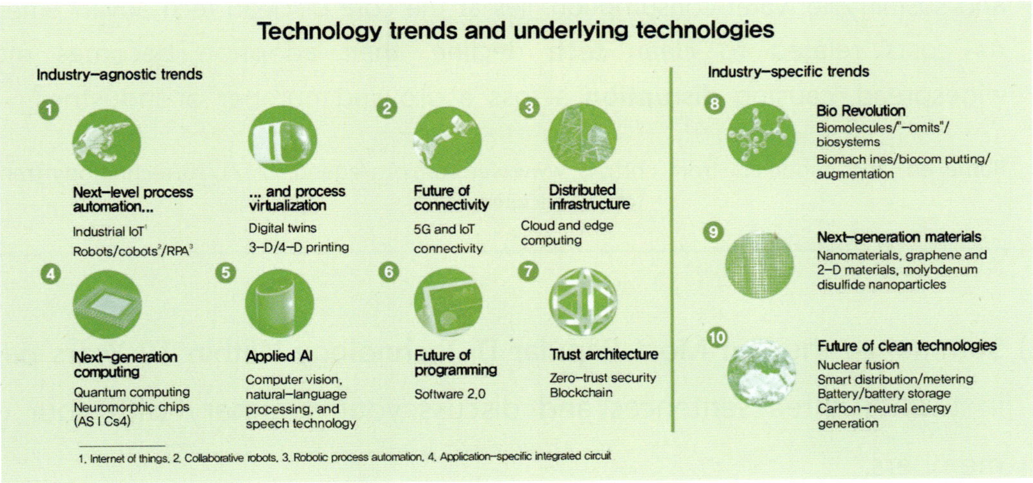

These advancements will impact both individuals and organizations. McKinsey forecasts that by 2025, more than 50 billion **gadgets** and devices are expected to be connected to the Industrial Internet of Things (IoT), powered by faster digital connections, including 5G. Moreover, process automation, 3D printing, and robots will generate around 79.4 zettabytes of data per year. A distributed IT infrastructure will also encompass hybrid-cloud or multi-cloud platforms, making it more accessible to devices, enhancing speed, saving costs, and bolstering cybersecurity defenses.

Next-generation computing involves numerous far-reaching developments, from quantum AI to fully autonomous vehicles. Applied artificial intelligence (AI) stands out as one of the most significant tech trends, becoming increasingly sophisticated and giving rise to tech-based tools for training machines to recognize patterns and take action based on their detections. Additionally, software 2.0 could lead to the creation of software applications and result in AI-driven applications that enable rapid scaling and **diffusion** of new data-rich capabilities.

However, criminals in cybersecurity will **redoube** their efforts, and trust architecture will aid in the battle against cybercrime, aiming to reduce the operating and capital **expenditure associated** with cybersecurity. Simultaneously, the bio revolution, propelled by advancements in AI and DNA **sequencing**, may bring substantial progress in gene therapies and highly personalized medicines.

Lastly, next-generation materials will enable various market sectors, such as energy, transportation, health, pharmacy, semiconductors, and manufacturing, to transform with notably higher efficiency in diverse, **as-yet-untouched** application areas. Furthermore, the future of clean tech trends, encompassing renewable energy, cleaner and greener transport, energy-efficient buildings, and sustainable water consumption, lies at the core of clean tech advancements. As costs related to clean tech decline, their adoption becomes more widespread, causing **disruption** across a growing number of industries.

Retrieved and modified from: https://www.weforum.org/agenda/2021/10/technology-trends-top-10-mckinsey/

1) Summarize the **Ten Most Popular IT Technology Within 10 Years** passage in two or three sentences and discuss your summary with your group members.

Tips – How to summarize: Summary is the short version of paraphrasing original text.

[1] Read the resources, identify the main points and **underline the keywords**.

[2] With appropriate **transition words** (e,g, first, second, third, to conclude, etc,) recreate the structure of writing within five to seven sentences.

[3] **Paraphrase** the main points of the text with similar expressions using different words and phrases.

CONTENT READING RESOURCE 2

Pre-reading Activity

Technology Hype and The Basic Ethics

Read the definitions of the key vocabulary found in the example paragraph. Fill in the blanks with the correct form of the words in bold.

fueled (v) – driven or powered by
perception (n) – way of understanding
immersive (adj) – feels very real
resolution (n) – image clarity
disillusionment (n) – feeling of disappointment
garnered (v) – collected or earned
implementation (n) – putting into action
anticipated (adj) – expected beforehand
overestimation (n) – guess too high
inflated (adj) – increased unrealistically

1. The company had an ________ of how popular their product would be.
2. The graphics on this game are so ________; it feels like I'm really there!
3. Many users faced ________ when they found out the app wasn't as good as expected.
4. The startup's success was ________ by a lot of media coverage.
5. Your ________ of how easy coding is might not be accurate.
6. The value of the cryptocurrency seemed ________, not reflecting its real worth.

7. The ________ of the new software took longer than we thought it would.
8. If you buy a screen with higher ________, the image will be clearer.
9. The software update ________ a lot of positive reviews.
10. The ________ demand for our new product was high, but sales were low.

Reading Activity

Technology Hype and The Basic Ethics

"Technology hype" refers to **inflated** expectations and **overestimation** of the abilities or timelines for the application and adoption of technology. When a new technology is introduced, it garners significant attention and public interest. Hype can be **fueled** by media coverage, public **perception**, marketing efforts, and industry trends. However, such hype can create a gap between the current state and capabilities of the technology and the expectations associated with it.

Here are several notable examples of technology hype throughout history:

Firstly, in the 1990s, virtual reality (VR) technology seemed capable of transporting users into **immersive** virtual worlds. Unfortunately, limitations in early VR related to **resolution**, graphics, and user experience resulted in a failure to achieve widespread adoption, leading to **disillusionment**.

Additionally, around 2012-2013, 3D printing **garnered** considerable attention and hype. It was believed that users could manufacture complex objects at home using this technology. While 3D printing has made significant advancements in prototyping and healthcare, limitations in speed, cost, and material capabilities led to the deflation of the initial hype.

Furthermore, Blockchain technology and the Internet of Things (IoT) gained immense hype, yet real-world **implementation** and adoption of these new technologies have been slower than **anticipated**.

hype cycle for emdrgint tech, 2022

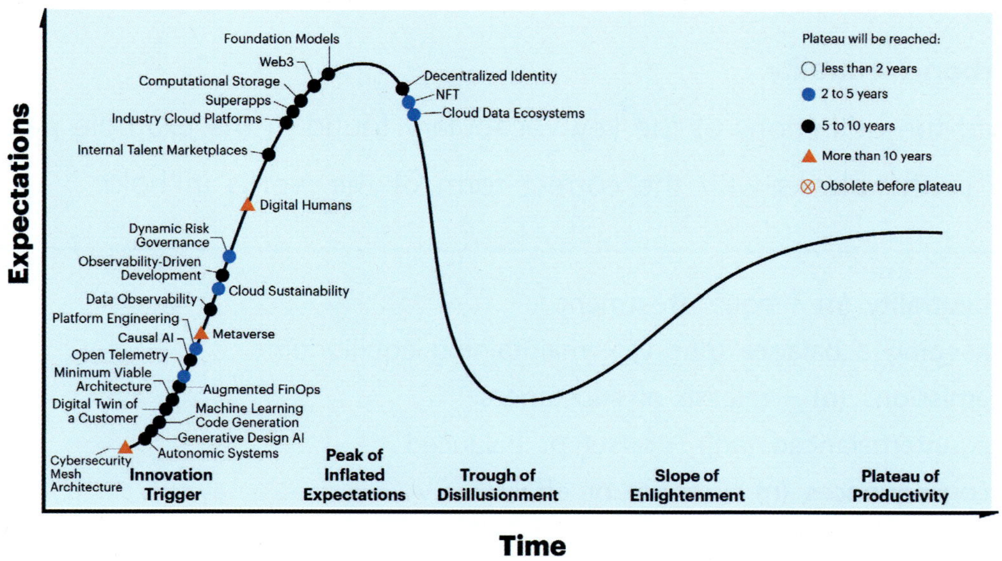

Source: Gartner

In conclusion, it is advisable for technology users to approach technology hype with a critical mindset. Evaluating the actual capabilities and limitations of a technology is crucial, rather than relying solely on overestimated claims, as most technologies lack the value or potential initially attributed to them. Understanding the limitations and conducting realistic evaluations of these technologies are essential for maintaining balanced perspectives.

2) Summarize the **Technology Hype** passage in two or three sentences and discuss your summary with your group members.

CONTENT READING RESOURCE 3

Pre-reading Activity

Carbon Neutrality

Read the definitions of the key vocabulary found in the example paragraph. Fill in the blanks with the correct form of the words in bold.

neutrality (n) – equal treatment
keeping a balance (phr. v) – maintaining equilibrium
emissions (n) – release of substances
counterbalanced (adj) – offset or balanced
consequences (n) – results or effects
acidification (n) – making more acidic
biodiversity (n) – variety of life
laid down (phr. v) – established or set
legislation (n) – laws or rules
essential (adj) – absolutely necessary

1. ________ around data protection is becoming more important.
2. Lowering ________ from data centers is a goal for many tech companies.
3. Net ________ ensures all data on the internet is treated the same.
4. A good internet connection is ________ for remote work.
5. If you ignore online security, there may be serious ________.
6. ________ between speed and security is important for any network.
7. The new software update was ________ by several bug fixes.
8. Reducing ________ of the ocean is not a direct concern for most IT companies.
9. ________ in a coding team means having people with different skills.
10. New guidelines for data privacy were ________ by the company.

Reading Activity

Carbon Neutrality

With the implementation of the European Climate Law, the EU has committed to achieving carbon **neutrality** by 2050. But what does this actually entail?

Carbon neutrality essentially involves **keeping a balance** between carbon **emissions** and their absorption in carbon sinks. By extracting carbon dioxide from the atmosphere and achieving net zero emissions, the goal is to make all global greenhouse gas (GHG) emissions **counterbalanced**.

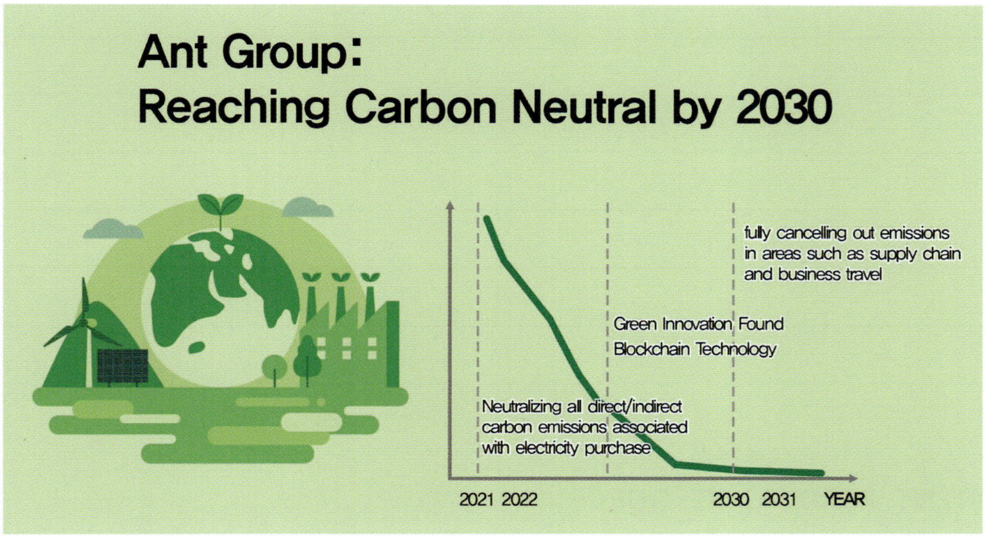

The **consequences** of rapid changes in our climate include rising sea levels, ocean **acidification**, and loss of **biodiversity**. As a result, limiting global warming to 1.5 degrees Celsius has been established as the safety threshold by the Intergovernmental Panel for Climate Change (IPCC).

This target, **laid down** in the Paris Agreement and endorsed by 195 countries, forms the basis for the European Commission's European Green Deal —a flagship initiative designed to steer Europe towards climate neutrality by 2050. The binding **legislation** to achieve these objectives is the European Climate Law.

To sum up, carbon sinks play a pivotal role in absorbing more carbon than they release. Natural carbon sinks primarily include soil, forests, and oceans, which collectively have the capacity to remove between 9.5 and 11 gigatonnes of CO_2 annually. This is significant, given that global CO_2 emissions reached 37.8 gigatonnes in 2021. Therefore, an **essential** step towards achieving climate neutrality is to substantially reduce carbon emissions.

Retrieved and modified from: https://www.europarl.europa.eu/news/en/headlines/society/20190926STO62270/what-is-carbon-neutrality-and-how-can-it-be-achieved-by-2050

3) Summarize the **Carbon Neutrality** passage in two or three sentences and discuss your summary with your group members.

____

____

____

____

____

____

____

CONTENT READING RESOURCE 4

Pre-reading Activity

Hydrogen Energy & Material

Read the definitions of the key vocabulary found in the example paragraph. Fill in the blanks with the correct form of the words in bold.

pollutants (n) – harmful substance
decarbonization (n) – cutting carbon emissions
commitment (n) – firm dedication
cost-effective (adj) – good value for cost
flammable (adj) – easily catches fire
vector (n) – a path of transferring
oxidation (n) – chemical change with oxygen
intermittent (adj) – not constant

initiatives (n) – new plans or strategies
utilizing (v) – make practical and effective use of

1. The company's ________ to cybersecurity is its top priority.
2. ________ power outages can disrupt online services.
3. Several new green tech ________ were launched this year.
4. Some tech companies aim to reduce their level of ________ levels for a greener future.
5. ________ of data centers aims to reduce their carbon footprint.
6. Using cloud storage can be more ________ than local servers.
7. Make sure to keep ________ materials away from server rooms.
8. ________ can cause damage to electrical circuits over time.
9. Malware is often delivered through a ________ like an email attachment.
10. The company was not fully ________ its workforce.

Reading Activity

Hydrogen Energy & Material

Hydrogen energy holds significant importance in the future of human existence and has played a pivotal role in addressing energy **sustainability** and usability.

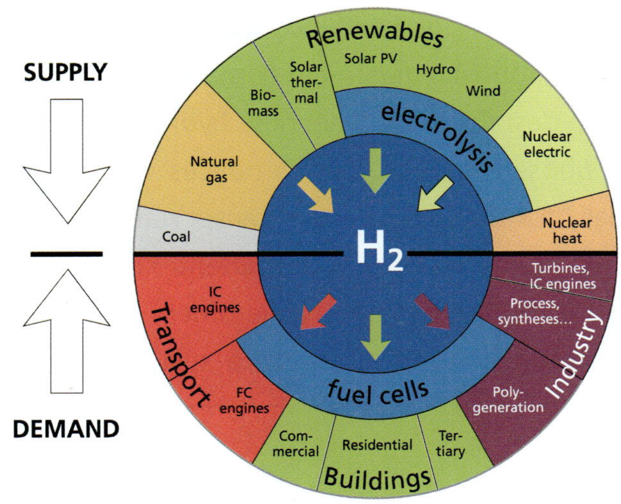

Retrieved and modified from: https://pubs.rsc.org/en/content/articlehtml/2008/jm/b805758n

First and foremost, hydrogen is a clean energy source that does not produce **pollutants** when utilized in fuel cells to generate electricity. **Utilizing** renewable energy sources such as water electrolysis makes hydrogen a sustainable, clean, renewable, and environmentally friendly energy option.

Secondly, hydrogen can serve as a versatile energy storage solution. It can be captured and stored for later use, thereby enabling a more stable energy supply. Furthermore, this form of energy finds diverse applications including fuel for transportation, powering fuel cell vehicles, industrial processes, heating, and power generation.

Thirdly, hydrogen has the potential to play a significant role in **decarbonization** efforts. By substituting fossil fuels in various sectors, hydrogen can contribute to reducing greenhouse gas emissions, combating climate change, and enhancing air quality.

In addition, hydrogen energy has found use in a wide array of research and investment initiatives. Governments, industries, and research institutions worldwide are progressively investing in hydrogen-related research, development, and infrastructure. This **commitment** underscores the recognition of hydrogen energy as a promising solution for a sustainable and low-carbon future.

While hydrogen energy offers substantial potential, challenges persist in achieving widespread usability due to production limitations and infrastructure constraints for storage, transportation, and distribution. Therefore, the development of cost-effective and efficient production methods, along with improvements in cost and efficiency, remains crucial.

Furthermore, the primary method of producing hydrogen from water requires **cost-effective** electricity sourced from renewable sources to ensure environmental benefits. Due to its highly **flammable** nature, appropriate safety measures are imperative for handling, storage, and transportation. Ensuring safe practices and robust infrastructure is essential for broader adoption.

To conclude, despite the challenges, hydrogen stands as a carbon-free energy **vector**, whose **oxidation**, only produces water. It garners considerable interest, especially for the future of the transportation industry and the storage of excess power generated by **intermittent** sources. Increasing research, technological advancements, and government **initiatives** will support its development, ultimately contributing to a sustainable and clean future.

4) Summarize the **Hydrogen Energy & Material** passage in two or three sentences and discuss your summary with your group members.

____

____

____

____

____

____

____

CONTENT READING RESOURCE 5

Pre-reading Activity

Future Batteries

Read the definitions of the key vocabulary found in the example paragraph. Fill in the blanks with the correct form of the words in bold.

energy density (n) – power per size
longevity (n) – long life
compatibility (n) – works together
prospective (adj) – likely or expected
faster charging speed (phr.) – quicker power gain
frequent (adj) – often happening
advantageous (adj) – favorable, beneficial
unexpectedly (adv) – without warning
capital (n) – money for investment
interest rate (n) – loan cost percent

1. Smartphones with a ________ are very popular these days.
2. The ________ on the loan for our new servers is quite high.
3. The ________ of this laptop is better than most models on the market.
4. A high ________ battery can store more power for its size.
5. The company raised ________ to invest in new technologies.

6. Make sure to check the ________ of the software with your operating system.
7. We are launching a survey to learn about ________ customer needs.
8. ________ software updates are needed to keep your system secure.
9. Using cloud storage is ________ for remote work.
10. The server crashed ________, causing a lot of problems.

Reading Activity

Future Batteries

Future car batteries must meet several key criteria which include **energy density**, charging speed, life cycle and **longevity**, safety, cost, environmental impact, and manufacturing **compatibility** to become popular and widely adopted within **prospective** car industries.

For example, higher energy density is crucial as it enables batteries to store more energy, leading to longer driving ranges within a given volume or weight. **Faster charging speed** is highly desirable to reduce charging times and enhance convenience for vehicle owners. A long life cycle that allows batteries to endure a large number of charge-discharge cycles, resulting in an extended lifespan, can minimize the need for **frequent** replacements. This, in turn, makes the batteries more cost-effective and environmentally sustainable.

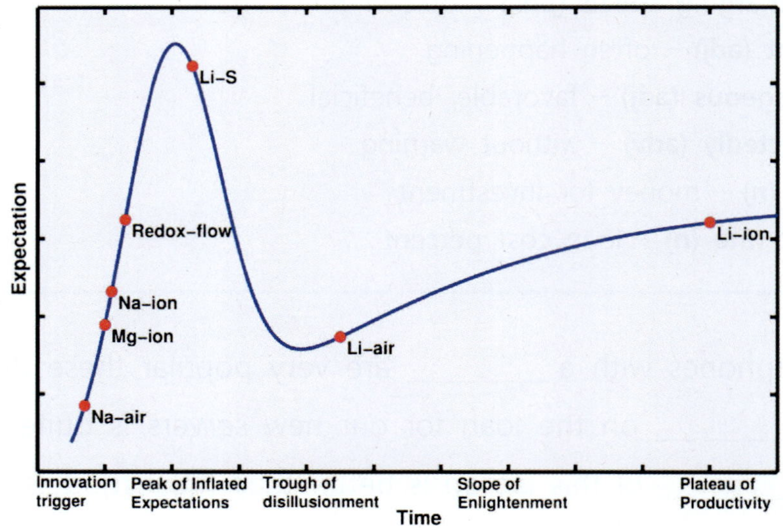

In scenarios where the economy **unexpectedly** deteriorates and expected returns aren't realized, investment losses may occur. During such times, if excessive external **capital** is introduced, the risk of investment loss further escalates due to the **interest rate**. In summary, it's important to note that using these batteries is advantageous when the expected return on investment surpasses the **interest rate** cost of borrowing.

5) Summarize the **Future Battery** passage in two or three sentences and discuss your summary with your group members.

____

____

____

____

____

____

____

CONTENT READING RESOURCE 6

Pre-reading Activity

Hydrogen Car vs. Electric Car

Read the definitions of the key vocabulary found in the example paragraph. Fill in the blanks with the correct form of the words in bold.

range (n) – the extent or distance between two points, often used to describe the maximum distance a vehicle, aircraft, or weapon can travel or operate without refueling or recharging.
refueling (v) – the act of replenishing a vehicle, machine, or equipment with fuel, typically to enable it to continue operating.
emitting (v) – releasing gases, particles, or substances, often pollutants, into the atmosphere as a result of human activities or natural processes.
exhausts (n) – the systems, typically consisting of pipes and a muffler, through which waste gases from an engine are expelled, and the gases themselves.

consumption (n) – the act of using up or utilizing resources, such as energy, goods, or services, often measured in terms of quantity or volume.
definitely (adv) – without a doubt; in a clear and certain manner, expressing a high degree of certainty or assurance.
infrastructure (n) – the basic physical and organizational structures and facilities (such as buildings, roads, transportation, and utilities) needed for the functioning of a society, business, or area.
sufficient (adj) – adequate or enough to meet a specific need, requirement, or standard; not lacking in quantity or quality.

1. The factory's ______________ of carbon dioxide had a significant impact on climate change.
2. The efficient ____________________ of electricity can lead to cost savings and reduced environmental impact.
3. We have a _____________ supply of food for the weekend camping trip.
4. The electric car has an impressive __________ of 300 miles on a single charge.
5. She is ____________ attending the conference next week.
6. Investment in ___________________ improvements can enhance economic development and quality of life in a region.
7. The car's ____________ system was in need of repair due to a leak.
8. The airplane landed at the airport for ______________ before continuing its journey.

Reading Activity

Hydrogen Car vs. Electric Car

Electric and hydrogen cars are often regarded as the top choices when it comes to factors like driving **range**, efficiency, environmental impact, power sources, and the availability of **refueling** or recharging stations. These types of vehicles stand out for their ability to operate without directly **emitting** carbon pollutants from their **exhausts**. Battery electric vehicles (BEVs) rely on Li-Ion batteries for power, while hydrogen cars use hydrogen fuel cells. It's worth noting that hydrogen fuel cells can be 100% renewable and environmentally

Hydrogen Car

Electric Car

friendly, whereas the production and **consumption** of materials like lithium and cobalt in electric vehicles can have negative environmental consequences.

However, in terms of driving range, hydrogen cars offer a superior range of 400 to 600 miles and boast a quick refueling process whereas electric vehicles typically provide a range between 150 to 375 miles. This difference is due to the energy efficiency of hydrogen-powered vehicles, which face challenges in the complex conversion of hydrogen gas into electricity for vehicle operation. Battery-powered electric vehicles, on the other hand, are highly energy-efficient, utilizing approximately 80% of the total energy for propulsion, making them **definitely** the more efficient choice.

Moreover, there's a marked contrast in **infrastructure** availability for these two types of vehicles. While electric vehicles benefit from thousands of readily available and **sufficient** charging stations worldwide, hydrogen vehicles suffer from a lack of refueling infrastructure. Refueling a hydrogen-powered vehicle is quick, taking only 5 to 10 minutes to fill the high-pressure hydrogen tank, whereas electric vehicles require 4 to 8 hours for a full charge.

In summary, the advantages of hydrogen cars encompass zero harmful emissions, swift refueling, and extended driving range, although they tend to be expensive and less efficient with limited refueling infrastructure. In contrast, electric cars are convenient, dependable, and offer widespread recharging options, albeit with a somewhat less eco-friendly image than one might initially expect.

Retrieved and modified from: https://bacancysystems.com/blog/hydrogen-vs-electric-cars#:~:text=Electric%20and%20hydrogen%20cars%20are%20considered%20the%20best%20options%20that,an%20electric%20or%20hydrogen%20car.

6) Summarize the **Hydrogen Car vs. Electronic Car** passage in two or three sentences and discuss your summary with your group members.

____

____

____

____

____

____

____

CONTENT READING RESOURCE 7

Pre-reading Activity

What AI Can Do for Humans at Present and the Future

Read the definitions of the key vocabulary found in the example paragraph. Fill in the blanks with the correct form of the words in bold.

state (n) – the particular condition that someone or something is in at a specific time.
potential (n) – the inherent or unrealized ability, quality, or capacity that someone or something may possess.
higher education (n) – formal education beyond the secondary (high school) level, typically provided by colleges, universities, and other post-secondary institutions.
excel (v) – to be extremely good at something.
autocomplete (n) – a feature in software or applications that predicts and suggests words or phrases as users type, making text input more efficient.
commonplace (adj) – something that is ordinary, widely known, or frequently encountered; lacking in novelty.
impaired (adj) – weakened, damaged, or diminished in quality or function, often in the context of physical or mental abilities.
disinformation (n) – false or misleading information deliberately spread to deceive or manipulate people, often for political, social, or propaganda purposes.
exposed (adj) – placed in a situation where something is visible, open to view, or vulnerable to outside factors.

regulatory (adj) – relating to rules, regulations, or laws that govern and control various activities or industries.

1. In order to _____ in your field you must apply yourself with dedication.
2. The young artist has great __________ for success in the art world.
3. In today's digital age, smartphones have become a __________ technology.
4. His __________ vision made it difficult for him to read small print.
5. Many students pursue ________ to obtain a college degree.
6. Detecting and countering ___________ campaigns is a challenge in the age of social media.
7. ____________ in search engines can help users find information quickly.
8. The __________ authority oversees safety standards in the pharmaceutical industry.
9. The house was __________ to the harsh elements during the storm.
10. The _________ of the company's finances was very concerning to shareholders.

Reading Activity

What AI Can Do for Humans at Present and the Future

Barbara Grosz, in her 2003 remarks, discusses the current **state** of artificial intelligence (AI) and its **potential** impacts on various aspects of our lives, including personal experiences, society, healthcare, and, **higher education**, both now and in the future.

Presently, AI systems **excel** in handling vast amounts of data, often in specific domains. For instance, AlphaZero achieved mastery in the game of Go through self-play. AI technologies have become commonplace in everyday life, offering features like grammar checks, **autocomplete** suggestions, automatic organization of personal photos, and speech recognition for a wide audience.

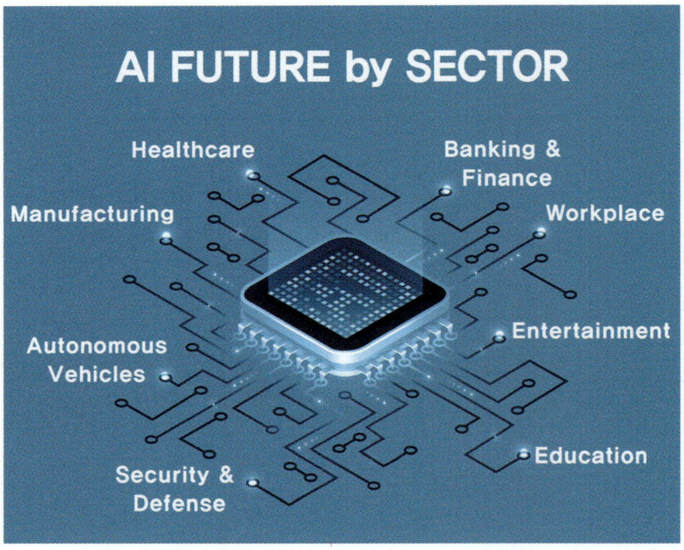

In addition, AI's potential applications in healthcare are substantial, too. It can aid in drug discovery, offer decision support by presenting treatment options, and provide practical assistance such as lane-keeping in driving or generating text-to-speech from images for the visually **impaired**. AI tools have also entered the mainstream, raising concerns about information and **disinformation** control, as people receive personalized news, social media content, and entertainment through search and ranking algorithms.

Similarly, from an educational perspective, children are **exposed** to AI when they engage with content on platforms like YouTube or browse photo albums. In higher education, computer science students are prompted to consider the ethical and safety implications of AI. They must learn to communicate across disciplinary boundaries to address concepts like safety, equity, and fairness, which can be challenging to quantify.

Moreover, AI has primarily been used for administrative tasks such as billing and surgery scheduling. The adoption of AI for improving patient care, while a significant aspiration, faces hurdles due to limited legal, **regulatory**, and financial incentives, as well as various disincentives. Nonetheless, AI tools, such as risk scoring and alert systems, are gradually finding their way into healthcare.

To sum up, balancing innovation with essential safeguards is a complex challenge, and the development of mechanisms for AI accountability may be a critical innovation in this context.

Retrieved and modified from: Source: https://seas.harvard.edu/news/2021/10/present-and-future-ai

7) Summarize the **What AI Can Do for Humans at Present and the Future** passage in two or three sentences and discuss your summary with your group members.

CONTENT READING RESOURCE 8

Pre-reading Activity

Why Cloud Data Can Lead the Future Industry

Read the definitions of the key vocabulary found in the example paragraph. Fill in the blanks with the correct form of the words in bold.

scalability (n) – the ability of a system, process, or organization to handle an increased workload or demand efficiently without a significant decrease in performance or the need for a complete redesign.
innovation (n) – the process of introducing new ideas, methods, products, or technologies to create a positive change or improvement in various aspects of life, business, or society.
integrity (n) – the quality of being whole and complete.
cost-effectiveness (n) – the measure of achieving desired results or benefits while minimizing costs or expenses, ensuring the efficient allocation of resources.
deployments (n) – the process of positioning, installing, or employing resources, personnel, or equipment to perform a specific task or function.
enhancements (n) – improvements, modifications, or upgrades made to something to increase its quality, performance, or capabilities.
stringent (adj) – characterized by strict, precise, or rigorous standards, requirements, or regulations that demand a high level of compliance and

precision.

flexibility (n) – the ability to adapt, change, or adjust easily to different situations, needs, or circumstances without losing efficiency or effectiveness.

1. __________ in a work schedule allows employees to balance work and personal commitments.
2. The military __________ of troops to the border was in response to a security threat.
3. The ______ of the data is vital for consumer trust and belief.
4. Technological ____________ has transformed the way we communicate and access information.
5. The _______________ of the new manufacturing process led to increased profitability.
6. The ____________ of the cloud computing platform allowed it to accommodate a growing number of users seamlessly.
7. The software developer released regular updates and ___________ to fix bugs and add new features.
8. The company had to meet __________ safety regulations to operate in the chemical industry.

Reading Activity

Why Cloud Data Can Lead the Future Industry

Eric Schmidt, the former CEO of Google, is credited with coining the term "cloud computing" at a conference in 2006. Since then, the cloud computing industry has experienced significant growth, with its value increasing from $371 billion to over $832 billion by 2025. There are several compelling reasons why cloud computing is crucial for businesses in 2024 and beyond such as scalability, growth, cost-effectiveness, security and flexibility.

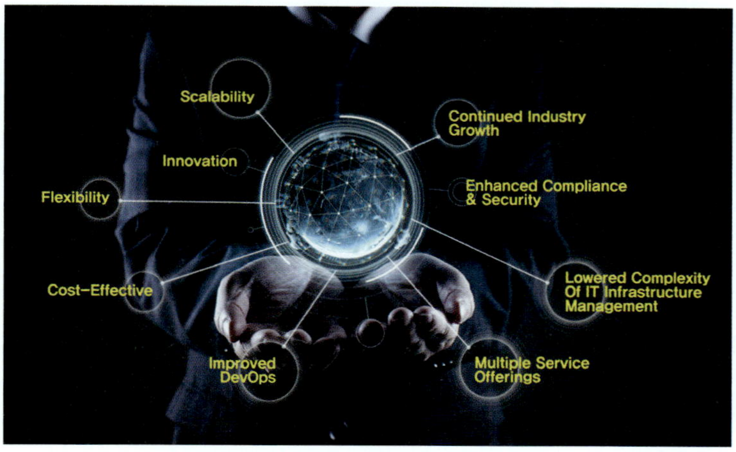

First, one of the key advantages of cloud computing is its inherent **scalability**, enabling businesses to easily and swiftly adjust their IT solutions to match the processing power of their hardware setup and manage technical resources.

Second, cloud computing is closely linked to business growth. Leveraging the cloud as an infrastructure for **innovation** can lead to improved performance, cost reduction, and increased agility. For instance, in the realm of IoT product development, companies are achieving innovation at a pace made possible through the use of cloud computing.

Third, **cost-effectiveness** is a primary driver for the importance of cloud computing in business. DevOps, with its emphasis on improved solution **deployment** quality and speed, is a significant benefit, thanks to the flexible communication processes that enable traditionally isolated teams to collaborate throughout the development cycle, along with the obvious business operations **enhancements** the cloud provides.

Fourth, major cloud service providers are enterprise-level entities known for their **stringent** security, compliance, and data protection standards. This is especially important for organizations operating in tightly regulated industries, such as healthcare, government, pharmaceuticals, and defense, where adherence to specific compliance requirements is crucial for safeguarding application and data **integrity**.

Furthermore, the **flexibility** of cloud computing allows businesses to avoid heavy investments in a single, potentially risky project that may or may not contribute to business growth.

To conclude, the availability of various cloud deployment models, including public, private, hybrid, and community, is driving most organizations to adopt a hybrid approach, making the cloud a significant resource for business success.

8) Summarize the **Why Cloud Data Can Lead the Future Industry** passage in two or three sentences and discuss your summary with your group members.

____

____

____

____

____

____

____

CONTENT READING RESOURCE 9

Pre-reading Activity

Electrica Die Sorting (EDS) in Semiconductor Manufacturing Process

Read the definitions of the key vocabulary found in the example paragraph. Fill in the blanks with the correct form of the words in bold.

semiconductor (n) – a material with electrical conductivity that is intermediate between that of conductors and insulators, often used in electronic devices.
package testing (n) – the evaluation of a semiconductor chip's performance and quality after it has been assembled and packaged.
defective (adj) – not functioning correctly or having flaws; in the context of semiconductor chips, chips that do not meet quality standards.
probe card (n) – a device with tiny pins that come into contact with a semiconductor wafer to transmit electrical signals and perform tests.
efficiency (n) – the ability to accomplish a task with minimal waste of time, energy, or resources.
yield rates (n) – the percentage of high-quality semiconductor chips in relation to the total number of chips on a single wafer.
flawless (adj) – perfect, without any defects or imperfections.
segregate (v) – to separate or set apart items based on specific characteristics or qualities.
rectify (v) – to correct or remedy a problem or defect.

proportion (n) – the comparative relationship of one thing to another in terms of quantity or size. Top of Form

1. A __________ is an essential component in most electronic devices, serving as a bridge between conductors and insulators.
2. What type of testing is conducted to evaluate a semiconductor chip's performance after it has been assembled and packaged? It's called __________.
3. The quality control team identified several __________ chips that did not meet the required standards during the inspection.
4. During semiconductor testing, a __________ is used to establish contact between the tiny pins and the wafer.
5. To improve the manufacturing process __________, it's important to identify and remove faulty chips at an early stage.
6. __________ is a key metric in semiconductor production, indicating the proportion of high-quality chips on a wafer.
7. The goal of semiconductor production is to achieve a __________ product, free from defects or imperfections.
8. In order to __________ the issue, the engineers had to carefully examine the design and manufacturing steps.
9. The process of __________ the defective chips allowed the production line to run more smoothly.
10. The __________ of high-quality chips relative to the total chip count on a wafer is a critical performance indicator in the semiconductor industry.

Reading Activity

Electrica Die Sorting (EDS) in Semiconductor Manufacturing Process

$$\frac{\text{Total number of functional chips produced}}{\text{Number of designed chips}} \times 100 = \text{Yield}$$

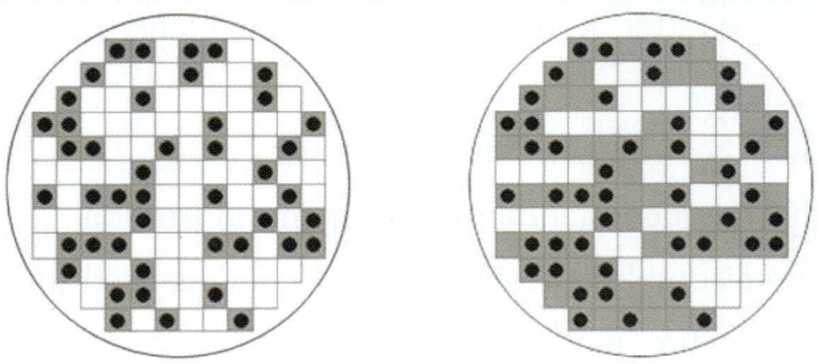

(a) About 60% yield (b) About 30% yield

In the final stages of semiconductor chip production, various tests, including EDS, package testing, and final quality testing, are essential to identify and separate defective chips. EDS is conducted once the wafer is finished, package testing occurs after chip assembly and packaging, and final quality testing is performed just before release from the consumer's perspective.

EDS, in particular, is the initial step in a series of tests to guarantee the flawless quality of semiconductor chips. It takes place between the FAB step (where electrical circuits are etched onto the wafer) and the packaging step (where the chip starts to resemble the final product). EDS primarily assesses the electrical characteristics to ensure that each individual chip meets the required quality standards.

The objectives of EDS include (1) identifying and segregating defective chips at the wafer level, (2) rectifying defective chips, (3) addressing issues discovered during the FAB or design stages, and (4) preemptively removing defective chips to enhance the efficiency of subsequent packaging and testing processes.

This process involves several steps: first, examining the electrical characteristics to confirm the desired quality level for each chip; second, repairing chips with fixable defects and marking chips that are beyond repair; and third, eliminating faulty chips from further processing to boost overall process efficiency. EDS is critical for improving semiconductor yield rates, which indicate the proportion of high-quality chips compared to the total chip count on a single wafer, serving as a direct measure of semiconductor productivity. These four steps can be summarized as follows: (1) Electrical Test & Wafer Burn In (ET Test & WBI), (2) Hot/Cold Test, (3) Repair/Final Test, and (4) Inking.

In conclusion, the EDS process involves making the wafer come into contact with a probe card, with numerous small pins on the card touching the wafer and transmitting electrical signals to identify and separate defective chips.

Retrieved and modified from: https://news.samsung.com/global/eight-major-steps-to-semiconductor-fabrication-part-8-electrical-die-sorting-eds

9) Summarize the **Electrica Die Sorting (EDS) in Semiconductor Manufacturing Process** passage in two or three sentences and discuss your summary with your group members.

CONTENT READING RESOURCE 10

Pre-reading Activity

Artificial intelligence, big data, cloud computing and connectivity

Read the definitions of the key vocabulary found in the example paragraph. Fill in the blanks with the correct form of the words in bold.

intricately (adv) – in a complex and detailed manner, often involving many interconnected elements or parts.
collaborate (v) – to work together with others on a shared project or task.
innovations (n) – the introduction of new ideas, methods, products, or processes that lead to positive changes or advancements.

symbiotic (adj) – involving a mutually beneficial relationship or interaction between different components or organisms.
derive (v) – to obtain or extract something from a source, often implying the generation of valuable insights or information.
infrastructure (n) – the underlying framework or basic physical and organizational structures needed for the operation of a system or society.
optimize (v) – to make something as effective or efficient as possible, often involving the best utilization of resources.
anomalies (n) – deviations from the norm or expected patterns, typically indicating irregularities or unusual occurrences.
predictive (adj) – relating to the ability to make forecasts or anticipations about future events or outcomes.
transformative (adj) – capable of bringing about significant and positive changes, often on a profound scale.

1. The __________ relationship between AI and big data drives many technological advancements.
2. Innovations in technology often result when diverse teams __________.
3. To __________ valuable insights from the data, AI algorithms play a crucial role.
4. Claire __________ crafted the delicate jewelry, paying meticulous attention to every tiny detail.
5. The company's recent __________ in renewable energy have the potential to revolutionize the industry.
6. The ability to __________ cloud resources can lead to cost savings and better performance.
7. The __________ analytics software helped the business forecast customer behavior with impressive accuracy.
8. The __________ changes brought by these advancements are reshaping entire industries.
9. The government is investing in upgrading the country's __________, including roads, bridges, and public transportation.
10. The __________ in the experimental data raised questions about the reliability of the measurements.

Reading Activity

Artificial intelligence, big data, cloud computing and connectivity

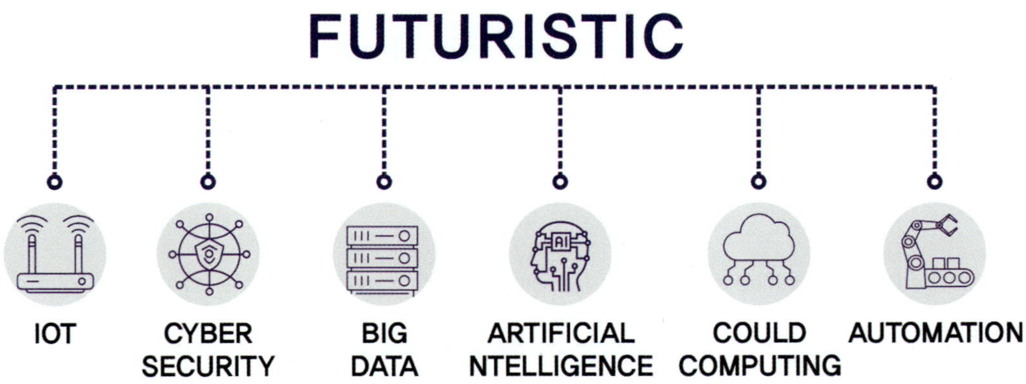

Artificial Intelligence (AI), big data, cloud computing, and connectivity are **intricately** linked and often **collaborate** to drive progress and **innovations** in the realms of data infrastructure, cloud technology, connectivity, the Internet of Things (IoT), and feedback mechanisms. Big data primarily represents the vast volume of structured and unstructured data sourced from various outlets. AI relies on extensive datasets to train models and **derive** valuable insights, making big data the driving force behind AI algorithms, empowering them to recognize patterns, make predictions, and generate intelligent responses.

AI encompasses various techniques, such as machine learning, deep learning, natural language processing, and computer vision. These techniques involve processing and analyzing big data to unveil patterns, detect **anomalies**, and formulate predictions or decisions. Cloud computing offers scalable and readily available access to computational resources, storage, and services via the internet. It provides the essential **infrastructure** for processing and storing large datasets efficiently. The cloud allows organizations to leverage substantial computing power, parallel processing, and distributed storage for AI training and implementation.

Connectivity, particularly through the Internet of Things (IoT), plays a pivotal role in collecting and transmitting data from sensors, devices, and systems. IoT devices generate extensive data, which contributes to big data, and AI algorithms analyze IoT data for real-time insights, predictive maintenance, and autonomous decision-making. Cloud platforms often serve as the foundation for managing and processing IoT data.

The **symbiotic** interconnectedness of AI, big data, cloud, and connectivity creates a feedback loop that generates insights, **optimizes** cloud resources, enhances connectivity, and improves IoT devices. The data generated by IoT devices and interactions with cloud services further enrich big data, which, in turn, fuels continuous learning and enhancement for AI algorithms.

In summary, AI, big data, cloud computing, and connectivity form a mutually beneficial ecosystem where each element depends on and elevates the others. They collaborate to harness the potential of data, process it effectively, and enable intelligent decision-making, **predictive** analysis, and **transformative** applications across diverse domains.

Retrieved and modified from: https://canlink.co.zw/blog/why-big-data-iot-ai-and-cloud-are-converging/ & https://www.researchgate.net/figure/The-relationship-among-IoT-Big-Data-and-Cloud-Computing_fig2_341166746

10) Summarize the **Artificial intelligence, big data, cloud computing and connectivity** passage in two or three sentences and discuss your summary with your group members.

____

____

____

____

____

____

____

CONTENT READING RESOURCE 11

Pre-reading Activity

Types of Data: Big Data, Small Data, Open Data vs. Closed Data

Read the definitions of the key vocabulary found in the example paragraph. Fill in the blanks with the correct form of the words in bold.

encompassing – Including or comprising a wide range or variety of different elements or aspects.
manageability – The quality or capability of being easily controlled, organized, or handled.
necessitating – Requiring something as necessary or essential for a particular purpose.
adeptness – Proficiency or skill in a particular area, demonstrating expertise or capability.
thorough – Complete, detailed, or exhaustive in considering all aspects of something.
integration – The act or process of combining or coordinating separate elements into a unified or coherent whole.
contingent – Dependent on something else, conditional, or subject to specific circumstances.
amenable – Willing or open to considering suggestions or ideas, adaptable or responsive.
profound – Having deep insight, knowledge, or understanding; showing great depth or intensity.
empowers – To grant authority or provide the capability or means to achieve something, enabling someone or something to take action or make decisions.

1. A __________ understanding of the principles is required for success in this field.
2. The success of the project is _____________ upon securing additional funding.
3. The team needs to demonstrate ________ in adapting to new challenges.
4. The organization aims to __________ its employees by offering training programs.
5. The course material is comprehensive, ___________ various topics.
6. The expansion of the company's operations is ____________ a comprehensive review of its infrastructure to accommodate the increased demand.
7. ___________ of the new software system requires careful planning and execution.
8. The _____________ of the system largely depends on its user-friendly interface.

9. Achieving the ________ insights necessary for innovation requires extensive research.
10. The success of the presentation was __________ to some last-minute changes.

Reading Activity

Types of Data: Big Data, Small Data, Open Data vs. Closed Data

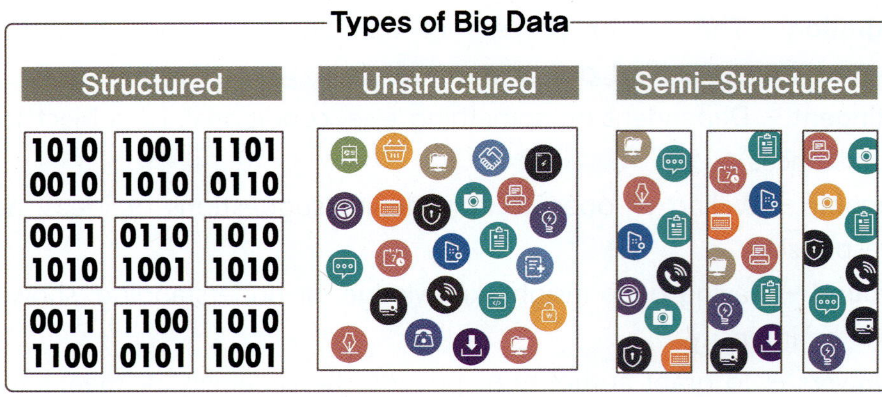

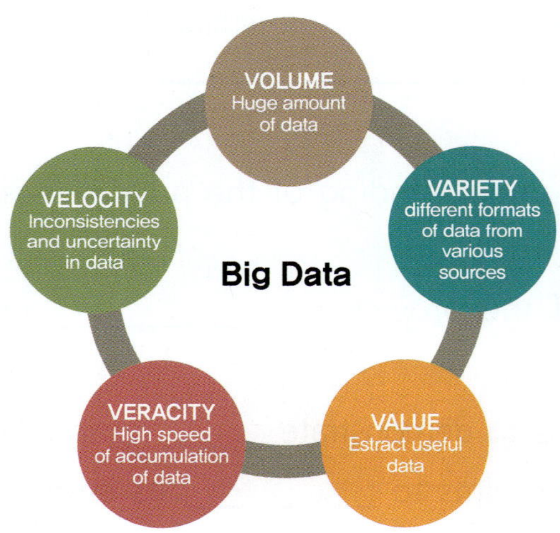

Future IT personnel must possess expertise across varied data types, **encompassing** closed, small, big, and real-time data, **contingent** on their availability and **manageability**. Closed data comprises confidential information crucial for organizations, encompassing sensitive business records and trade secrets, **necessitating** a **profound** understanding of security protocols, privacy laws, and ethical implications. In contrast, small data denotes compact datasets **amenable** to traditional database processing, often targeted towards specific applications without the need for sophisticated big data methods.

Big Data and small data

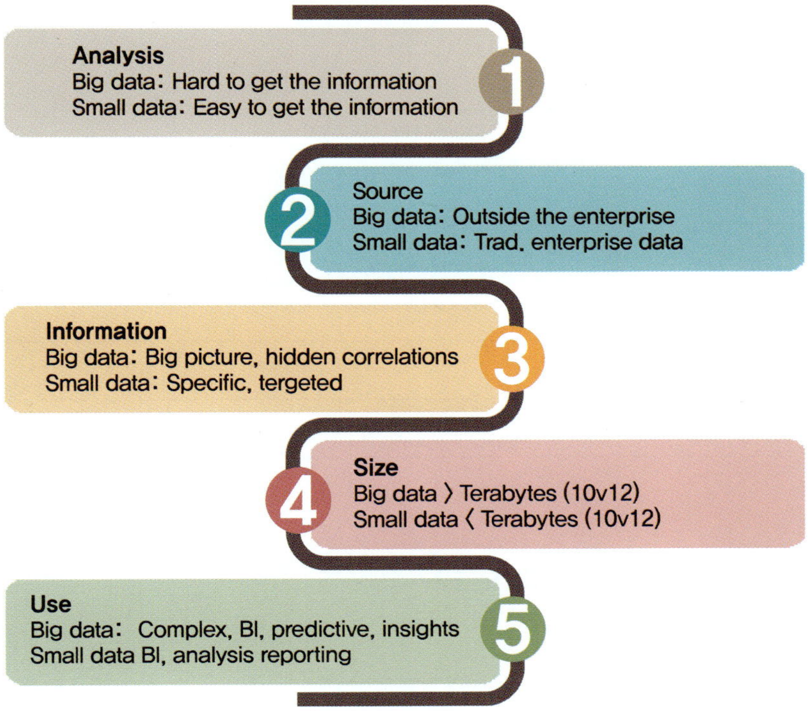

On the other hand, big data constitutes extensive and intricate datasets demanding advanced tools like Hadoop and Spark for **thorough** analysis due to their high volume, velocity, and diversity. Open data signifies publicly accessible datasets, involving government and research data, necessitating IT professionals to grasp open data sources and **integration** methods. Real-time data, processed promptly upon creation, requires **adeptness** in technologies like stream processing and event-driven architectures for effective analysis. Sensor data, gathered from diverse devices, demands familiarity with connectivity and integration protocols to ensure effective utilization in applications.

In summary, adeptness in diverse data types **empowers** future IT personnel to address varied data needs, execute appropriate data management strategies, and harness data's potential for significant insights and innovation.

Retrieved and modified from: https://www.selecthub.com/big-data-analytics/types-of-big-data-analytics/ & https://www.javatpoint.com/big-data-characteristics

11) Summarize the **Types of Data: Big Data, Small Data, Open Data vs. Closed Data** in two or three sentences and discuss your summary with your group members.

____

____

____

____

____

____

____

CONTENT READING RESOURCE 12

Pre-reading Activity

AI in Bio and Medical Field

Read the definitions of the key vocabulary found in the example paragraph. Fill in the blanks with the correct form of the words in bold.

expediting: Speeding up a process or making it happen more quickly.
scrutinize: To examine or inspect carefully and thoroughly.
prudent: Exercising careful, sound judgment in practical matters; wise and cautious in decision-making.
irregularities: Deviations or abnormalities from what is considered normal or expected.
revolutionizing: Causing a significant, fundamental change or reformation
diagnostic: Relating to the identification of a disease or condition by analyzing symptoms or data.
biomedical: Relating to the application of the principles of the natural sciences, especially biology and physiology, to clinical medicine.
discerning: Displaying good judgment or keen insight; perceptive or showing discrimination.
proactive: Acting in anticipation of future problems, needs, or changes.
predict: To foretell or forecast something based on present indications or signs.

1. The advancements in technology are ________ the industry practices, bringing in new methodologies.
2. They meticulously ________ the documents to ensure compliance with the regulations.
3. The accountant discovered some ________ in the financial report that needed further investigation.
4. The company introduced new software aimed at ________ the process of data analysis.
5. In the hospital, the doctor used various ________ tests to confirm the patient's condition.
6. Her ________ skills allowed her to spot the critical flaws in the experimental procedure.
7. Meteorologists can use weather patterns to help ________ future storms.
8. Being ________ in preventing potential risks is essential for a successful business.
9. The fire department's ability to ________ helps prevent unexpected disasters.
10. It's always ________ to assess the risks before making any investment decisions.

Reading Activity

AI in Bio and Medical Field

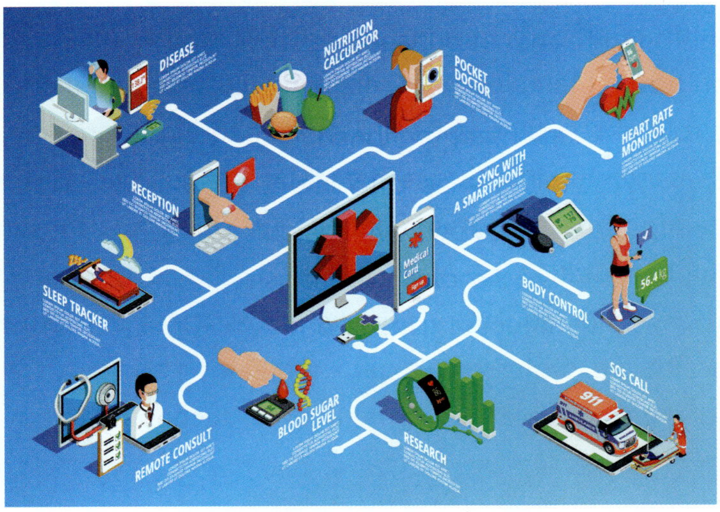

IT-driven Artificial Intelligence (AI) harbors the potential to induce substantial changes within the medical and bio sectors, **revolutionizing** facets of healthcare, research, and personalized medicine, encompassing medical diagnosis, drug discovery, precision medicine, disease monitoring, and data analysis. Firstly, AI algorithms exhibit the ability to **scrutinize** medical imagery like X-rays, MRIs, and CT scans, contributing to disease detection and diagnosis. Notably, AI-based algorithms display promise in accurately **discerning irregularities** in lung cancer screening images, enhancing **diagnostic** accuracy for improved patient outcomes.

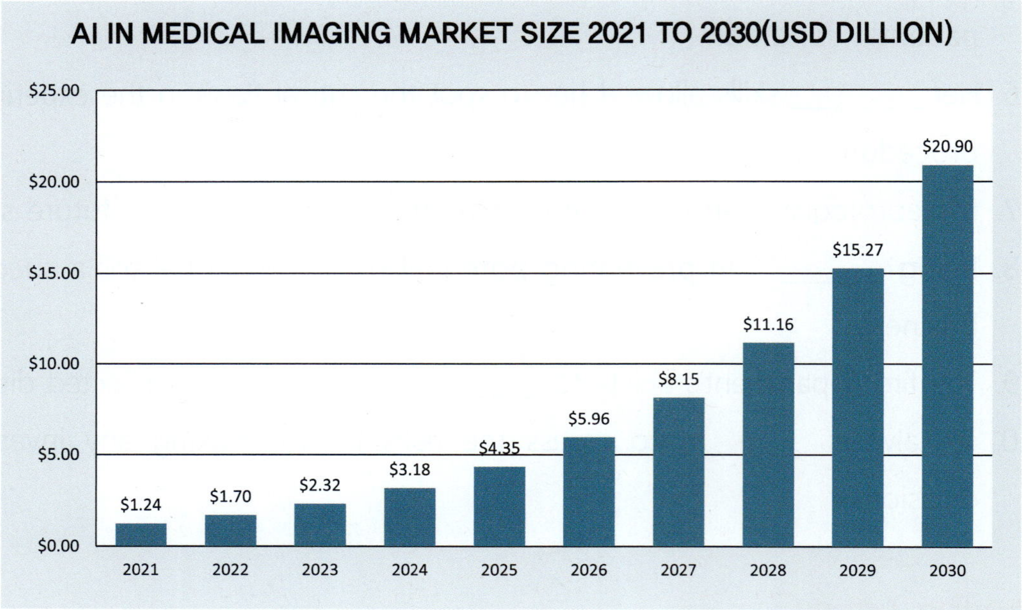

sourece: www.precedenceresearch.com

Moreover, AI contributes to **expediting** the drug discovery process by sifting through extensive **biomedical** data, identifying patterns and correlations to **predict** drug efficacy, repurpose existing drugs, and pinpoint potential targets for novel therapies, thus enabling customized medical approaches. Lastly, AI's role in real-time patient data monitoring, examining vital signs and symptoms, assists in early disease detection, prediction of disease progression, and facilitating **proactive** interventions. By doing so, to summarize, more **prudent** implementation of AI in the medical and bio sectors, considering ethical, privacy, and regulatory aspects, necessitates collaboration among AI experts, healthcare professionals, and regulatory bodies to ensure the safe, effective, and responsible deployment of AI technologies.

12) Summarize **AI in Bio and Medical Field** in two or three sentences and discuss your summary with your group members.

[Chapter 2]
Outlining a Final Group Project

DISCUSSION

1. Once the group project topic is selected, as a group, discuss and fill in the blanks with the topic of your final group project. Then select **three most important ideas you want to develop** for your final group project.

2. In addition, consider the following points.

1) Explain how the topic is being applied or can be applied to improve our actual lives or any industrial site.

2) Explain how start-up company could be created using the information from the reading. Consider the possible obstacles and concerns people might have in this start-up company.

3) Explain the advantages and disadvantages of the topic.

4) Explain where it can be contrasted/contrasted with the topic.

5) Explain any possible causes and effects, problem and solution, or evaluation and prediction, etc.

3. Using your preferred resource, research as many important examples as possible and prepare for the good visual materials and supporting ideas as you learned in the previous Units.

Topic: ______________________________

Main Argument for Your Final Group Project

Topic Sentence for Supporting Argument 1:

Topic Sentence for Supporting Argument 2:

Topic Sentence for Supporting Argument 3:

LEARNING OBJECTIVES	IN THIS UNIT STUDENTS WILL ...
PERFORMANCE & TASK	create a successful presentation slides by integrating effective design and clear text in order to strengthen the impact of their spoken delivery.
CRITICAL THINKING SKILLS 1	assess the organizational structure of exemplary presentations by examining their main components in doer to construct well-organized presentations of their own.
CRITICAL THINKING SKILLS 2	explain various types of visual materials by considering their benefits in presentations in order to enhance the clarity of their own presentations.
COMMUNICATION SKILLS	deliver effective project presentations by practicing and incorporating both verbal and non-verbal delivery techniques.
WRITING SKILLS	evaluate their classmates' presentations in written format by identifying strengths and weaknesses in content, language, and delivery.

UNIT 10

Effective English Presentations in Academic & Professional Settings

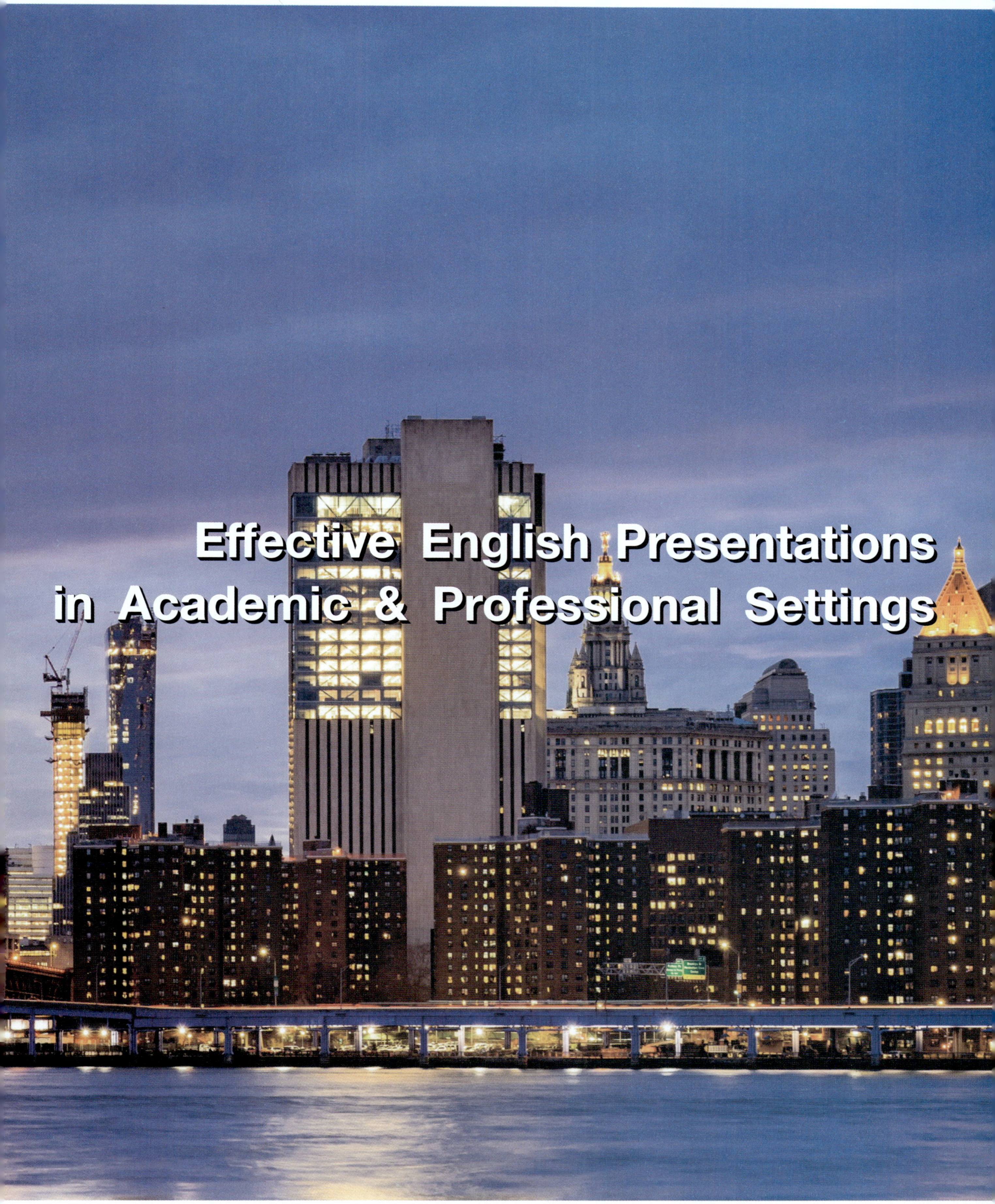

[Chapter 1]
Organization and Management of Presentations

BRAINSTORMING

Discussion

This unit explains effective English presentation organization. With your group members, discuss different parts of an effective English presentation and list them below.

Video & Note-taking Activity

Watch the video clip about making a presentation like Steve Jobs. Write the key points about the presentations below.

Final Group Project Organization

This unit is for preparing your group's final project based on the chosen **major-related issue,** and the following shows the final group project presentation organization.

The Organization of the Project

I. Introduction

1) Greeting the audience
2) Giving a hook
3) Statement of the purpose
4) Outlining main ideas in each topic sentence ①, ②, ③

II. Body Paragraph 1

1) Topic Sentence ① + Supporting Sentences ① + Concluding Sentence ①
Transitional Expressions ①

III. Body Paragraph 2

2) Topic Sentence ② + Supporting Sentences ② + Concluding Sentence ②
Transitional Expressions ②

IV. Body Paragraph 3

3) Topic Sentence ③ + Supporting Sentences ③ + Concluding Sentence ③
Transitional Expressions ③

V. Conclusion

1) Rephrasing the main ideas in each Topic Sentence ①, ②, ③
2) Thanking the audience
3) Inviting questions from the audience
4) Finishing with a final comment

Presentation Organization 1: Introduction

Introduction Components & Expressions

1) Greet and introduce yourself as a presenter.

– Good afternoon. Thank you for coming to my presentation.
  I am Peter Kim majoring in Computer Science.

2) Get the attention of the listener by including a hook statement (surprising facts, hot issues, problems, statistical data, famous quotes, proverbs, stories, or personal experiences).

– Have you ever heard/seen about...?
– Have you ever wondered why...?
– According to the statistics,
– Recent study shows that...
– Now, I have been interested in...

3) Introduce the purpose.

– The purpose of the presentation is to explain *the fuel efficiency of a hydrogen car.*
– The purpose of this presentation is to explain three environmental issues facing the world today that require immediateattention.
– This presentation aims to discuss *the change of currency for the past ten years.*

4) Give the audience a clear outline of what you will talk about.

– The outline of the presentation is as follows: First,... (Body 1) Second/ Next,... (Body 2), Finally,... (Body 3)
– There are three issues/matters that I'd like to discuss today. The first involves climate change, the second is water pollution, the third is natural resource loss.

TIPS

*** Rank the importance of your three key points and order them as such:**
Body 1 – Second most important point
Body 2 – Third important point
Body 3 – The most important point

Check-up Questions

1. Read the following and choose the correct answer that cannot be a hook statement.

   ① statistical data ② famous quotes

   ③ proverbs ④ using synonyms

2. Fill in the blank with an appropriate word or phrase.

   ① The __________ of the presentation is to discuss three advantages of using AI in computer engineering.

   ② There are three points that I'd like to __________ today.

Presentation Organization 2: Body 1, 2, & 3

Body Paragraphs Components & Expressions

1) Present one key point for each body paragraph.

- The first point for/against is...
- The second reason for/ against is that...
- The last but the most important point is...

2) Introducing important visual materials (diagrams, tables, graphs, etc.) **to support your point**

- This picture shows...
- Please look at this table to illustrate further.
- Let's take a look at this graph/video, which demonstrates...

3) Clarifying and explaining

- Let me explain it one more time.
- Let me make it more clear.
- To give a specific example,...

4) Starting and ending each section with a clear transition

- So far, I have presented... Now, I will move on to the next point.
- I have talked about... I will now present the last point...
- That wraps up my main points/arguments. (In conlusion,...)

Check-up Questions

1. Decide whether each of the following is true (T) or false (F). Write your answer in the space provided and then compare with your partner.

_____ ① Present the least important reason first.

_____ ② Do not use transition words when the key points are changed.

_____ ③ Present two key points for each body paragraph.

2. Which of the following expressions is not for clarifying and explaining body paragraphs?

① Let me make it more clear. ② Let me explain it one more time.

③ The second point against is that... ④ To give a specific example,...

3. Which of the following expressions is not for starting and ending each section with a clear transition of body paragraphs?

① That wraps up my main points/arguments. (In conlusion,...)

② I have talked about... I will now present the last point...

③ To illustrate further, please look at this table.

④ So far, I have presented... Now, I will move on to the next point.

Presentation Organization 3: Conclusion

Conclusion Components & Expressions

1) Rephrasing the main arguments and restating the outline

- To summarize the key/main points of my presentation,...
- In summary,... To sum up,...

2) Giving thanks to the audience: Closing the presentation

- Thank you for listening to my presentation.
- Thank you for your attention.

3) Inviting questions from the audience

– If you have any questions, please do not hesitate to ask.
– The floor is now open for questions.

TIPS

* Be prepared to deal with some unexpected questions/responses.
* If you do not understand the audience's question, ask for repetition.
  – If you don't mind, could you repeat the question?
  – Would you mind repeating the question?

4) Concluding with final remarks

– If there are no more questions, this is the end of the presentation. Thank you very much again.
– If there are no more questions, I will wrap up my presentation. Thank you very much for listening.

Check-up Questions

Answer the following question to check your understanding of conclusion components and expressions.

1. Fill in the blank with an appropriate word or phrase.
   ① To ___________ the key/main points of my presentation,...
   ② If you have any questions, please do not __________ to ask.
   ③ Would you mind _________ the question?

2. Choose the expression that can be used for conclusion components.

① So far, I have presented... Now, I will move on to the next point.
② I have talked about... I will now present the last point...
③ Please look at this table to illustrate further.
④ The floor is now open for questions.

Writing the Final Group Project Script

Complete the final group project presentation script for the finally selected topic. After that, receive feedback from the professor.

Topic: ________________________

I. Introduction

1) Greeting

____

____

____

____

2) Hook

____

____

____

____

3) Statement of the Purpose

____

____

____

____

4) Outline of Main ideas in each Topic Sentence ①, ②, ③

____

____

____

____

____

____

____

Ⅱ. Body Paragraph 1

1) Topic Sentence ① + Supporting Sentences ① + Concluding Sentence ①
Transitional Expressions

Ⅲ. Body Paragraph 2

2) Topic Sentence ② + Supporting Sentences ② + Concluding Sentence ②
Transitional Expressions

IV. Body Paragraph 3

3) Topic Sentence ③ + Supporting Sentences ③ + Concluding Sentence ③ Transitional Expressions

V. Conclusion

1) Rephrasing the Main Ideas in Each Topic Sentence ①, ②, ③

2) Thanking the Audience

3) Inviting Questions from the Audience

4) Finishing with a Final Comment

[Chapter 2]
Making Effective Presentation Materials

BRAINSTORMING

Analyze and write your opinion about the positive and negative features of each slide sample in the table. Next, share your ideas with your partner.

Slide Sample 1

* Machine learning (ML)

- Research focuses on understanding and reating "learning" strategies
- Methods that employ data to improve performance on a particular set of tasks
- Considered to be a part of artificial intelligence.

Slide Sample 2

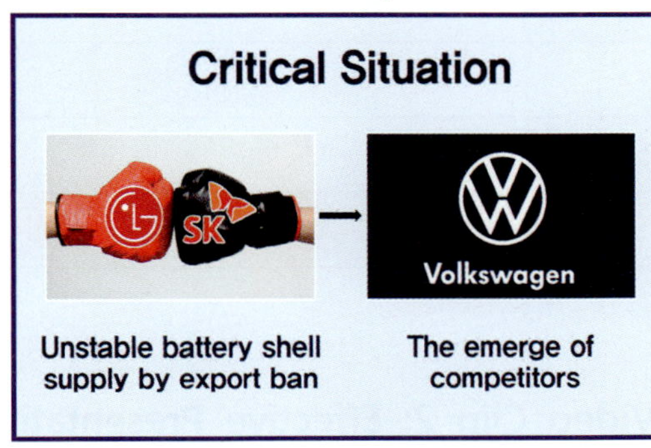

	Slide Sample 1	Slide Sample 2
1) Positive points		
2) Negative points		

Video & Note-taking Activity

Watch the following video clips about English presentation slides. Write down the key points.

Video Clip 1: Effective Presentation Slides

Video Clip 2: Effective Presentation Slides

Effective Presentation Materials: Strategies (1)

1) Organization

- In the beginning of your presentation, introduce an interesting hook to get the attention of the audience (e.g. visuals, etc.).
- Include an outline of your presentation at the beginning.
- Organize slides in a logical way.
- Include a summary of the presentation at the end.

2) Key Points of PowerPoint Content

- Include one key point per slide.
- Do not write every detail. Write only key words and important phrases in the slides.
- Write 6~8 lines per slide and about 6 words per line.
- Include meaningful visuals.
- Use appropriate tables and graphs but not too many.
- Insert transitional slides in-between different issues.

Check-up Question

Answer the following question to check your understanding of PowerPoint organization and content.

1. Fill in the blank with an appropriate word or phrase for the organization and content of PowerPoint.

   ① In the beginning of your presentation, introduce an ________________ to get the attention of the audience (e.g. visuals, etc.).

   ② Use appropriate tables and graphs but not ____________.

   ③ Write ____________ per slide and about __________ per line.

Effective Presentation Materials: Strategies (2)

Font Types and Sizes of the PowerPoint Slides

- Select appropriate font types. Use Arial, Tahoma or Verdana. Do not use Times New Roman which is more appropriate for small text.
- Use a big enough font size appropriate for the screen you are using.
- Do not use all CAPITAL LETTERS for titles and the text as they are too difficult to read.
- Make important text bold for emphasis.
- Avoid italics if possible. If you do need to use italics for emphasis, make the italicized words bold.
- - Avoid using too many bullet points.

Slide Design

- Show sharp contrast between the font color on the slide and the background slide color.
- Insert appropriate video materials and sound effects. Avoid using them too much.

Check-up Questions

Answer the following question to check your understanding of the font types and sizes of the PowerPoint slides.

1. Fill in the blank with an appropriate word or phrase for the font types and sizes of PowerPoint.
   ① Do not use all ________________ for titles and the text as they are too difficult to read.
   ② Avoid ______ if possible. If you do need to use _____ to emphasize, make the ______ words bold.
   ③ Show _________ between the font color on the slide and the background slide color.

2. Read the following and choose the wrong answer for key points of font types of the PowerPoint slides.
   ① Avoid using too many bullet points.
   ② Make important text bold for emphasis.
   ③ Use Times New Roman font types for the PowerPoint slides.
   ④ Use Arial, Tahoma or Verdana font types for the PowerPoint slides.

3. Read the following and choose the wrong answer for key points of slide design of the PowerPoint.
   ① Insert appropriate video materials.
   ② Show sharp contrast between the font color on the slide and the background slide color.
   ③ Insert appropriate video materials.
   ④ Insert many sound effects as much as possible.

4. Based on the explanation about effective English presentation slides, analyze the following slide samples.

Slide Sample 1

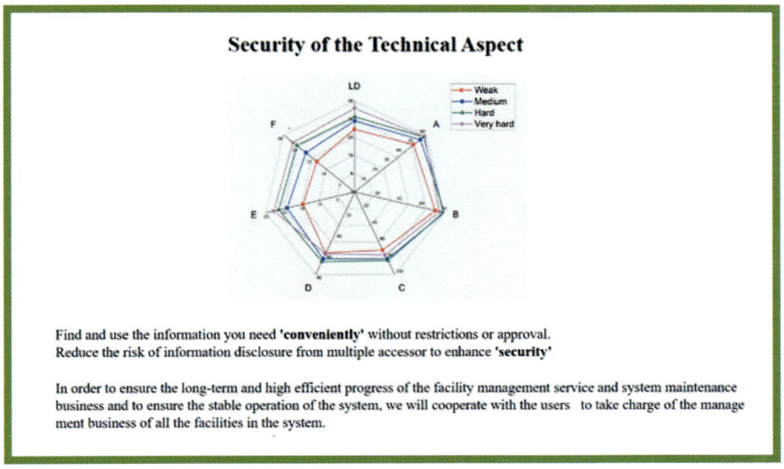

1) Is the slide sample above effective? Why or why not?

____

____

____

____

2) Write suggestions to improve the slide.

Slide Sample 2

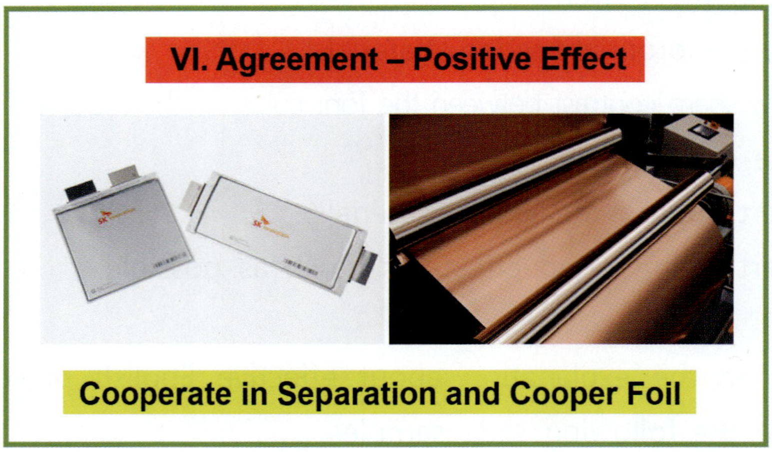

3) Is the slide sample above effective? Why or why not?

4) Write suggestions to improve the slide.

[Chapter 3]
Presenting Different Types of Data

Describing Graphs

Carefully read the following sample answer showing how to describe a vertical bar graph.

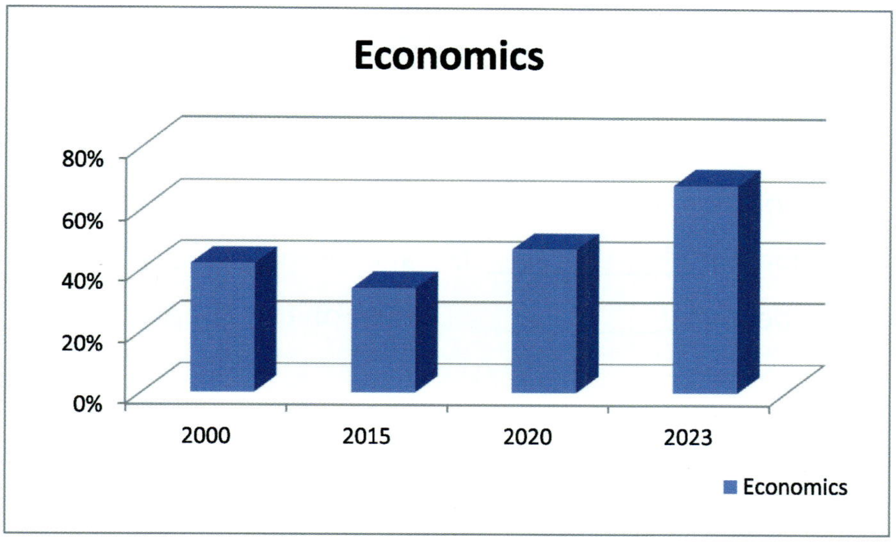

1) Topic of the Graph

This bar graph shows a comparison of economic majors applying to BPA Public Corporation from 2000 to 2023.

2) Describe the Horizontal Axis (X) and Vertical Axis (Y) of the Graph

The vertical axis shows the number in percentages of economic majors applying in a given year. The horizontal axis shows the year in which they applied.

3) Describe the Specific Details of the Graph

As you can see from the graph, 2015 had the lowest number of applicants, which was a 10% drop from 2000. Since 2020 though, there has been a steady rise of applicants who have majored in economics.

4) Conclusion

In conclusion, we can expect that the number of applicants applying to BPA Public Corporation who have majored in economics will increase in the next five years.

Check-up Question

Answer the following question to check your understanding of describing graphs.

1. Fill in the blank with an appropriate word or phrase for describing graphs.
   ① Describe the ___________ (X) and Vertical Axis (Y) of the Graph.
   ② Describe the ___________ Details of the Graph.

Presenting Various Diagrams: Charts and Graphs

1) Introduce the topic of the graph or pie chart and the specific type of graph (e.g., line or bar graph, etc.).

- This graph/pie chart represents/shows...
- The topic of this graph is the percentage of Chat GPT use by MS university students from 2022 to 2024.

2) Describe what the X (vertical) and Y (horizontal) axes represent on this graph.

- The horizontal axis shows the year from 2022 to 2024. The vertical axis shows the percentage use of Chat GPT by students.
- The vertical axis represents the hours of Chat GPT use.

3) Describe the specific details of the graph (for a pie chart, write the most important points; the largest ones are first and move on in decreasing order of importance).

– As you can see from the graph, there has been an increase in the percentage of students who use Chat GPT, specifically from March 2023 to May 2023 compared to March 2022 to May 2022.
– As you can see on the left of the graph,...
– At the bottom of the graph,...
– According to the pie chart, an online Zoom class, at 72%, is the most popular activity.../takes up the highest proportion of Internet use in 2022.

4) Conclusion

– In conclusion, we can expect that the percentage of students using Chat GPT will increase.

Check-up Question

Answer the following question to check your understanding of describing graphs.

1. Fill in the blank with an appropriate word or phrase for describing graphs.
   ① Introduce the ______ of the graph or pie chart and the specific type of graph (e.g., line or bar graph, etc.).
   ② Describe the specific details of the graph (for a pie chart, write the most important points; the _________ ones first and move on in decreasing order of importance).

Expressions to Describe the Degrees of Change in a Chart or Graph

Expressions to Describe the Graphs or Charts' Degree Shift

1) Increase

(1) Verb: increase, grow, rise, improve, expand, go up,

(2) Noun: increase, growth, rise, improvement, expansion, gain

– Most IT companies expect a sharp increase/growth/gain in the year...

– The number of electronic cars will see a gradual increase...

2) Decrease

(1) Verb: decrease, decline, drop, fall, reduce, go down, get worse

(2) Noun: decrease, decline, drop, fall, reduction, sharp fall, downturn

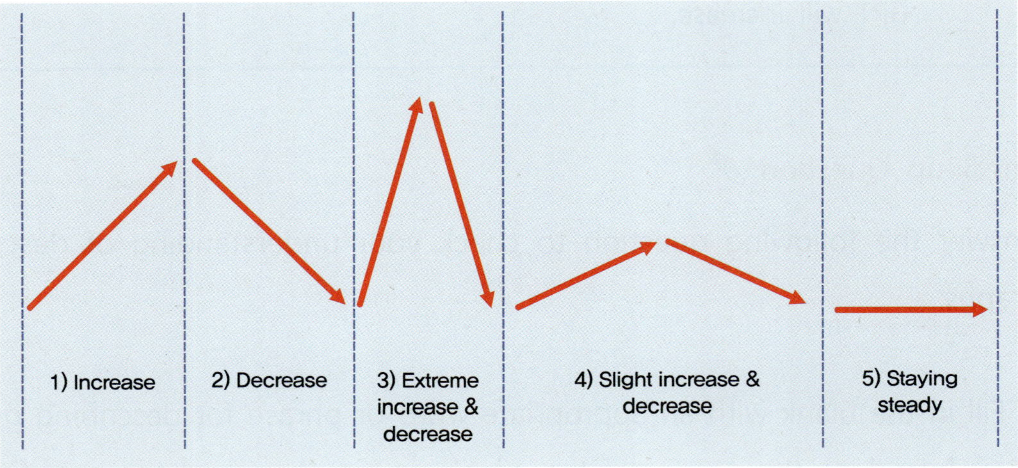

3) Extreme increase and decrease

(1) Verb: increase *sharply/drastically*, rise *sharply/drastically*
decrease *sharply/drastically*, drop *sharply/drastically*

(2) Noun: a *sharp* increase, a *sharp* decrease

(3) Adjective: sharp, drastic, extreme

(4) Adverb: sharply, drastically, extremely, significantly

– There was a sharp increase in the year...

– There was a drastic decrease in the year...

4) Slight increase and decrease

(1) Verb: increase *continuously/steadily*
decrease *continuously/steadily*

(2) Noun: a gradual increase, a gradual decrease
(3) Adjective: continuous, gradual, steady, slight
(4) Adverb: continually, gradually, steadily, slightly
- There was a continuous increase in the year...
- There was a gradual decrease in the year...

5) Staying steady (= steadily)
(1) Verb: remains steady, maintains the same, stays the same, etc.
(2) Noun: maintenance
(3) Adjective: steady, stable, unchanged, the same

Check-up Questions

For the following questions, choose the right answers.

1. Choose the words to describe an extreme increase.

① drop sharply ② improve gradually
③ rise sharply ④ maintain same

2. Choose the words to describe a slight increase.

① maintain constantly ② fall sharply
③ rise drastically ④ increase steadily

3. Choose the words to describe staying steady.

① drop drastically ② expand sharply
③ fall extremely ④ maintain stable

Expressions to Describe the Numerical Data in a Chart or Graph

Expressions to Describe the Numerical Data

For reading decimal numbers, say the period as 'point'. After the decimal point, *use single numbers, such as* 'three point two' (= 3.2). Another way is to express as a fraction. For example, one hundredth (0.01).

1) Numbers with a Decimal Point

- 0.5 – Zero Point five
- 0.02 – Point oh two / Point zero two / Zero point zero two
- 0.0003 – Point oh oh oh three / Zero point zero zero zero three
- 8.35 – Eight point three five (NOT eight point thirty-five) /
  Eight and thirty five hundredths
- 2.0004 – Two point zero zero zero four
- 13.357 – Thirteen point three five seven

2) Numbers with Commas (Thousand → Million → Billion → Trillion)

- 200,000 – Two hundred thousand
- 15,000,000 – Fifteen million
- 4,000,000,000 – Four billion
- 200,000,000,000 – Two hundred billion
- 3,000,000,000,000 – Three trillion

Check-up Questions

For the following, write the correct answers.

1. Write down how to read the following numbers with decimal points.

   ① 0.25 ______________________________

   ② 0.034 ______________________________

   ③ 12.003 ______________________________

2. Write down how to read the following numbers.

   ① 997,000 ______________________________

   ② 7,540,000 ______________________________

   ③ 28,000,000 ______________________________

Expressions to Describe Approximation and Years in a Chart or Graph

1) Using Approximations for Long Numbers

When a number is too long, and the specific number is not important, it is possible to read approximately. In this case, use the expressions for **approximations (almost, nearly, about, approximately,** etc.).

– 989,225 – Nine hundred (and) eighty nine thousand/ two hundred/ and twenty five
– Almost a million

– 1,101,257,489 – One billion, one hundred and one million,/ two hundred and fifty-seven thousand,/ four hundred and eighty-nine
– About one billion

2) Reading Years

– Before 2000: 19/70 – Nineteen seventy
19/88 – Nineteen eighty-eight

– After 2000: 2005 - Two thousand (and) five
2035 – Twenty thirty five / Two thousand (and) thirty five

Check-up Questions

Answer the following questions to check your understanding of describing numbers in a chart or graph.

1. Fill in the blank with an appropriate word or phrase for describing numbers in a chart or graph.
   ① When the number is too long, and the specific number is not important, it is possible to read approximately. In this case, use the expressions for ___________.

2. Which of the following words is not for describing approximations?
   ① about ② almost
   ③ on ④ approximately

Expressions to Describe Fraction Data

Different Expressions to Describe Fraction Data

1) Use different expressions, like proportions, percentages, fractions, etc.

- the proportion of/the percentage of
- a small minority/a large number of employees
- a significant number of employees
- over a quarter of employees
- less than a fourth

2) Vary your language by changing percentages to fractions or ratios

- 20% → a fifth
- 25% → a quarter
- 60% → three-fifths
- 80% → four-fifths
- 48% → just under/nearly a half
- 78% → just over/approximately three quarters

3) Change percentages to proportion/number/amount/majority/minority

- 5% → a very small number
- 10%~15% → a minority
- 65%~75% → a significant proportion
- 75%~85% → a very large majority

4) How to read fractions

- 1/4 – A fourth/One fourth/A quarter
- 3/4 – Three fourths/Three quarters
- 1 1/3 = 4/3 – Four thirds/One and one third
- 2 3/4 – Two and three-fourths or Two and three quarters

Check-up Questions

For the following questions, write the right answers.

1. Write down how to read the following fractions.

① 3/4 ______________ ② 8/10 ______________

③ 2⅘ ______________

2. Change each of these words into fractions.

① three fifths ______________ ② five sevenths ______________

③ six ninths ______________

ACADEMIC WRITING SKILLS

Writing Activity: Presenting Visual Content

Explain and describe the following figures below.

1) Vertical Bar Graph: Tech Giants Were All about AI this Earnings Season

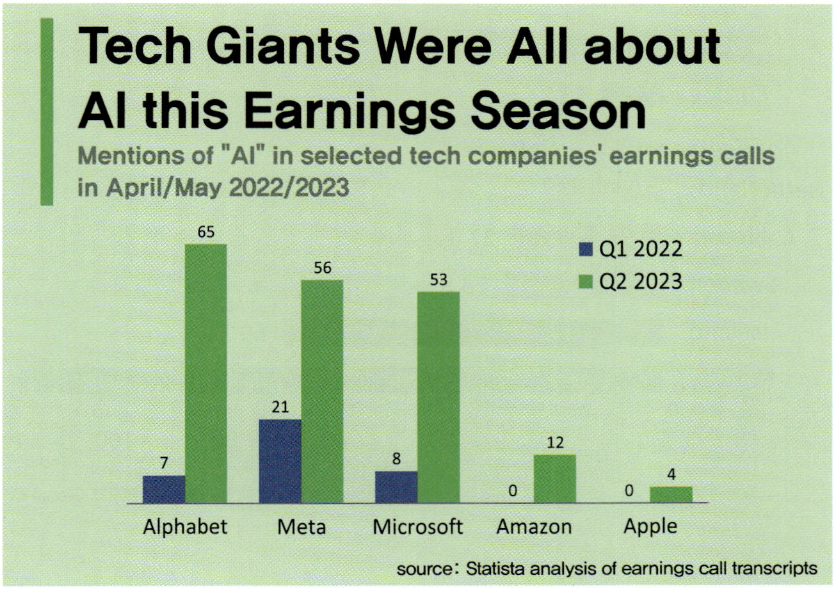

2) Horizontal Bar Graph: Plug-in electric car ownership per capita in selected top selling countries and regional markets as of December 2021

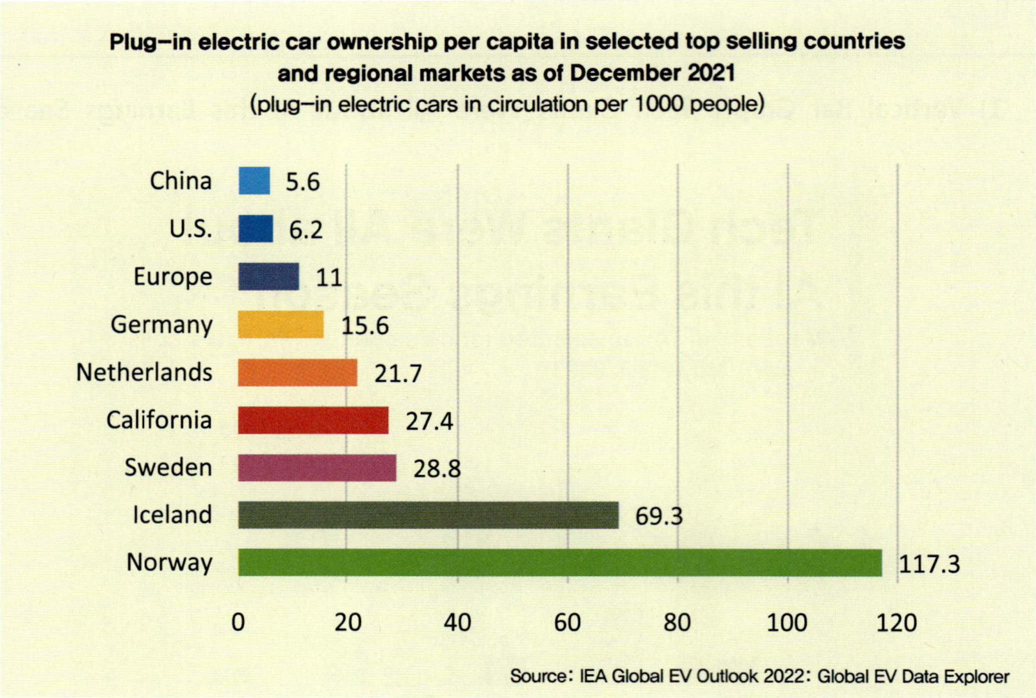

3) Graph: Global Mobile Network Data Traffic (Per Month)

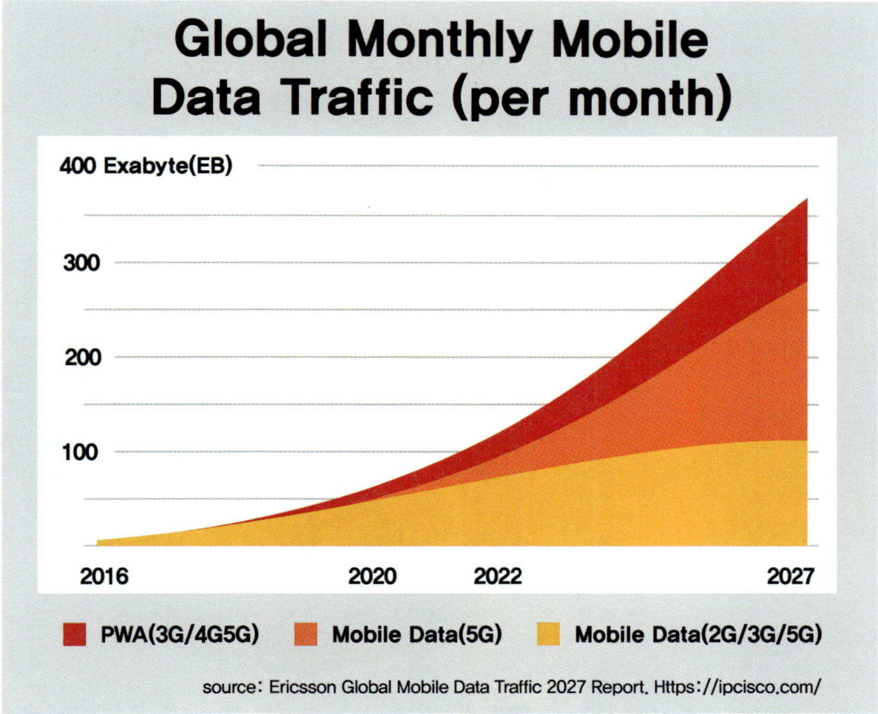

4) Pie Graph: The Typical Basket of Goods and Services

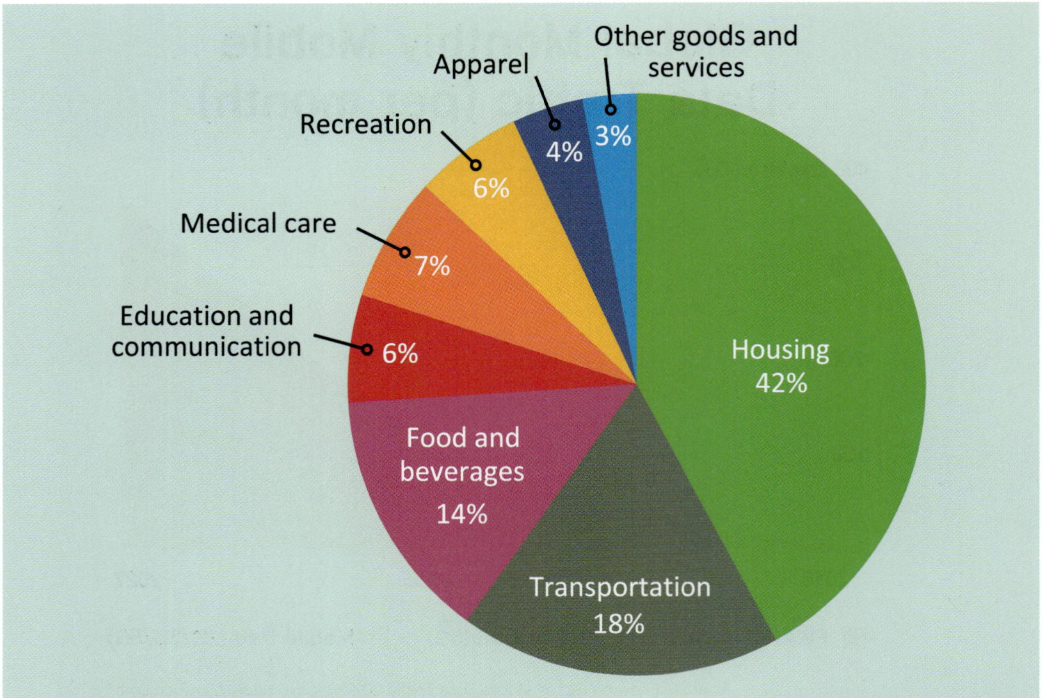

source: Retrieved and modified from Principles of Economics, 5e, pp. 533. Mankiw, N. G. (2008). Cengage Learning

Preparing for the PowerPoint Slides

Based on the final version of the script, plan PowerPoint slides using the given table and have **a professor's feedback**.

PowerPoint Slides	
1)	2)
3)	4)
5)	6)
7)	8)
9)	10)
11)	12)

[Chapter 4]
Evaluating Group Project

Checklist Rubric for the Group Project

For evaluating group project, check the given checklist. Count points for the group project content and structure, and write specific reasons. Put **a check (V)** for each of the following English project check questions.

I. Project Content/Structure (10%)		(−) 1	2	3	4	(+) 5
1. Intro duction	1) Greeting					
	2) Hook					
	3) Purpose of the Project					
	4) Outline the Main ideas in each Topic Sentence ①, ②, ③					
2. Body Paragraphs 1, 2, & 3	1) TS ① + SSs + CS Transitional word					
	2) TS ② + SSs + CS Transition word					
	3) TS ③ + SSs + CS Transitional word					
3. Conclusion	1) Rephrasing the Main ideas in each Topic Sentence ①, ②, ③					
	2) Thanking the audience					
	3) Inviting Questions from the Audience					
	4) Finishing with a Final Comment					
Content Total Points (50/5=10): ______________ (Not at all-1/ little-2/ Somewhat –3/ Much-4/ Very much-5)						
Write specific reasons for the points given to other groups.						

II. Project Delivery, Attitude, & English (10%)	(−) 1	2	3	4	(+) 5
1. Non-verbal (Attitude)					
1) Smiling Face & Confidence					
2) Eye contact w/ the audiences					
3) Natural hand gestures					
4) Right posture of the body					
5) Delivery speed (not too fast & too slow)					
2. Verbal (Delivery)					
6) An appropriate volume					
7) A consistent and comfortable tone of voice					
8) An appropriate speed and good pauses					
9) Intonation & not monotonous					
3. English Related					
10) English Fluency					
11) English Accuracy (pronunciation & grammar)					
Delivery Total Points (50/5=10): ______________ (Not at all-1/ little-2/ Somewhat –3/ Much-4/ Very much-5)					
Write specific reasons for the points given to other groups.					

Evaluation of the Group Project

As audiences, write the main points of the group project. In addition, based on the evaluation rubric of the project, evaluate the positive and negative points of the contents and key points, and also about delivery. Write any suggestion to improve projects.

[1] [Group Project #1: ______________________________]

	Positive Features	Negative Features
PPT slides		
Presentation		
Main points		
Other helpful comments		

[2] [Group Project #2: ______________________________]

	Positive Features	Negative Features
PPT slides		
Presentation		
Main points		
Other helpful comments		

[3] [Group Project #3: ____]

	Positive Features	Negative Features
PPT slides		
Presentation		
Main points		
Other helpful comments		

[4] [Group Project #4: ____]

	Positive Features	Negative Features
PPT slides		
Presentation		
Main points		
Other helpful comments		

[5] [Group Project #5: ______________________________]

	Positive Features	Negative Features
PPT slides		
Presentation		
Main points		
Other helpful comments		

References:

(1) 21 of the mst important technologies that changed the world
https://www.usatoday.com/story/money/2020/01/09/21-most-important-inventions-of-the-21st-century/40934825/

(2) 3D printing & healthcare 관련 통계, 데이터 및 그림 출처
https://www.gminsights.com/industry-analysis/healthcare-3D-printing-market?gclid=EAIaIQobChMIqonAmNur8gIVOtSzCh3VdwHUEAAYASAAEgLeevD_BwE

(3) Augemented Reality 관련 내용, 통계, 데이터 및 그림 출처
https://mobidev.biz/blog/augmented-reality-future-trends-2018-2020

(4) Lithium ion battery & market —Supporting Details 출처
https://www.forbes.com/sites/arielcohen/2021/02/11/what-batteries-will-power-the-future/?sh=1d8c511941c0
https://www.eletimes.com/top-10-lithium-ion-battery-manufacturers-in-the-world
https://pulsenews.co.kr/view.php?year=2021&no=316115

(5) K-pop and it's influence on the world
https://www.queensjournal.ca/story/2019-01-14/pop-culture/the-global-influence-of-k-pop/

(6) https://www.bbc.com/culture/article/20190529-how-did-k-pop-conquer-the-world

저자 약력

책임저자 정성희 교수

- 현 숭실대학교 베어드교양대학 글로벌소통과 언어 주임교수
- 현 숭실대학교 창의뮤지컬영어연구소 소장, CTE 총괄 기획 책임
- 현 ESP학회 편집 이사, KATE, 팬코리아영어교육학회 이사
- 미국 오하이오 주립 대학교 (Ohio State University), 영어교육 석사, M.A.
- 미국 오하이오 주립 대학교 (Ohio State University), 영어교육 박사, Ph.D.
- 전문분야: 영어교육 교수방법론, 영어 쓰기 및 말하기, 멀티미디어영어교육, 커리큘럼 개발
- 민족 사관고등학교 영어 교사
- EBS 강의
- 용인 한국외국어대학교 부설고등학교 영어 교사
- 덕성여자 대학교 교양영어 초빙교수
- 중앙대학교 CIEP 초빙교수
- NEAT (National English Ability Test) 채점위원, 출제 위원
- 전 숭실대학교 베어드교양대학 조교수, MAEP & CTE 총괄 기획 팀장
- 논문 및 저서

  CTE for IT, Computer Science, Bio & Natural Science Majors (2015-2016) 책임저자
  CTE 시리즈 공동저자
  MAEP for Communication Skills in Global Business & Finance (2015-2016) 책임저자
  영어교육 교수방법론, ESP 쓰기 말하기 및 플립러닝 영어교육관련 연구논문 다수

공동저자 송은혜 교수

- 현 숭실대학교 베어드교양대학 글로벌소통과 언어 부교수
- 영국 워윅대학교 (University of Warwick), English Language Studies and Methods 석사, M.A.
- 영국 리즈대학교 (University of Leeds), TESOL 박사, Ph.D.
- 전문분야: 영어교육교수방법론, 멀티미디어 영어교육 방법론, English Speaking Area
- 경희대학교 국제캠퍼스 교양학부 객원교수
- 한양사이버대학교 실용영어학과 조교수
- 한양대, 숙명여대, 성균관대 TESOL 대학원 강의
- MATE (Multimedia Assisted Test of English) Speaking Area 채점위원
- 멀티미디어언어교육학회 학술이사
- 한국외국어교육학회 이사
- 현대영어교육학회 감사 및 현 섭외이사
- 논문 및 저서

  영어교육교수방법론 & 멀티미디어영어교육관련 분야 연구논문 다수
  'Screen English', '아주 많이 행복한 영화영어', 'Grammar for Writing in English' 공동저자,
  CTE for Professional Communication Skills (2015-2016) 책임저자
  CTE 시리즈 공동저자
  MAEP for Communication Skills in Global Business & Finance (2015-2016) 공동저자

공동저자 복은임 교수

- 현 숭실대학교 베어드교양대학 글로벌소통과 언어 부교수
- 고려대학교 교육학 전공 (영어교육학 부전공), B.A. Ed.
- State University of New York at Potsdam, General Education 석사, M.S. Ed.
- State University of New York at Buffalo, Literacy Education 박사, Ph.D
- 전문분야: ESL 청소년 리터러시교육, 온라인 미디어를 이용한 외국어 교육, 다모드 리터러시 (Multimodal Literacies)
- State University of New York at Buffalo 리터러시 교육 대학원 강의
- 논문 및 저서
  온라인 공간에서의 ESL 청소년들의 리터러시 발달 관련 분야 연구논문 다수
  CTE for Foreign Companies (2015-2016) 책임저자
  CTE for Engineering Majors (2015-2016) 책임저자
  CTE 시리즈 공동저자
  MAEP for Communication Skills in Global Business & Finance (2015-2016) 공동저자

Career Track English

2024년 2월 27일 초판 1쇄 발행
2025년 8월 20일 초판 2쇄 발행

저자 정성희 · 송은혜 · 복은임
감수 베어드교양대학 글로벌 소통과 언어 원어민교원

발행인 유수경
발행처 도서출판 영민
등록 2001. 7. 16 제1-2888호
주소 서울시 성북구 보문로 26길 18 201동 1202호
전화 02-904-7204
팩스 02-921-7202

ISBN 978-89-6341-448-5 93740
정가 29,000원